Conveyancing Law

Jean Se

C000050938

The M & E Handbook Series

Conveyancing Law

P H Kenny
LLB, Dip Crim, LLM Solicitor
Head of Department, School of Law,
Polytechnic of Newcastle upon Tyne

C M Bevan
LLB (Bristol) Solicitor
Lecturer in Law,
University of Exeter

Third Edition

Pitman Publishing
128 Long Acre, London WC2E 9AN

A Division of Longman Group UK Limited

First published 1980
Second edition 1983
Third edition 1986
Reprinted 1988, 1989

British Library Cataloguing in Publication Data

Kenny, P. H.
  Conveyancing law. – 3rd ed. – (M. & E. handbooks)
  1. Conveyancing – England
  I. Title   II. Bevan, C. M.   III. Series
  344.2064'38   KD979

ISBN 0-7121-0755-X

Founding Editor: P. W. D. Redmond

Printed and bound in Great Britain by
Richard Clay Ltd, Bungay, Suffolk

Contents

Part three   Conveyancing in particular transactions

Preface

This HANDBOOK has been revised to take account of changes in the syllabus for the Law Society Finals examination. This has resulted in new chapters dealing with some aspects of landlord and tenant law and leasehold conveyancing.

The text covers conveyancing law in sufficient depth for students preparing for undergraduate law examinations, the Solicitors New Finals examinations, and the Institute of Legal Executives examinations.

It deals with the academic aspects of conveyancing law, but the many references to particular problems and illustrations from recent cases should give something of the practical feel of the subject. For this reason it is hoped that the book will be especially useful for those students taking the Solicitors New Finals examinations who presently find difficulty obtaining an overall grasp of this area of the law.

With the formation of the Council for Licensed Conveyancers, we have kept the needs of these new entrants to the conveyancing business in mind while preparing this new edition. The emphasis on conveyancing practice will make this a handy, up-to-date reference guide to everyone working in this area.

Separate treatment has been given to four topics in order to emphasise particularly practical difficulties and to cover many points not found in the larger textbooks. These topics are mortgages in conveyancing, leaseholds in conveyancing, purchase of the freehold reversion and compulsory sales.

Registered land conveyancing is given a full treatment. The

opportunity is taken to illustrate a number of practical points and, in this way and by reference to typical forms in use, bring the subject to life for the student.

A glossary of terms is included in Appendix 1 to help the reader who comes fresh to conveyancing law and who can very frequently find the terminology a source of considerable confusion.

Opportunity has been taken to reflect more accurately the style of the now no longer "new" Law Society Finals course. Appendix 5 includes as well as questions from an LL.B exam paper a question paper set in the Law Society Finals together with notes on how to prepare a successful answer. The Law is stated as at Epiphany 1986.

Land Registration Bill 1986

As this text is in the press a short Land Registration Bill is in Parliament which will almost certainly become the Land Registration Act 1986 and have the following effect:

Chapter 25 (**15–17**) Conversion of Title

  (i) Good leasehold, qualified freehold or qualified leasehold can be upgraded to absolute leasehold on any application by the proprietor *or* provided the Registrar is satisfied as to the title.

  (ii) Possessory freehold or possessory leasehold can be upgraded to absolute freehold or good leasehold respectively on any application when the Registrar is satisfied as to the title or if the land has been registered for 12 years if the proprietor is in possession.

Chapter 26 (**7**); (**21**)

    The situation is rationalised so that leases for 21 years or less are overriding interests and long leases are registrable.

    So the following changes are made:

    (i) Compulsory first registration takes place on the grant of a lease of 21 years or more or the assignment of a lease with more than 21 years to run (s. 2 LPA 1986).

    (ii) Inalienable leases are registrable (s. 3 LRA 1986).

    (iii) S. 70 (1) (k) LRA 1925 is amended so that leases not at a rent or at a premium can be overriding interests under that paragraph (s. 4 LRA 1986).

Chapter 27:4

The Minor Interests Index is abolished (s. 5 LRA 1986).

Ss. 174 & 212 Insolvency Act 1985 replace s. 42 Bankruptcy Act 1914 and s. 172 Law of Property Act 1925 respectively. These new sections are not yet in force. When they are brought into effect it should be noted that by Schedule 9 paragraphs 20 and 24 a conveyance executed before ss. 174 & 212 come into force will only be set aside if the Conveyance would have been set aside under the old law. The new law will only apply in its entirety to conveyances executed after that date.

The Latent Damage Bill 1986 proposes that the limitation period for negligent actions resulting in latent damage should be *either* six years from the date of the negligent act *or* three years from the date when the plaintiff knew of the material facts about the damage and knew that the damage was attributable to the defendant's negligence. Knowledge is defined as knowledge which the plaintiff might reasonably be expected to acquire from observable or ascertainable facts including facts ascertainable with expert advice if the plaintiff should, as a reasonable person, have sought such advice (cf. the discoverability test in *Sparham-Souter* v. *Town & Country Development Ltd.* 1976). The effect will be to overrule *Pirelli General Cable Works Ltd.* v. *Oscar Faber & Partners* (1983).

The bill also proposes a 15-year 'long-stop' period. A plaintiff will be barred from starting an action more than 15 years from the date of the negligent action whether or not damage has occurred.

P H Kenny
C M Bevan
May 1986

Note on reprint: The Land Registration Act 1986 came into force on 1 January 1987. The Insolvency Act 1985 was largely replaced by the Insolvency Act 1986 which came into force on 29 December 1986. The Latent Damage Act 1986 came into force on 18 December 1986.

1988

List of abbreviations

AEA	Administration of Estates Act 1925
ALA	Acquisition of Land Act 1981
AL(AP)A	Acquisition of Land (Authorisation Procedure) Act 1946
CP(VD)A	Compulsory Purchase (Vesting Declaration) Act 1981
EPA	Enduring Powers of Attorney Act 1985
H&BCA 1984	Housing and Building Control Act 1984
LCA	Land Charges Act 1972
LLCA	Local Land Charges Act 1975
LPA	Law of Property Act 1925
LRA	Land Registration Act 1925
LRefA	Leasehold Reform Act 1967
LR(E&E)R	Leasehold Reform (Enfranchisement and Extension) Regulations 1967
LR(N)R	Leasehold Reform (Notices) Regulations 1967
LRR	Land Registration Rules 1925
L&T 1954	Landlord and Tenant Act 1954 Part II
LS	Law Society's General Conditions of Sale (1980 Edn, 1984 revision)
NC	National Conditions of Sale (20th Edn, 1981)
PEA 1977	Protection from Eviction Act 1977
RA 1977	Rent Act 1977
SLA	Settled Land Act 1925
T&C	Town and Country Planning Act 1971

Table of cases

Part one

Introduction to conveyancing

1

Conveyancing in context and an outline of procedures

Conveyancing in context

1. The subject-matter. LPA 1925, s. 205 defines a "conveyance" as including a mortgage, charge, lease, assent, vesting declaration, vesting instrument, disclaimer, release and every other assurance of property or of an interest therein by an instrument except a will. "Convey" has a corresponding meaning. The law of conveyancing is concerned with the legal mechanism whereby the ownership of land (freehold or leasehold) or of an interest in land is transferred from one person to another.

2. The nature of conveyancing. Of all law subjects commonly studied at college, conveyancing is probably the most practical in nature and the least suited to being studied in a purely academic context. The following paragraphs are intended to give some guidance on bridging the gap between the academic and the practical sides of the subject.

3. Importance of practical knowledge. Conveyancing is about how to transfer ownership in land, about the rights of the parties at different stages in real property transactions, and about their respective positions if things should go awry in the course of the transaction. In studying the law and procedure in this area it is important to try to develop a "feel" for the way things "actually happen". The following may help the student:

   (*a*) practitioners' books (*see* **4**);

(*b*) forms used in practice (*see* 5);

(*c*) Land Registry practice notes (*see* 6);

(*d*) practice itself (*see* 7).

4. Practitioners' books. These works are particularly useful in conveyancing in that they contain funds of information that no textbook can ever provide. Students can usefully look at the precedents they contain and the notes explaining the reason for the inclusion of particular clauses and variations in precedents. Particularly useful for the student to look through are volumes 18 and 19 of the *Encyclopaedia of Forms and Precedents* which deal with the sale of land. Neither should the student shrink from the weightier professional texts such as *Emmet on Title* or *George on Sale of Flats* (these and other published works mentioned in the text are listed in the Bibliography in Appendix 3) which will help to give the student the "flavour" of the subject from the solicitor's standpoint. Also of interest to students are practitioners' journals. The would-be solicitor is well advised, for example, to become a regular reader of the Law Society's *Gazette*. Its correspondence column, editorial comment and articles, if regularly read, will help the student understand current trends and concerns in practice.

5. Forms used in practice. There are many references in the text to forms used by conveyancers, and countless more forms are found in practice. The keen student will seek out the parts of textbooks (e.g. the large appendixes in Ruoff and Roper, *Registered Conveyancing*) where specimen forms are printed and perhaps photocopy some of the official forms and use them in hypothetical exercises to see how they work. In the same way forms, particularly those referred to often (standard forms of contract, preliminary enquiries, local search forms and so on), can readily be obtained, if not from a friendly solicitor, then very cheaply from the law stationer who will be found in every medium-sized to large town. These forms will be invaluable in aiding the student to "see" the subject for himself.

6. Land Registry practice notes. The Land Registry publishes a set of practice notes on various aspects of registered land conveyancing. These are designed to assist solicitors in carrying out their work and are simply, clearly and authoritatively written. No aspiring solicitor should fail to equip himself with a set—available free of charge by writing to any District Land Registry.

7. Practice itself. Finally, of course, conveyancing must be learned in the field. The solicitors final examination now makes a more serious attempt at practical instruction, but the conveyancer must always gain most understanding from exposure to the real world of practice. The student who gleans some experience of practical conveyancing by working in an office, or through a holiday job, or even by persuading a solicitor friend to let him read through some conveyancing files and have a shot at drafting his own documents, will be greatly helped in feeling confident that he can properly come to grips with the subject.

The academic framework of conveyancing

8. Previous knowledge required. One of the surprising things (to non-lawyers) is that the study of law is generally not "progressive". Each subject is taken as separate and discrete. This is emphatically not so in the study of conveyancing law and practice. The student must build on several subjects in which a competent understanding is essential. These are outlined in **9–12** below.

9. Land law. The student must have a thorough understanding of the principles he has studied in land law. If areas of weakness are felt the student would be well advised to strengthen these *before commencing* his conveyancing studies. An explanatory work such as Dalton's *Land Law* or Riddall's *Introduction to Land Law* can be used for this purpose.

10. Contract law. The conveyancer and the conveyancing student are constantly involved in questions of contract law and a large part of their work is simply the detailed examination of one or other species of contract. Accordingly a thorough grasp of the principles of contract law is required. Particularly important are formation of contract, formalities of written contracts, misrepresentation and remedies for breach of contract.

11. Equity and trust law. Especially important are the equitable remedies, but a background understanding of the entire area is useful to the would-be conveyancer.

12. Other areas. Conveyancing law verges on a number of other areas of law. Some understanding of succession is necessary in dealing with transactions involving personal representatives. The same consideration makes a knowledge of company law useful in dealing with the position of companies in conveyancing transactions. Other subjects such as planning law, local government law and revenue law are touched upon but no specialist knowledge can be expected from the student.

The two systems of conveyancing

13. Introduction. In England and Wales the method of conveyancing to be used in any particular case depends on whether or not the title to the land has been registered under the Land Registration Acts 1925–71. Where the land has not been registered, it is subject to the older system of unregistered conveyancing, described in Part Two. Under this system a vendor's title is traced through the title deeds disposing of the property. If the land has been registered, it is subject to the system of registered conveyancing, described in Part Four. Under this more modern system title to land is proved by entry of the vendor's name on the official register of title and perusal of the title deeds is dispensed with.

Many of the topics covered in Part Two are also particularly relevant to registered conveyancing, notably those in Chapters 2–8 and Chapter 15.

In dealing with the system of registered conveyancing, the student must constantly have in mind the fact that the traditional rules of contract law and land law apply and thus that the system is *essentially* procedural.

14. Land Registry search. To discover if the title to the land is registered a search should be made in the index map and parcels index of the Land Register using Form 96. The search will disclose whether there is any caution or priority notice affecting the land (*see*

27:**14** and 12:**12**) and also whether the land is in a compulsory area of registration, and if so whether the title has been registered. The form is sent to the appropriate District Land Registry serving the area within which the land is situated. (An explanatory leaflet detailing the areas served by each District Registry can be obtained from any District Registry.) It should be remembered that even if the land is not within an area of compulsory registration, in certain circumstances land may be voluntarily registered (*see* 26:**19**), so a search should always be made.

15. Qualified persons. By virtue of the Solicitors Act 1974, s. 22, only solicitors were entitled to prepare conveyances etc. for reward. There were and still are certain unimportant exceptions for barristers, public officers and those employed to copy documents. Now, by virtue of the Administration of Justice Act 1985, there will be a further class of qualified conveyancers — licensed conveyancers. Where the term solicitor or conveyancer is used in the text, it may be assured to include licensed conveyancers.

Representation of the parties to a conveyance

16. Legal requirements. No party to a conveyance is required by law to employ a qualified person to act for him. On the other hand no person other than a solicitor may hold himself out as such (Solicitors Act 1974, Part I). Further only a qualified person may prepare certain documents "in expectation of any fee, gain or reward".

Ordinarily each party will be represented (and must be strongly advised so to be represented) by his own solicitor. There are now strict restrictions on the same firm of solicitors acting for "both sides" in a conveyancing transaction (*see* Rule 2 of the Solicitors' Practice Rules, *see* Appendix 6).

17. Mortgagees. Nowadays the bulk of domestic purchases (and also a very large proportion of commercial transactions) take place with the assistance of a simultaneous mortgage. This means that a separate person will sometimes act for the mortgagee, although frequently the purchaser's conveyancer will be allowed by the mortgagee to act for him also.

Outline of conveyancing procedures

18. Introduction. The outline in the following table explains the main steps in chronological order in a sale of unregistered land. (For differences in registered land, *see* 25:5–8, and 28:3–14.)

Outline of conveyance procedures

Purchaser	Vendor
1. Make local searches and enquiries of local authorities.	
2.	Draft contract in duplicate and send both to purchaser.
3. Raise enquiries before contract.	
4.	Reply to enquiries before contract.
5. Examine replies and return one copy of contract when approved.	Agree contract.
6. Sign contract, exchange parts and pay deposit.	Sign contract, exchange parts and obtain deposits.
7.	Send abstract of title to purchaser.
8. Examine abstract of title and raise requisitions.	
9.	Reply to requisitions on title.
10. Draft conveyance, assignment or transfer and send to vendor for approval.	
11.	Approve conveyance, assignment or transfer and return to purchaser.
12. Engross conveyance.	
13.	Prepare and send completion statement to purchaser.
14. Sign conveyance in escrow and send to vendor.	
15. Make land charges search.	
16.	Vendor executes conveyance.

Purchaser	Vendor
17. Attend on completion: examine abstract of title against title deeds and documents, pay balance of purchase monies and obtain necessary title deeds.	Attend on completion: produce all relevant title deeds and documents, hand over those the purchaser is entitled to and obtain balance of purchase monies.
18. Fill in "particulars delivered" form and deliver it with duty and conveyance to Inland Revenue stamp office.	
19. On receipt of stamped conveyance send it with other title deeds and documents to purchaser or at his order.	

Progress test 1

1. Define what is meant by the law of conveyancing. (**1**)

2. What other areas of law should the student of conveyancing have an understanding of? (**9–12**)

3. What are the two systems of conveyancing? (**13**)

4. What is the Form 96 and where is it sent? (**14**)

5. Whose duty is it to draw up the contract for the sale of the land? (**18**)

6. Who draws up the conveyance? (**18**)

7. What is sent and by whom to the Inland Revenue stamp office? (**18**)

8. Who receives a completion statement? (**18**)

9. What does the purchaser's solicitor do with the title deeds and documents after the conveyance has been stamped? (**18**)

Part two
Unregistered conveyancing

2
Pre-contract enquiries and searches

Introduction

1. Types of enquiries and searches. Before the purchaser commits himself to buying the property, i.e. before contracts are exchanged, he will wish to know as much as he can about it. The following searches and enquiries should be made to this end.

(a) Enquiries before contract (*see* **2–4**).
(b) Local land charges search (*see* **5–8**).
(c) Enquiries of the local authority (*see* **9–12**).
(d) Index map search (*see* **13**).

Where appropriate the following should also be made.

(e) Commons Registration Act Search (*see* **14**).
(f) National Coal Board search (*see* **15**).
(g) Enquiries of British Rail, statutory undertakers and planning authorities (*see* **17**).

Enquiries before contract

2. Subjects covered. These enquiries of the vendor are intended to deal with matters that the vendor is not obliged to disclose to the purchaser (*see*, for example, *Re Forsey and Hollebone's Contract* (1927): no duty on vendor to disclose a matter registered as a local land charge) but which may provide vital information in relation to the purchase of the property. Matters normally raised include:

(*a*) boundaries, often a source of trouble, and any disputes affecting the boundaries;

(*b*) easements and covenants;

(*c*) services enjoyed by the property, such as gas, water, electricity and drainage;

(*d*) guarantees or other agreements relating to the fabric of the building;

(*e*) agreements relating to the maintenance of any road over which rights of access to the property are enjoyed;

(*f*) whether there is any agreement or bond for constructing and adopting the road on which the property is situated;

(*g*) adverse rights affecting the property which are not apparent upon inspection and interests of those in actual occupation;

(*h*) planning considerations;

(*i*) fixtures and fittings;

(*j*) whether there has been any breach of a restriction affecting the property.

If a newly built property is being sold, the purchaser will wish to know if the vendor is going to pay for the drainage system to be connected to the public sewer. Where the house is leasehold, information will be requested about the lease and the lessor.

3. Forms used. Standard printed forms are used in many cases to raise these enquiries and if this procedure is followed care should be taken to delete those enquiries which are inappropriate. There is no point in asking about the lease if the property is freehold! It may be necessary to add enquiries to the printed form arising from the draft contract or other features of the transaction. For example, is the property liable to flooding? Is the wiring in good condition? Or enquiries about the central heating or other services.

4. Vendor's replies. The vendor is not obliged to answer the enquiries but if he does not do so there is always the possibility that the purchaser will not continue with the sale. However, solicitors invariably frame replies qualified by such phrases as "so far as the vendor is aware" or "to the best of our knowledge and belief".

Unqualified replies are rarely forthcoming unless the purchaser is prepared to make an issue of it.

The replies that the vendor gives are not of themselves terms of the contract, so that an incorrect reply will not give rise to an action for breach of contract or warranty. It may, however, be an actionable misrepresentation under the Misrepresentation Act 1967 (*see* 8:**8–13**).

It should be noted that the printed forms carry a clause disclaiming liability for the accuracy of the replies. It was stated in *Walker* v. *Boyle* (1982) that the clause did not prevent the answers from being representations of fact.

In *Djan* v. *Daloroto* (1979) the purchaser successfully sued the defendant basing his claim, *inter alia*, on a misrepresentation in the answer given in reply to an enquiry as to whether any notices relating to the property had been served on the defendant vendor.

A new sentence has been added to the clause as follows: "These replies are given on behalf of the vendor and without responsibility on the part of his solicitors their partners or employees". To be effective this will have to satisfy the test of reasonableness in the Unfair Contract Terms Act 1977. This clause was added after *Wilson* v. *Bloomfield* (1979) which suggests that a purchaser may be able to sue a vendor's solicitor in negligence because of an incorrect reply.

Local land charges search

5. The local land charges register. LLCA 1975, s. 3 (which came into force on 1st August 1977) requires district councils, London borough councils and the City of London Corporation to maintain a local land charges register for their area. Local land charges can be divided into two broad categories:

(*a*) financial charges on the land for work carried out by the local authority;
(*b*) restrictions on the use of the land.

The register is divided into twelve parts:

(*i*) general financial charges;
(*ii*) specific financial charges;
(*iii*) planning charges;

    (*iv*) miscellaneous prohibitions and charges;

    (*v*) charges for improvement of ways over fenlands;

    (*vi*) land compensation charges;

    (*vii*) new town charges;

    (*viii*) civil aviation charges;

    (*ix*) open-cast coal mining charges;

    (*x*) listed building charges (buildings of special historical or architectural interest);

    (*xi*) light obstruction notices;

    (*xii*) (land) drainage scheme charges.

All charges are enforceable by the local authority except (*viii*) and (*ix*), which are enforced by statutory bodies, and (*xi*) which is enforced by private individuals.

6. The search. A purchaser should search in all parts of the register and this can be done by either a personal or an official search.

(*a*) *Personal search.* The purchaser (or his agent, a term which includes his solicitor) attends at the council offices and upon payment of the prescribed fee, personally searches the register (LLCA 1975, s. 8). The charges are registered against the land concerned, not against the estate owner's name as is the case with land charges. The correct postal description of the land is usually sufficient to identify it.

Personal searches are not often used because the right of compensation (*see* 8) is narrower than with an official search. It is used if it is necessary to have the result of the search quickly, because the purchaser wishes to exchange contracts in a short space of time.

(*b*) *Official search.* LLCA 1975, s. 9 provides that an official search may be made of the register. A requisition for a search and for an official certificate of search is sent to the Registrar of Local Land Charges for the area within which the land is situated, together with the necessary fee. The search is undertaken by the Registrar's staff and the result is sent to the purchaser in the form of an official certificate signed by the Registrar and dated. This will state either that there are no subsisting entries relating to the property or that there are a certain number of entries and that copies of the entries are attached to the certificate.

The Registrar may require a plan of the land as well as the postal address. A separate search is made for each parcel of land being purchased, i.e. for each piece of land in separate occupation or separately rated at the date of the search or each building or part of a building so occupied or rated.

7. The effect of registration. Registration of a local land charge is deemed to be notice of the charge to all persons for all purposes. To be validly registered not only must the charge be entered in the register, but it must also be in the correct part of the register. As registration is notice, the purchaser will be bound by the charges whether or not he searches the register.

8. The right to compensation. If an official search fails to reveal a registered charge or a charge is in existence at the date of the search which the local authority has failed to register (the latter covers both failure to register it at all and registering it in the wrong part of the register) the local authority is liable to compensate the purchaser for any resulting loss. This right to compensation is based on the principle that failure to register a local land charge does *not* affect its enforceability against the purchaser.

Where a personal search has been effected, compensation is paid only for loss resulting from the failure of the local authority to register a charge either at all or in the correct part of the register (LLCA 1975, s. 10). (If the purchaser or his agent negligently searches the register and fails to note a properly registered charge it is not the fault of the local authority! An agent in such circumstances may well be faced with an action for negligence.)

It should be noted that the statutory right to compensation only applies if the search is made before contracts are exchanged.

Enquiries of the local authority

9. Introduction. A search in the local land charges register will reveal only those matters which are capable of registration. There are many other matters of concern to the purchaser not disclosed by the search and further enquiries are therefore required to elicit relevant information from the local authority. The enquiries are sent to the appropriate district council or London borough and include any necessary enquiries of the local county council, e.g. questions relating to motorways and trunk roads. They accompany the local land charges search.

10. The form. The Law Society, the metropolitan authorities, and county and district councils have approved a standard form for use in this context. "Con. 29 England and Wales" is used for all authorities outside the London boroughs, a slightly different Con. 29 being used for the London boroughs.

11. Exclusion clause. Both forms contain a clause which states that neither the local authority nor their officers are legally responsible for the replies given to the enquiries, unless they are negligent.

In *Coats Patons (Retail) Ltd* v. *Birmingham Corporation* (1971) the effect of a similar exclusion clause was considered by the court. The difference between the two clauses was that in the *Coats* case there was no admission of responsibility where negligence was present. It was stated in that case that a contract was made between the applicant and the corporation when the form was sent in and the authority was obliged to make appropriate enquiries before supplying the answers. If, on the facts (as was the case), the authority was liable for breach of contract, the exclusion clause fell to the ground, as this was a fundamental breach. The claim in negligence was upheld, the exclusion clause having no bearing, as it was not drafted in terms that would cover negligence.

The present position is that if there is negligence on the part of the authority or its officers, there is no dispute but that the authority is liable. With regard to a claim in contract against the authority, the effect of the Unfair Contract Terms Act 1977 is that an exclusion clause must be fair and reasonable (*see* 8:**13**) if it is to be valid. Even if it does satisfy this test, if the breach is of a fundamental nature, the exclusion clause *may* fall to the ground. It is a question of construction in each case.

12. The enquiries. Many of the enquiries relate to planning matters (*see* Chap. 3), while other standard enquiries deal with the question of whether the roads which abut the property have been adopted by the local authority or are in private ownership. This leads to the question of who is liable to maintain or make up the roads when they are in private ownership. Enquiry will be made to see if the local authority has agreed to adopt the road with or without any cost to those whose properties front on to the road. The developer of a site may enter into an agreement under the Highways Act 1980. s. 38, whereby he furnishes a bond to defray any costs which may be incurred in the making up of the road. If the road has been made up and the cost has to be borne by the frontagers, the sum is a charge on the property and registrable as a land charge in part (*ii*) of the local land charges register (*see* 5).

Other enquiries relate to schemes for new roads which may affect the property, the location of sewers and water pipes, and whether the property is within an area of compulsory registration of title, a smoke control area or a slum clearance area.

In Part II of the form are enquiries which will only be answered if the purchaser places his initials against a particular enquiry. Matters covered include various planning matters (*see* Chap. 3), location of gas pipes within 100 feet (31 metres) of the property, and whether a noise abatement zone order has been made for the area which includes the property. For rented properties, enquiries will be made as to whether there is a certificate of disrepair in force, and whether the house has been registered as being in multiple occupation.

Other additional enquiries may be added by the applicant, which will be answered at the council's discretion.

Other searches

13. Search in the index map and parcels index of the Land Register. The purpose of this search is explained in 1:14. If the land has been registered the title number will be disclosed and whether it is registered freehold or leasehold. Registered rent-charges are also disclosed by the search.

14. Commons Registration Act search. The Commons Registration Act 1965 imposed a duty on county councils to keep a register relating to village greens and common land and interests over them, e.g. easements, *profits a prendre* and mineral rights. In *G*.

& K. Ladenbau (UK) Ltd v. *Crawley and De Reya* (1978) it was said that where a solicitor is acting for a purchaser who is buying land on which no buildings have been erected and with which he is not personally familiar, he may in certain circumstances be guilty of professional negligence if he fails to make a Commons Registration Act search and this results in loss to the purchaser. On the facts of this case the solicitor was negligent.

Where the search is made, the purchaser will wish to consider the result of the search before proceeding further.

15. National Coal Board search. The request for the search is sent to the Area Coal Board office. Where the property is situated in an area where there has been extensive coal mining it is important to know if this has affected the site the purchaser is buying, not only because of problems such as subsidence (which can also affect the method of construction, e.g. raft foundations are often constructed in such areas rather than the normal type of foundations), but also because it will reveal future works.

The search will disclose:

(*a*) past workings and the subsidence caused thereby (if any);

(*b*) proposed future workings and any estimated subsidence;

(*c*) the proximity of open-cast workings.

16. Enquiries of other bodies. In appropriate circumstances enquiries will be made of a variety of other bodies, for example:

(*a*) British Rail if there might be any rights of way or other easements or interests relevant to railway workings;

(*b*) statutory undertakers such as the Electricity or Gas Boards where their activities or conduits might affect the purpose for which the land is being bought;

(*c*) planning authorities generally when the proposed development of other land might affect the purchaser (*see also* 3);

(*d*) In particular areas particular enquiries may be necessary, e.g. as to past or present tin mines in Cornwall and salt mines in Cheshire;

(*e*) Enquiries of rent assessment committees or rent officers relating to registered rents under the Rent Act 1977.

17. Search in the Land Charges Register. At one time it was customary to make this search before contracts were exchanged as well as immediately before completion (*see* 12:**19**). The effect of LPA 1969, s. 24 is that it is no longer essential to search before contracts are exchanged. This section states that when any question arises as to whether a purchaser knew, at the date of entering into the contract, of a registered land charge (not being a local land charge), then the question is to be decided by reference to his actual knowledge.

If the purchaser has made a search before contracts are exchanged then he is deemed to have knowledge of any charge revealed by the search. It may be that the purchaser will wish to know about such matters before he enters into the contract, e.g. if there is a Class F land charge registered against the matrimonial home by the wife of the vendor who refuses to remove it after contracts have been exchanged, which could involve the purchaser in expense and delay before the matter is concluded.

In practice this search is rarely made at this stage.

Progress test 2

1. What sort of matters are often the subject of an enquiry before contract? (**2**)

2. How many parts is the local land charges register divided into? What type of charge can be enforced by a private individual? (**5**)

3. What is meant by a personal search of the local land charges register and what is the disadvantage of this method? (**6, 8**)

4. In what circumstances will a local authority be obliged to compensate a purchaser who has searched the local land charges register? (**8**)

5. What are enquiries of local authorities and which local authorities deal with the enquiries? (**9**)

6. How would you find out if the property being purchased was or was not in a slum clearance area? (**12**)

7. When would you make a Commons Registration Act search? (**14**)

8. Why would you make a National Coal Board search? (**15**)

9. Is it necessary to search in the Land Charges Register at this stage? (**17**)

3

Enquiries relating to planning matters: the legal background

In advising a client a solicitor will obviously have to take account of the planning legislation which affects all use of real property. In order to do this he will need to make enquiries about the planning situation of the land. This chapter outlines the legal background to the enquiries he should make.

Development

1. Definition of development. T&C 1971 provides that planning permission is necessary for the development of land. Section 22 defines "development" as the carrying out of building, engineering, mining or other operations in, on, over or under land or the making of any "material change" in the use of any buildings or other land. Building operations include rebuilding, structural alterations of or additions to buildings, and other operations normally undertaken by a person carrying on business as a builder. Engineering operations include the formation or laying out of means of access to highways. T&C 1971, s. 20 declares the following to be "material changes":

(*a*) the use as two or more separate dwellings of any buildings previously used as a single dwelling;

(*b*) the deposit of refuse or waste materials except in a hole already used for that purpose;

(*c*) the display of advertisements on the outside of a building not normally used for that purpose.

In any other situation it is a question of fact and degree as to whether the change is material. The governing factor is a comparison with the previous use of the land or building.

2. Work that is not development. T&C 1971, s. 20 states that the following are *not* development:

(*a*) Works which affect only the interior of a building or which do not materially affect the external appearance of a building.

(*b*) Certain road works.

(*c*) Inspection of public services.

(*d*) The use of any building or other land within the curtilage of a dwelling house for any purpose incidental to the enjoyment of the dwelling house as such.

(*e*) The use of any land for the purpose of agriculture or forestry (including afforestation) and the use for any of these purposes of any buildings occupied together with land so used.

(*f*) In the case of buildings or land used for a purpose of any class specified in an order made by the Secretary of State under that section, the use thereof for any other purpose of the same "use classes" (*see* **3**).

3. Use classes. The order referred to in **2**(*f*) is the Town and Country Planning (Use Classes) Order 1972 which lists eighteen separate use classes. A change within a use class, e.g. from a grocer's shop to a furniture shop, is not development. If there is a change from one class to another, e.g. from a grocer's shop to an estate agent's office, there is no automatic rule that this is development; it is subject to the normal rule of material change.

4. Permitted development. Article 3 of the Town and Country Planning General Development Order 1977 as amended contains twenty-three separate categories of development for which blanket permission has been granted by the Secretary of State. Therefore individual applications for permission are not required in any case which falls within one of the listed categories. It should be remembered that this does not mean that the Building Regulations under the Public Health Act 1961 have been complied with, so that an application to deal with this still has to be made to the local planning authority.

Categories mentioned in the order include the following.

(*a*) *Class I*—development within the curtilage of a dwelling house. Generally, an existing house may be improved, altered or enlarged under permitted development so long as the cubic content of the original building is not increased in the case of a terrace house by 50 cubic metres (m^3) or 10 per cent, which ever is the greater, *or* in any other case by 70 cubic metres (m^3) or 15 per cent, which ever is the greater, subject to a maximum of 115 cubic metres (m^3) for all types of houses. This allows the erection of garages, sheds, etc.

(*b*) *Class II*—the painting of the exterior of a house and the erection of gates, fences, walls or other means of enclosure provided they do not exceed 2 metres in height or 1 metre where abutting a road used by vehicles.

The local planning authority can make a direction under Article 4 of the Town and Country Planning General Development Order depriving a landowner of this right to permitted development (question 8 of Con. 29—*see* 2:**10**). This may be done when granting express planning permission by inserting a condition which has the effect of a direction. It may also be done in circumstances where the development would be permitted except that it involves making or altering the access to a trunk or classified road or which would obstruct the view of drivers using the highway so as to create a danger. Should the landowner wish to develop the land in any way he will have to make a formal application for planning permission, rather than being able to take advantage of the permitted development order.

Development plans and structure plans

5. **Introduction.** These topics are covered in question 7 of Con. 29.

6. **Development plans.** The development plan consists of a structure plan drawn up by the county planning authority and approved by the Secretary of State, and various district plans drawn up by the relevant district planning authorities. Once the structure plan has

been approved, it is the duty of the county planning authority to consider whether the local plans conform with it.

7. Structure plans. Introduced by T&C 1971, these take the form of written statements plus diagrams showing the planning policies for the area in general terms. For example, the plans will show if a piece of land is required for a highway or government purposes, thus allowing the blight notice procedure to be implemented. This procedure gives the landowner the right to compel the local authority to buy the property at a price which ignores the planning blight.

8. Local plans. These were also introduced by T&C 1971, and they fill in the detail of the structure plans. There are three types:

(a) district plans—the primary guide for the area;

(b) action area plans—areas selected for intensive redevelopment within the next ten years (the purchaser should bear in mind the possibility of a compulsory purchase order);

(c) subject areas—showing in detail the authority's proposals for a particular use of land.

Planning permission, refusals and restrictions

9. Register of planning applications. (T&C 1971, s. 34.) Part I of the register deals with those applications which are pending, while Part II contains details of applications which have been decided, together with the results of the applications. The importance of the register is the fact that it gives details of any conditions which attach to the planning permission (question 11 of Con. 29). This can be said to be of less importance since 1st August 1977 as LLCA 1975, which came into force on that date, states that a condition prohibiting or restricting the use of land is a local land charge if imposed on or after that date. Therefore a search in the local land charges register should disclose the condition. However, such an entry will not disclose the full details of the condition, so that the register of planning applications should always be searched even when it is known that the planning permission was granted after 31st July 1977.

10. Revocation, modification and discontinuance orders.
Express planning permission can be revoked or modified. Compensation for loss resulting from such action should be claimed within six months of the order being made. A discontinuance order can discontinue the use, impose a condition or require the alteration or removal of a building or works. All three types of order are subject to the approval of the Secretary of State.

11. Tree preservation orders. (T&C 1971, s. 60.) Such an order may refer to an individual tree or a group of trees and is subject to the approval of the Secretary of State. The usual form that the order takes is that it prevents the tree being cut down or lopped without permission unless it is in a dangerous state or dying. If the tree is cut down in defiance of an order or because it is dying, the owner of the land must replace the tree unless the planning authority waives this right. (Question 9 of Con. 29.)

12. Compensation paid under T&C 1971, s. 169. This compensation is paid when a decision of the Secretary of State has restricted the existing use development of the land, e.g. land zoned for industrial development, but planning permission is refused for a new factory. It should be noted that compensation is not always payable. The fact that compensation has been paid could affect any price payable under a compulsory purchase order.

13. Listed buildings. (T&C 1971, s. 54.) The Secretary of State may list a building of special architectural or historical interest without advance notice. (See, for example, *Amalgamated Investment Property Co.* v. *John Walker* (1976). The purchaser entered into a contract to buy an old warehouse for £1¾ million for redevelopment purposes. It was worth £¼ million as it stood. After contracts were exchanged the building was listed and as a result demolition required "listed building consent". The purchaser was bound by the contract.)

A purchaser will be concerned to see if any work has been carried out in contravention of these controls or if a notice has been served requiring that a building be returned to its original state. If a listed building is not being properly maintained a repair notice can be served and, if necessary, a compulsory purchase order made. (Questions III and V of Con. 29.)

The local planning authority may serve a building preservation notice relating to a building which they believe should be listed, and which is in danger of demolition or alteration. The notice lasts six months unless the decision about its listing is confirmed by the Secretary of State. During the duration of the notice the listed building controls operate. (Question 13 of Con. 29.)

14. Time limits. When express planning permission is granted a time limit is set within which development must start. In relation to a full permission, it must start within five years from the granting of the permission. If instead of requesting full permission a successful application is made for outline permission, then the application for detailed permission must be received within three years of the grant of outline permission and development must start within five years of such a grant or within two years of the approval of the details, whichever is the later (T&C 1971, ss. 41 and 42).

15. Completion notices. If development has begun but has not been finished within the five-year period and will not be completed within a reasonable time thereafter, the local planning authority may serve a completion notice terminating the planning permission after the expiration of a further period being not less than twelve months from the date of service of the notice. Work actually carried out before termination is legal (T&C 1971, s. 44).

Enforcement

16. Enforcement notices. (Question 6 of Con. 29.) Under T&C 1971, s. 87, an enforcement notice may be served following a breach of planning control either because a condition has been broken or because development has been carried out without permission. Notice is served on the owner and occupier and anyone else who has interest in the land which is materially affected by the notice. (*See Stevens* v. *London Borough of Bromley* (1972)—notice invalid unless served on all interested parties.) If the breach occurred before 1st January 1964 no action can be taken. For breaches which have occurred since 1st January 1964, notice may be served at any time and still be valid, except in the following three cases where notice must be served within four years of the breach if it is to be valid:

(*a*) the carrying out of operations constituting development;

(*b*) failure to comply with a condition relating to the carrying out of such operations;

(*c*) the change of use of a building to use as a single dwelling house.

(*See Thomas David (Porthcawl)* v. *Penybont RDC* (1972).)

17. The form of the notice. (T&C 1971, s. 87.) The notice must specify the following:

(*a*) The alleged breach of planning control.

(*b*) The steps required to remedy it.

(*c*) The period for compliance with the notice beginning with the date on which the notice is to take effect.

(*d*) The date when the notice is to take effect, being not less than twenty-eight days after service.

18. Appeals. Before the notice comes into force anyone on whom it has been served may appeal to the Secretary of State on any of the following grounds (T&C 1971, s. 88).

(*a*) Planning permission ought to be granted or the condition discharged.

(*b*) The matters alleged do not constitute a breach of planning control.

(*c*) Four years have elapsed since the breach occurred (only relevant for those cases mentioned in **16**(*a*)–(*c*)).

(*d*) Where (*c*) does not apply, that the breach occurred before 1st January 1964.

(*e*) The enforcement notice was not properly served.

(*f*) The steps required exceed what is necessary to remedy the breach.

(*g*) The specified period for rectification falls short of what should reasonably be allowed.

19. The stop notice. While an appeal is pending the enforcement notice has no effect. T&C 1971, s. 90 as amended by the Town and Country Planning (Amendment) Act 1977 permits the local planning authority to serve a stop notice to prevent the carrying on of any activity which is, or is included in, a matter alleged by the notice to constitute the breach of planning control. A stop notice cannot prohibit the use of land as a caravan site for a person's only or main residence nor a building as a dwelling house. Neither may it prohibit the continuation of any activity which commenced more than twelve months before, unless the activity is incidental to building, mining or other operations.

20. Established use certificate. Where it is clear that no action can be taken for a past breach an application can be made to the local planning authority for an established use certificate which is conclusive against the planning authority when obtained.

Progress test 3

1. X wishes to demolish his house. Is this development? (**1**)
2. Give two examples of a material change of use. (**1**)
3. Y intends to knock down the dividing wall between his kitchen and his living room. Does he need planning permission? (**2**)
4. A's house has a cubic content of 1,000 cubic metres, and he is about to erect a garage in the garden. How big can it be while still remaining permitted development? (**4**)
5. What is a development plan? (**6**)
6. What is the effect of a tree preservation order? (**11**)
7. B was granted outline planning permission on 1st April 1977, and detailed permission was granted on 1st April 1979. What is the latest date by which B must start development? (**14**)
8. On what grounds may a person on whom an enforcement notice has been served appeal to the Secretary of State against it? (**18**)
9. When can the local planning authority serve a stop notice? (**19**)

4

Defective premises

Surveyors

1. Purchaser's surveyor. The purchaser, in addition to making the appropriate searches, must ensure that the building is structurally sound before committing himself to buying it. The purchaser may inspect the building with the permission of the vendor, but unless he is an expert in this field, there will be many things that he will miss about the condition of the building. He could, therefore, hire a qualified surveyor to inspect and report on his findings.

If this surveyor is negligent in preparing his report and as a result loss is suffered by the purchaser, the latter will have a claim against the surveyor for breach of contract and, in tort, under the rule in *Hedley Byrne & Co.* v. *Heller & Partners* (1964) (*see* 8:**11**). However, it is normal practice for an exclusion clause to be inserted into the report purporting to exclude liability for negligence. This clause must now be read in conjunction with the Unfair Contract Terms Act 1977, ss. 2 and 3. A clause which attempts to exclude liability for death or personal injury is totally void and liability for other loss can only be excluded in so far as this is reasonable (*see* 8:**13**).

2. The building society surveyor. Most domestic purchases are made with the assistance of a mortgage from a building society. Before it agrees to advance monies on a property, the building society will have the property surveyed. This does not mean that the purchaser should rely on this survey and not carry out his own survey. The building society is interested in the property only as

security for the mortgage. If the house is for sale at £25,000 and a
mortgage of £15,000 is requested, all the society is concerned with is
whether the house will be good security for £15,000.

**3. Claims for loss against a surveyor instructed by a building
society.** In the case of *Yianni* v. *Edwin Evans* (1981) a purchaser
successfully recovered damages from a surveyor who had missed
obvious structural defects when carrying out a valuation report for a
building society. The purchaser did not see this report or have his
own survey conducted. It was held that the surveyor did owe a duty
of care to the purchaser because he knew or ought to have known
that 90 per cent of mortgagors do not obtain an independent survey
and rely on the building society report. A warning by the building
society that an offer to advance monies did not constitute a warranty
that the purchase price was reasonable and that he should obtain his
own survey did not prove contributory negligence on the part of the
purchaser. For an example of a reasonable disclaimer by a building
society, see *Stevenson* v. *Nationwide B.S.* (1984).

Some building societies now offer to have a joint survey carried
out on behalf of itself and the purchaser or have a policy of disclosing
its report to the purchaser. In both cases the surveyor would owe a
duty of care to the purchaser.

Common law protection

4. Warranty of good work. A purchaser who is buying a house
which is in the course of construction has the benefit of a warranty of
good work and proper materials so that the house is fit for human
habitation (see *Jennings* v. *Taverner* (1955) and *Hancock* v. *B. W.
Brazier (Anerley)* (1966)). This protection does not extend to
subsequent purchasers nor to purchasers who buy houses after they
have been constructed.

5. Latent defects in buildings. This topic has been dealt with in a
number of cases in recent years. One problem, that has attracted
judicial attention, is when does time start "to run" in such cases
under the Limitation Acts? In *Pirelli General Cable Works Ltd* v.
Oscar Faber & Partners (1983) the House of Lords held that time

started to run when the material physical damage came into existence and not when the damage was or should have been discovered by a reasonable man. Thus it disapproved of the "discoverability" test in *Sparham-Souter* v. *Town & Country Development Ltd* (1976).

The Pirelli case concerned negligence by consultant engineers but the same principle will apply to negligent builders, engineers or local authorities. The duty is owed to the owners of the land as a class. (*See* Preface.)

6. Duty of local authority: the Dutton case. In 1972 the Court of Appeal in *Dutton* v. *Bognor Regis UDC* decided that the local authority had breached its statutory duty under the Public Health Act 1936 to examine the plans of the house properly and also its duty to inspect the foundations of the house to ensure that they complied with the local by-laws.

However in *Anns* v. *London Borough of Merton* (1977) it was held that a local authority was not under a duty to inspect the foundations but it did owe a duty of care when deciding whether to inspect foundations and if an inspection was carried out, failure to do so properly would give rise to an action for breach of statutory duty. The scope of the *Anns* decisions was narrowed by the House of Lords in *Peabody Foundation* v. *Sir L. Parkinson & Co.* (1984). A local authority did not owe a duty of care for economic loss suffered by building developers for the local authority's failure to ensure that building work complied with plans approved by them. The duty was owed to occupiers and members of the public to safeguard them from dangers to health and safety. Further, since the plaintiffs were directly responsible for failure to comply with plans, it would not be fair to impose a duty on the local authority. The *Peabody* case was applied in *Investors in Industry Commercial Properties Ltd* v. *South Bedfordshire District Council & Others* (1986).

Statutory protection

7. Defective Premises Act 1972. This Act imposes a duty to build properly. The duty is owed by a person taking on work for or in connection with the provision of a dwelling and is owed to a person ordering the dwelling and to every person who acquires an interest (legal or equitable) in the dwelling. The duty is to see that the construction work is carried out in a workmanlike or professional manner with proper materials so that the premises are fit for human habitation (s. 1).

It applies not only to builders but also to architects and other professional persons "taking on work for or in connection with the provision of dwellings". The Act came into force on 1st January 1974 and it may be enforced by subsequent purchasers.

8. Exclusion for approved schemes. The operation of s. 1 may be excluded if there is a scheme covering the property which is approved under s. 2 of the Act. In this situation the purchaser's rights in respect of defective premises are to be found in the scheme and *not* in the Act. The National House Builders Scheme (*see* below) run by the National House Builders Council (NHBC) is the only one approved under s. 2.

The National House Builders Scheme

9. Form of agreement under the scheme. The details of the cover given by the scheme are set out in the agreement which is signed by the individual builder and the purchaser of the house. This agreement was redrafted in 1975 and again in 1979. As there are some differences between the two versions, it is important to note which form of the agreement is sent to the purchaser. The 1979 agreement is for use in respect of houses registered with the Council after 18th April 1979.

10. Outline of the 1979 agreement. Builders who are registered with the Council (not all builders are as it is not compulsory), must offer to enter into the NHBC agreement with the purchaser(s) of dwelling houses.

The 1979 edition of the agreement states that the agreement is made by the first purchaser on behalf of himself and his successors in title. This is an attempt to resolve the difficulty of whether or not the agreement can be assigned to a subsequent purchaser. The NHBC rules have for some time contained a provision that the vendors of the property are prohibited from taking objection in proceedings or otherwise to the fact that the benefit of the agreement has not been assigned (i.e. expressly assigned) to the person making the claim. Subsequent purchasers appear to be protected as a result. It should be noted that it has been argued that the agreement comes within LPA 1925, s. 78 as one where the benefit of the agreement runs with the land and that therefore a subsequent purchaser would be able successfully to sue the builder even where there has been no express assignment to him.

11. Terms of the agreement. The agreement warrants that the house is or has been built in a workmanlike manner, that it is built of proper materials so that it is fit for human habitation and that it complies with the NHBC regulations, which include and extend the Building Regulations (the latter apply to all dwelling houses and are enforced by the local council).

12. The ten-year certificate. A house covered by the agreement will qualify for a ten-year certificate issued by the NHBC. During the first two years from the date of issue, the builder is liable to make good any defects due to non-compliance with NHBC regulations. The NHBC will satisfy any arbitration award or judgment if the vendor fails to do so. The first two years are called the initial guarantee period.

13. The structural guarantee period. The remaining eight years are referred to as the structural guarantee period. During this time the NHBC will reimburse the purchaser the cost of remedying major damage caused by any defect in the structure or by subsidence, settlement or heave, provided that there is no other insurance at the time of the claim to cover the cost. Major damage is defined by the agreement as "damage to the dwelling requiring complete or partial rebuilding or repair work". Examples of this are dry rot affecting the structure of the house, and cracks in foundations built on shrinking clay. Wet rot, a leaking gutter or defects in a porch or drive are not major defects.

14. Liability of the builder outside the two-year period. The agreement states that if any work undertaken by the vendor/builder in the initial guarantee period to remedy a defect caused by a breach of the NHBC requirements fails to remedy the defect or damage, the *vendor/builder* shall remain under a continuing liability to remedy such a defect or damage even after the expiration of the initial guarantee period.

For example, a certificate is issued in June 1979 and the purchaser informs the builder in writing in September 1979 that there are cracks in the foundations. The builder discovers that this is because the foundations are not of the correct depth. He simply cements over the cracks and says it is a result of settlement. In June 1981 the kitchen floor disappears because of faulty foundations. Even though the two-year period has expired, the builder, rather than the NHBC, is liable to make good the damage and remedy the defect.

Progress test 4

1. Is it worth while for a purchaser to employ a surveyor to report on the condition of the property, if he is buying the property with the aid of a building society mortgage? (**1, 2**)

2. A bought a house in the course of construction and two years later he sold it to B. What protection if any have A and B at common law regarding the structure of the house? (**4, 5**)

3. M bought a house which had been built seven years before she completed the sale. She has discovered cracks in the walls which are the result of faulty foundations. Who can she sue, if anybody? (**5, 6**)

4. What difference would it make to A and B in question (2) if the events took place after 31st December 1973? (**7**)

5. What is the only approved alternative to the rights given to the purchaser under the Defective Premises Act 1972? (**8**)

6. Describe the warranties contained in a National House Builders Scheme agreement. (**11**)

7. Under a ten-year certificate who is liable to repair minor defects to the property? (**12, 13**)

8. Under a ten-year certificate who is liable to remedy major defects to the property? (**12, 13**)

5
Formation of the contract

Form of the contract

1. **The contract.** As with any other contract, there must be an offer and an acceptance, an intention to create legal relations, and consideration must be present. A contract for the sale of land can be differentiated from other contracts by reason of:

(*a*) the requirements of LPA 1925, s. 40(1) (*see* **2**);

(*b*) the equitable doctrine of specific performance (*see* 15:**11–15**);

(*c*) the duty of the vendor to prove his title to the property (*see* 9:**1–3**).

2. **Requirements of LPA 1925, s. 40(1).** This subsection states that no action may be brought upon any contract for the "sale or other disposition of land or any interest in land, unless the agreement upon which such action is brought, or some memorandum or note thereof, is in writing, and signed by the party to be charged or by some other person thereunto by him lawfully authorised". These requirements are explained in detail in **3–16** below.

3. **"Sale or other disposition".** This includes a mortgage, disclaimer, release, assent, devise and bequest (LPA 1925, s. 205(1)(ii)).

4. **"Land or any interest in land".** Contracts for the sale of freehold land or for the granting and assigning of leases are clearly within s. 40. The following are some areas which are perhaps less clear.

(*a*) *Interests in land* covers easements and profits, as well as *fructus naturales*, i.e. crops which grow naturally on the land, such as timber and grass (unless the contract states that they are to be severed before or on sale). *Fructus industriales*, i.e. annual crops grown commercially such as potatoes and wheat, are not within the definition of "interests in land".

(*b*) *Fixtures*, i.e. those things which are attached to the land and so become part of it, are within s. 40.

(*c*) *Interests in the proceeds of a trust for sale* of land are also covered by this section (*Cooper* v. *Critchley* (1955)).

(*d*) *A contract to lease furnished rooms* can be contrasted with a contract to provide lodgings, i.e. where the lodger does not have the right of exclusive occupation of any particular room(s). The former contract must comply with s. 40, the latter is outside the scope of this section.

5. Legal cases relevant to s. 40.

(*a*) In *Steadman* v. *Steadman* (1973) it was held by the Court of Appeal that where there was a single contract but only one term of the contract related to the sale of land, s. 40 did apply to the whole contract. (This point was not dealt with in the House of Lords.)

(*b*) The case of *Daulia Ltd* v. *Four Millbank Nominees Ltd* (1978) concerned an agreement to enter into a written contract for the sale of land. The written contract, if entered into, would have been specifically enforceable and would therefore have created an equitable interest in land. It was held that LPA 1925, s. 40 would apply to the agreement to enter into such a contract.

The facts of the case were that the plaintiffs entered into an oral agreement with the defendants, whereby the defendants agreed to enter into a written contract for the sale of land to the plaintiffs, provided the plaintiffs attended at the defendants' offices with a draft contract in the terms already agreed and with a banker's draft for the amount of the deposit. The plaintiffs fulfilled the conditions but the defendants refused to enter into a written contract. The plaintiffs sought damages for breach of contract. The Court of Appeal agreed that there was breach of the oral contract. However, the contract came within s. 40. There was no written evidence of it and the plaintiffs' actions, rather than being acts of part performance, only suggested that the parties were about to enter into a contract. The appeal by the plaintiffs was dismissed.

The memorandum

6. "Some memorandum or note thereof". The contract does not need to be in writing. What is required is written evidence of it. If this is lacking, the contract is valid in all respects except that it is unenforceable by action. If a purchaser pays a deposit to the vendor under an oral contract and then refuses to complete, the vendor is entitled to forfeit the deposit. Should he be sued for its return, he can plead the oral contract as a defence (*Monnickendam* v. *Leanse* (1923)).

7. Existence of the memorandum. The memorandum does not have to be contemporaneous with the contract but it must be in existence before any action is brought on the contract (*Lucas* v. *Dixon* (1889)). It may even come into existence before the contract, as in *Reuss* v. *Picksley* (1886) where a written offer was sent which was orally accepted—the offer was the memorandum.

It does not matter that there was no intention that the document in question should form a memorandum within s. 40, for this is a question of evidence not intention. A note in an auctioneer's book, a letter to a solicitor and a receipt for a deposit have all been held to be sufficient memoranda. (*See* 22.)

8. Terms of the memorandum. To be a sufficient memorandum within s. 40 it must contain the following.

(*a*) *The names of the contracting parties* or a description of them so that they can be identified with reasonable certainty (*Potter* v. *Duffield* (1874)). To describe the vendor simply as "the vendor" will not suffice, but to describe him as "the owner" or "the proprietor" will be acceptable.

In *F. Goldsmith (Sicklesmere) Ltd* v. *Baxter* (1970) the plaintiff was described as Goldsmith Coaches (Sicklesmere) Ltd and it was held that although this was clearly an incorrect description of the plaintiff/vendor it did not give rise to any doubt that the plaintiff was the vendor.

Where an agent signs the memorandum, note should be taken of *Davies* v. *Sweet* (1962). In this case an agent signed a memorandum and there was nothing in the memorandum to show that he signed as an agent or who the principal was. Nevertheless the contract *was* enforceable directly against the principal.

(*b*) *The subject-matter—the property.* This also must be described in such a way that it can be identified with certainty. In *Plant* v. *Bourne* (1897) "twenty-four acres of land, freehold, at Totmonslow, in the parish of Draycott, in the County of Stafford", was a good description, once it had been established that the vendor had no other land there. Even "my house" would be sufficient if the vendor owned only one house. Ordinarily in domestic conveyancing the full postal address will suffice.

If no mention is made of the interest in the property being sold, it will be assumed to be an unencumbered freehold estate (*see Timmins* v. *Moreland Street Property Co. Ltd* (1958)).

(*c*) *The consideration.* The memorandum must state the consideration or the means through which it can be ascertained, e.g. "the purchase price is £2,500" or "the purchase price is the value of 10,000 shares in ICI as at 1st May 1980". By looking at the value of those shares as quoted on the Stock Exchange on the day mentioned the consideration can be ascertained.

(*d*) *Other material terms.* If there are any other material terms these must be reflected in the memorandum, e.g. if a date for possession has been agreed. Extrinsic evidence (i.e. external to the memorandum) cannot be given to vary or contradict the terms of a written contract but such evidence is admissible to show that the memorandum is incomplete through the omission of a material term, with the result that the memorandum cannot be pleaded in court. (*See Johnson* v. *Humphrey* (1946) for completion date omitted.) However, if the material term is exclusively for the benefit of the plaintiff, then the plaintiff can waive the term and enforce the contract without the term (*see Hawkins* v. *Price* (1947)).

If the omitted term, as in *Scott* v. *Bradley* (1971), is to the detriment of the plaintiff and he agrees to perform it, the court will enforce the contract. In this case the missing term was that the plaintiff would pay the legal costs of the vendor.

(e) *Material terms for leases.* Memoranda relating to leases must contain the date from which the lease is to run and the length of the lease (*see Harvey* v. *Pratt* (1965)), as well as the matters mentioned in (a)–(d)). The rent comes under (c).

9. "Signed by the party to be charged or by some other person thereunto by him lawfully authorised". LPA 1925, s. 40(1) states that only the defendant or his agent (*see* **13–16**) need have signed the memorandum. It is *not* necessary for the plaintiff to have signed it. If only one joint tenant has signed the memorandum then it cannot be enforced against both unless it can be proved that the one defendant/joint tenant who signed had authority to bind his co-tenant. If this authority is lacking, the signatory may be sued for breach of contract (*see Malhotra* v. *Choudhury* (1979)) or breach of warranty of authority.

"Signature" is given a wide interpretation and includes both initials and a signature by impressing a rubber stamp containing a facsimile of a signature on the memorandum. As to the position of the signature, in *Ogilvie* v. *Foljambe* (1817) it was held that so long as the name was inserted with the intention of giving effect to the document as a whole it did not matter where the signature appeared.

10. Joinder of documents. The situation may arise that, whereas there is no one document which is a sufficient memorandum, if two or more documents are read together they will constitute a memorandum. The documents can only be read together if the document signed by the party to be charged (the defendant) contains a reference, express or implied, to the other document or transaction. In *Griffiths* v. *Young* (1970) a letter signed by the vendor/defendant referred to a letter written by the purchaser/plaintiff such that the plaintiff was entitled to specific performance of the contract.

In the leading case of *Timmins* v. *Moreland Street Property Co. Ltd* (1958) the purchaser/defendant signed a cheque for the deposit, which was made payable to the vendor's solicitors. He received a receipt for the cheque signed by the vendor and containing the information required to be a sufficient memorandum. The vendor sued for the purchaser's breach of contract and sought to read the cheque (the document signed by the party to be charged) together with the receipt. This could not be done as there was no express or implied reference from the cheque to the receipt. If the purchaser had brought the action so that the court would have looked first at the receipt, that could have been read with the cheque.

If the document signed by the defendant refers to an oral agreement, parol evidence is admissible to identify any other document which refers to the agreement. The two documents when read together, if they contain all the material terms, constitute a memorandum in writing (*see Fauzi Elias* v. *George Sahely & Co.* (1983)).

11. The "side by side" rule. The *Timmins* case (*see* **10**) has cast some doubt on what is known as the "side by side" rule as defined in *Sheers* v. *Thimbleby & Sons* (1897). In the latter case several documents signed by the defendant when placed side by side could be seen to refer to the same transaction and could be read together to form a memorandum. In *Burgess* v. *Cox* (1951) the defendant had signed only one of the documents but when placed side by side they manifestly referred to the same transaction with the result that the contract was enforceable by the plaintiff. It is not clear to what extent this principle may be relied on today.

12. Absence of an effective memorandum. As already noted (*see* **6**) the lack of a sufficient memorandum does not invalidate the contract but renders it unenforceable by action. A contract may be enforced by action despite the lack of a memorandum in the following circumstances.

(*a*) If the defendant does not expressly plead the absence of a written memorandum to satisfy LPA 1925, s. 40. In this case the courts will enforce the oral contract.

(*b*) If it is the defendant's fraud which has prevented the execution of a memorandum, for equity will not allow a statute to be used as an instrument of fraud. This is given its most widespread application in an act of part performance by the plaintiff (*see* **17–21**) and on a sale by the court, e.g. in executing a trust for sale (LPA 1925, s. 40(2)).

Agents

13. Agent's authority. If an agent signs the memorandum, he must have authority to do so, either express, implied or ostensible. If an agent has authority to enter into a contract of sale, he automatically has authority to sign a memorandum of sale. It is more likely that the contract will have been concluded by the principal and that the agent's authority is restricted to signing the contract. When the agent signs the contract he must indicate clearly that he does so as an agent by adding words such as "X as agent for Y". The agent can be sure then that he will incur no personal liability on the contract.

Some examples of agents are discussed in **14–16** below.

14. Auctioneers. When the property is sold by auction, the auctioneer has implied authority to sign a memorandum of sale on behalf of the vendor and of the purchaser. This occurs, normally, in the auction room immediately after sale. In *Chaney* v. *Maclow* (1929) the auctioneer signed the memorandum in his office an hour and a half after the sale, and it was held that he had authority to do so. In *Bell* v. *Balls* (1897) the auctioneer signed a week after the sale and this was held to be ineffective as by that time the auctioneer's authority had lapsed. In both these cases the auctioneer was signing on behalf of the purchaser and in order to be effective the signing must take place within a reasonable time of the sale so that it can be said to be part of the sale transaction.

The auctioneer's authority to act for the vendor lasts for a longer period of time, namely throughout the time that he has instructions to sell the property.

Under the general principles of agency, an agent cannot delegate his authority. Therefore if the auctioneer's clerk signs the memorandum, this is usually ineffective (*see Bell* v. *Balls* (1897)).

15. Solicitors. A solicitor when instructed to act in the sale of a property has no implied authority to sign a memorandum of sale. He may be given express authority to do so.

Following the case of *North* v. *Loomes* (1919), instructing a solicitor to act in the sale of land appears to give him implied authority to sign a memorandum of sale of an already *negotiated* contract.

In *Horner* v. *Walker* (1923) a letter signed by the lessee's solicitor enclosing an engrossment (fair copy) of the lease formed an adequate memorandum of sale, despite the fact that this was, in all probability, not the intention of the solicitor when he signed the letter.

16. Estate agents. In *Wragg* v. *Lovett* (1948) it was said that an estate agent has no implied authority to sign a contract of sale on behalf of a vendor who has instructed him to sell his property. He may have been given express authority to do so, in which case his signature is effective. He does not have any implied authority to bind the purchaser, but again he can be given express authority by the purchaser (*see Davies* v. *Sweet* (1962)).

The doctrine of part performance

17. Introduction. LPA 1925, s. 40(2) states that "this section . . . does not affect the law relating to part performance".

In *Chaproniere* v. *Lambert* (1917) there were said to be four conditions which must be satisfied before the doctrine could operate. The conditions are discussed in **18–21** below.

18. Reference to and consistency with contract. The acts by the plaintiff taken together must refer to some contract concerning land and must be consistent with the contract alleged to exist. This was how the requirement was explained in the case of *Kingswood Estate Co. Ltd* v. *Anderson* (1963). (Before that case the test was somewhat stricter in that the acts of part performance had to refer to the contract alleged and to no other title.) In the *Kingswood* case a widow agreed to leave her rented home, giving up her statutory protected tenancy, and moved into alternative accommodation provided by her landlords, Kingswood Estate Co. Ltd. It was agreed that she should have a life tenancy of the new flat. Later the landlord served a notice to quit, saying that she had a weekly tenancy only. In court they argued that her occupation of the flat, while it gave rise to the idea that she had a contract of tenancy, was equally referable to any sort of tenancy, whether weekly, monthly or otherwise, and so could not be said to be referable to a life tenancy and to no other. The Court of Appeal held that it was sufficient that it was consistent with the contract alleged to exist.

Entering into possession of the defendant's property with his consent is one of the most unequivocal acts of part performance. This must be distinguished from remaining in possession.

In *Wakeham* v. *Mackenzie* (1968) it was held that the actions of the plaintiff in leaving her council flat, moving into a widower's home, taking care of him and the house without payment, and paying some part of the household food and fuel costs, did necessarily refer to some contract and were consistent with the contract alleged that the widower would leave her the house in his will.

This case can be contrasted with that of *Maddison* v. *Alderson* (1883) where a housekeeper was paid initially but stayed on as an unpaid housekeeper, because, she said, her employer agreed to leave her the house in his will. Her action was held to be equivocal and explainable on several grounds other than there being a contract between her and her employer.

In *Rawlinson* v. *Ames* (1925) the defendant agreed to take a lease of a flat from the plaintiff and asked that certain alterations be carried out, which the plaintiff did. The defendant from time to time supervised the alterations and then refused to take the lease, pleading s. 40(1). The plaintiff was granted a decree of specific performance, as the acts were sufficiently referable to and consistent with the alleged contract.

The payment of money is sometimes said not to be capable of being an act of part performance. This is not accurate: it is, of itself, an equivocal action, but if accompanied by other actions can satisfy the courts. In *Steadman* v. *Steadman* (1974) (*see also* 5) an oral agreement was made between husband and wife whereby the wife agreed to transfer her interest in the matrimonial home for £1,500 to the husband, to have a maintenance order in her favour discharged, to accept £100 in settlement of all arrears due under the order and to have the balance discharged. The magistrates' agreement to the order was obtained (in so far as this was relevant), the husband paid the £100 and his solicitors prepared and sent a transfer form to the wife for the conveyance of her interest to the husband. She refused to sign it and pleaded that the contract was unenforceable under

LPA 1925, s. 40(1). The House of Lords ordered specific performance of the contract, stating that the payment of the £100, the announcing of the agreement to the magistrates and the preparation and sending of the transfer form were sufficient acts of part performance.

19. The statute may not be used as an instrument of fraud. The acts of part performance must be of such a kind that it would be a fraud on the part of the defendant to take advantage of the contract not being in writing. The acts of part performance must have been carried out by the plaintiff who has been induced or simply allowed by the defendant to alter his position for the worse, relying on the oral contract (*see Rawlinson* v. *Ames* (1925) above).

20. The contract must be specifically enforceable. The equitable remedy of granting a decree of specific performance is not available for every breach of contract and although often granted in relation to the sale of land, where every piece of land is said to be unique and therefore damages cannot be an adequate remedy, it is still a discretionary remedy and not available as of right (*see* 15:**11–15**). The remedy could be refused despite the existence of acts of part performance if it would cause undue hardship to the defendant (*see Patel* v. *Ali* (1984)), or because of a misrepresentation or because the plaintiff has not fulfilled his contractual obligations.

21. Evidence of the contract. There must be proper evidence that a contract has been concluded between the parties rather than incomplete negotiations. The acts of part performance allow parol evidence (or written evidence) of the existence of the contract and the terms of the contract to be admitted by the court. If the evidence does not prove these matters, then the doctrine cannot be relied upon.

In *Daulia* v. *Four Millbank Nominees Ltd* (1978) (for facts *see* **5**(*a*)) it was said that the plaintiffs' acts in performing the conditions of the vendors' offer (i.e. by attending at the vendors' office with the contract and banker's draft for the deposit) did not point to there being a contract between the parties but to these actions being carried out in contemplation of making a contract. The vendors' refusal was a refusal to enter into a contract and not a breach of contract.

"Subject to contract" agreements and conditional contracts

22. "Subject to contract" agreements. The existence of a contract depends, *inter alia*, on an unqualified acceptance of the offer. If the phrase "subject to contract" is used (or possibly one like it) then the intention of the parties is that although an "offer" is made and "accepted", neither of them is to be contractually bound until a formal contract has been agreed by the parties, signed and exchanged. Unless and until this happens either party is entitled to withdraw from the agreement and the purchaser is entitled to recover any deposit which he may have paid (*see Chillingworth* v. *Esché* (1924)).

This principle has been reaffirmed in *Tiverton Estates Ltd* v. *Wearwell Ltd* (1975) after some doubt was cast on the effect of the phrase "subject to contract" in *Law* v. *Jones* (1973). The classic interpretation of "subject to contract" was reaffirmed in *Alpenstow Ltd & another* v. *Regalian Properties plc* [1985], although on its exceptional facts, the court held that there was a binding contract.

However, in *Daulia* v. *Four Millbank Nominees Ltd* (1978) it was said that the decision in *Law* v. *Jones* was to the effect that if a letter was sent which was stated to be "subject to contract", then such a letter could not form a memorandum within LPA 1925, s. 40 as there was no contract to be enforced. If a later oral contract was concluded, however, and it was sought to enforce that contract, then the "subject to contract" letter was capable of forming a sufficient memorandum, if it contained the necessary details (*see* 8).

23. Waiver of the phrase "subject to contract". *Griffiths* v. *Young* (1970) illustrates this point. A solicitor's letter was sent subject to contract. A telephone call was made in which an unconditional offer was made and accepted. Although neither party appeared to realise it at the time, the court held that the telephone call had waived the phrase "subject to contract" and an oral binding contract came into force immediately which was evidence by a memorandum consisting of the previous correspondence between the parties, even though they thought the correspondence was subject to contract.

In *Cohen* v. *Nessdale* (1982) it was stated that the parties could remove the qualification "subject to contract" only if they both expressly agreed that it should be expunged or if such an agreement was to be necessarily implied.

24. Provisional agreements. In *Branca* v. *Cobarro* (1947) an agreement between the parties was expressed to be "a provisional agreement until a fully legalised agreement drawn up by a solicitor and embodying all the conditions herewith stated is signed". It is a question of construction as to what the effect of such an agreement is. In that case it was held to be a binding contract even though no formal contract was ever signed. Particular attention was paid to the word "until" as indicating an immediate, binding contract which was to remain binding unless and until it was superseded by a later agreement, which did not happen.

25. Conditional contracts. An agreement which is subject to contract and which is not a binding contract should be distinguished from a contract which is subject to a condition. In *Smith and Olley* v. *Townsend* (1949) the contract was subject to preliminary enquiries and searches and the purchaser's solicitor being satisfied on these matters. Care must be taken for in *Lee-Parker* v. *Izzet* (*No. 2*) (1972) the contract was subject to the purchaser obtaining a satisfactory mortgage, which was held to be void for uncertainty and avoided the contract. The effect of any condition is a question of construction in any particular case.

If a condition is inserted that the contract is conditional upon planning permission being obtained, a date should be inserted within which the permission must be obtained. If no time is specified the permission must be obtained within a reasonable time from the date of the contract.

If the condition is not fulfilled, the contract does not become binding and both parties are free from the agreement and the purchaser is entitled to recover any deposit he has paid.

A condition solely for the benefit of one party may be waived by him. In *Batten* v. *White* (1960) the vendor repudiated the contract at a time when the purchaser was still trying to obtain planning permission and before he was entitled to do so. The purchaser was allowed to waive the condition and sue for specific performance.

This can be contrasted with the decision in *West (Richard) & Partners (Inverness) Ltd* v. *Dick* (1969) where the contract was conditional upon planning permission being granted. Conditional planning permission was obtained, and the question was therefore "was the condition in the contract satisfied"? The answer was yes, unless the conditions attached to the permission were so burdensome as to prevent it being permission in any real sense of the word.

In *Aberfoyle Plantations* v. *Cheng* (1960) the contract was conditional upon the vendor obtaining new leases for part of the property comprised in the sale. In addition, the contract fixed a date for completion. The fixing of the date for completion meant that the condition had to be fulfilled by that date even though the condition was not stated to be of the essence of the contract. (*See* 6:35–38) for situations where time is of the essence in a contract.)

Procedures

26. Preparation of the contract. Where it is agreed by the parties that a written contract of sale shall be drawn up, as where the agreement is "subject to contract", this is done by the vendor's solicitor. After all, only he has access to the title deeds and other documents from which the contract is drafted. The draft contract is prepared in two parts and both parts are sent to the purchaser's solicitor for him to approve or amend as the case may be. The terms of the contract (*see* 6) are a matter for negotiation at this stage and both parties must agree to any proposed amendments. The final draft of the contract may be very different from that originally proposed, or it may be approved by the purchaser's solicitor as first drafted.

After agreement has been reached the purchaser's solicitor retains one copy of the draft contract and returns the other to the vendor's solicitor.

The next stage is for the vendor's solicitor to engross the contract in two parts. (In practice if there are no or few amendments to the draft contract, this may be used as the engrossment.) Both parts are sent to the purchaser's solicitor. He checks that the contract is correct and sends one part back to the vendor's solicitor.

27. Signing the contract. The vendor's solicitor obtains his client's signature to the contract, having satisfied himself that the vendor can convey what he said he can.

The purchaser's solicitor does the same, having checked the replies to his local searches and enquiries, made sure that a mortgage offer has been made and accepted, if appropriate, and examined again the replies to his enquiries before contract. (The enquiries and answers to these will have determined the final form of the contract.)

28. Exchange of contracts. Neither party is bound until the contracts have been exchanged. At one time exchange would take place by the purchaser's solicitor attending at the vendor's solicitor's office and actually handing over his part and receiving in exchange the vendor's part. A completion date would be agreed by the parties and a receipt given for any deposit paid by the purchaser. This is called "face to face" exchange and rarely occurs today. Exchange by post is now the normal method of exchange (*see* **29**).

29. Exchange by post. After signing the contract the purchaser's part of the contract together with a cheque for the deposit is posted to the vendor's solicitor. The purchaser's solicitor may insert the agreed completion date or leave it to be settled by the rules of common law or by the National Conditions of Sale or the Law Society's Conditions of Sale, where the contract is made in accordance with these standard forms of conditions (*see* 6: **14–28**). On receiving the purchaser's part of the contract, the vendor will date the contract and send off his part in exchange.

In *Harrison* v. *Battye* (1975) the plaintiff agreed to buy the defendant's house, subject to contract. A contract was agreed and the plaintiff's solicitor sent off his part of the contract to the vendor. The vendor's solicitor, by mistake, sent off to the plaintiff's solicitor the plaintiff's part of the contract, not the vendor's. It was held that there was no contract between purchaser and vendor because the two parts were not in the same terms (the deposit stated was different in each part). The effect of the clerical error in returning the wrong part was left open. (*Domb* v. *Isoz* (1979) suggested that trivial clerical slips may be overlooked.)

A similar point occurred in *Eccles* v. *Bryant & Pollack* (1948). The vendor's solicitor wrote to say that he was ready to exchange contracts. The purchaser posted his part but the vendor, who had signed his part of the contract, changed his mind and his part was never despatched. The purchaser was refused a decree of specific performance as there was no contract of which specific performance could be granted. The court did not decide when the contract comes into existence where the post is used. Is it when the last part is posted, which seems most likely, or when the last part is received by the purchaser? The Law Society's Conditions of Sale state that it is when the vendor posts his part or, if a document exchange is used, when deposited at the exchange (LS 10). The National Conditions of Sale say nothing on this matter.

30. Exchange by telephone. In *Domb & Another* v. *Isoz* (1979) CA it was said that a solicitor, acting for either a vendor or a purchaser of a house, who holds his client's signed part of the contract has ostensible authority to effect exchange of contracts. The exchange can be affected in any manner recognised by the law as amounting to exchange. Today a telephone call between the solicitors for the vendor and the purchaser purporting to exchange contracts would create a binding contract (*see* LS 10). Where a solicitor had ostensible authority to deliver that document to another solicitor, if he gives an undertaking to hold that document to the order of that other solicitor, this binding undertaking constitutes constructive delivery of the document. It was recommended by the Court of Appeal that this method should be carried out only by partners in the firm and that both parties should agree and record identical attendance notes. *See* Law Society's formulae for exchanging contracts by telephone/telex (Appendix 6).

31. One contractual document. As mentioned in **26**, the contract is usually engrossed in two parts, but there is nothing preventing it being engrossed in one part. The major difference is that in this case the contract comes into existence after both parties have signed it.

There is no exchange and indeed it is difficult to see how there could be.

In *Smith* v. *Mansi* (1963) both parties signed the contract and the vendor took it to their solicitor saying that he did not wish to be bound until he had rearranged the completion date with the purchaser. By mistake, the solicitor inserted the original completion date. A decree of specific performance was granted against the vendor. Exchange was unnecessary and the vendor could not unilaterally prevent it coming into force unless he had mentioned this to the purchaser before or at the time of signing. He could not later change his mind.

32. Registration of a contract of sale. A contract to convey or create a legal estate is registrable as a Class C(IV) land charge, an estate contract (*see* 12:**6**). If not registered it will be void against a purchaser of the legal estate for money or money's worth. Despite this, it is not normal practice to register such a charge unless there is likely to be a long delay between the date of the contract coming into force and completion or the purchaser has reason to suspect that the vendor may try to sell the same property to someone else. Nevertheless, failure to register the charge is prima facie negligence (*see Midland Bank Trust Co. Ltd* v. *Hett, Stubbs & Kemp* (1978)).

Progress test 5

1. What must a memorandum for the sale of land contain so that the contract is enforceable? (**8, 9**)

2. What is the "side by side" rule? (**11**)

3. To what extent can an auctioneer validly sign a memorandum on behalf of the vendor or purchaser? (**14**)

4. What conditions must be satisfied before the doctrine of part performance can operate? (**18–21**)

5. Can the payment of money ever be an act of part performance? (**18**)

6. Is an agreement which is "subject to contract" really a contract? (**22**)

7. X enters into a contract to sell his land to Y, which is subject to Y obtaining planning permission for domestic dwellings. How long

does X have to wait before he can assume that he is now free to sell his land to Z?   (**25**)

8. What is meant by exchange of contracts?   (**28–30**)

9. Is it usual to register a contract for the sale of land as a Class C(IV) land charge?   (**32**)

6
Contents of the contract

Introduction

1. Three parts of the contract. A written contract can be said to be in three parts:

(a) the particulars of sale (*see* **3–9**);

(b) the conditions of sale (*see* **10–28**);

(c) a memorandum to satisfy LPA 1925, s. 40 (*see* **5:6–12**).

2. Difference between the particulars and the conditions of sale. In *Torrance* v. *Bolton* (1872) the difference between the particulars and the conditions was said to be that the proper office of the particulars is to describe the subject-matter of the contract, and that of the conditions to state the terms on which it is sold. It should be clear that the word "condition" is used here in a different sense from when referring to a conditional contract (*see* **5:25**).

The particulars of sale

3. Description of the property. The division between the particulars and the conditions of sale is a matter of tradition and convenience, but it is usual for the particulars to deal with the land by giving a physical description of it and also of the interest which is being sold, e.g. "ALL THAT freehold property together with the dwelling house and outbuildings erected thereon situate and known as 10 Green Road, Newford in the County of Blackshire for an estate in fee simple free from encumbrances".

4. Physical description. Great care must be taken to describe the property accurately. In practice the description used in the conveyance to the vendor is often inserted into the contract. Even so, the solicitor should check that no change has been made to the property which makes that description inaccurate, e.g. if part of the property has been sold off. A substantial difference between the area of the property as stated in the contract and what it actually is can give the purchaser a right to rescind the contract (*see Watson* v. *Burton* (1956)). Lesser inaccuracies may lead to the vendor being obliged to accept a reduction in the purchase price. If measurements are part of the description, these must be accurate.

A plan may be attached to the contract as part of the description, and again this must be correct. In the case of *Re Lindsay and Forder's Contract* (1895) the plan was stated to be for identification purposes only but it was held that the purchaser was entitled to the whole of the land coloured in on the plan, notwithstanding that the plan was inaccurate. In *Lloyd* v. *Stanbury* (1971) it was pointed out that where the vendor is selling only part of his property, the need for a plan is that much greater so that both parties understand exactly what is the subject-matter of the sale.

If the description refers to a plan in a previous conveyance, it is not good practice simply to refer to it. A copy of that plan should be attached to the contract, after it has been ascertained that the plan is still accurate.

The scale of the plan must be appropriate to the transaction. The use of small-scale ordnance survey plans when selling plots of land or where a house is being split into flats is inadequate.

5. Description of the estate or interest. The description of the land includes not only the physical description but also that of the estate or interest in the land which is being sold. Unless anything to the contrary appears in the particulars, it is assumed that a fee simple in possession free from encumbrances is the subject of the sale (*see Timmins* v. *Moreland Street Property Co. Ltd* (1958)). The purchaser would be entitled to sue for breach of contract where the vendor is not able to convey or at his direction have conveyed the interest he has contracted to sell (*see* 15:**4–10**). A qualification to this rule is that if, at the date of making the contract, the purchaser knew that the vendor could only convey a lesser interest, despite what was said in the contract, he is entitled only to the lesser interest (*Timmins* v. *Moreland Street Property Co. Ltd* (1958)).

6. Freehold or leasehold? The particulars in a contract should disclose whether the property is freehold or leasehold.

7. Types of leasehold. If the property is leasehold, then it must be stated whether the vendor is assigning a head lease (i.e. where the lessor is owner of the freehold) or an underlease (i.e. where the lessor is a tenant of the owner of the freehold). In *Re Russ and Brown's Contract* (1934) it was incorrectly stated in the contract that the vendor was selling the unexpired residue of a lease, whereas it was an underlease. The purchaser was entitled to rescind the contract. In the later case of *Becker* v. *Partridge* (1966) a sub-underlease was described as an underlease, but *obiter* it was said that this was unlikely to justify rescission.

The importance of knowing if it is a lease, underlease or sub-underlease is that in the case of an underlease or sub-underlease, the purchaser will be aware that there is a possibility that his interest may be forfeited as a result of the actions or omissions of the head lessee (where he is buying an underlease) or the head lessee and the underlessee (where he is buying a sub-underlease), who are persons over whom he has no control.

When an underlease is being sold, the purchaser is entitled to be informed if the head lease contains property other than that which he is purchasing under the underlease, for the actions of the head lessee and of the other underlessees could give rise to a situation which might lead to forfeiture of the head lease and thus automatically bring to an end all underleases and sub-underleases. It will be remembered that LPA 1925, s. 146 (as amended by the Law of Property (Amendment) Act 1926, s. 1) gives the sub-tenant a right to apply to the court for relief against the forfeiture of his landlord's lease.

In *Becker* v. *Partridge* (1966) the purchaser of an underlease which related to a flat comprising part of a house was not told that the head lease covered the whole house, but in the circumstances the court felt that it was obvious that the head lease would do so and the purchaser's action failed.

A purchaser of an underlease should if possible inspect the headlease to see if it contains any provision rendering it liable for forfeiture, e.g.

(*i*) reservation of a ground rent higher than the total of the underlease ground rents;

(*ii*) provision for forfeiture on bankruptcy or liquidation;

(*iii*) other onerous covenants. (*See* further 19:**7–9**.)

8. Benefits passing with the land. Rights, such as easements, and restrictive covenants which are for the benefit of the land forming the subject-matter of the sale should be expressly referred to in the particulars of sale. When the property is conveyed to the purchaser, LPA 1925, s. 62 will come into operation, so that subject to any contrary intention expressed in the conveyance, all privileges, rights, easements and advantages appertaining or reputed to appertain to the land will pass to the purchaser. It should be noted that s. 62 does not apply to the contract, only to the conveyance.

9. Burdens affecting the land. The vendor is bound to disclose all latent defects affecting his title of which he knows. This includes any encumbrances affecting the property, e.g. restrictive covenants, easements and leases. These may be disclosed in the particulars or in the special conditions (*see* **13**). Where they are disclosed is of no particular significance, so long as they are disclosed. It is sometimes found that existing liabilities are referred to in the particulars and new liabilities in the special conditions—this is a matter of practice only. (*See also* 8:**14–18** for non-disclosure.)

The conditions of sale

10. Types of conditions. There are two types of conditions, special and general. Special conditions are those which are particular to an individual contract, e.g. when a certain day is fixed for completion (*see* **13**). The general conditions are those which have general application. The two sets of general conditions in common use are the National Conditions of Sale and the Law Society's Conditions of Sale (*see* Appendix 2 and **14–28**).

11. Open contracts. There is no obligation for either of the standard sets of conditions to be incorporated into the contract. A contract for the sale of land which expressly provides for nothing beyond describing the parties, the property and the price is an "open" contract. A contract may be totally open or partially open, because a particular point is not dealt with by the contract. Where the contract is open, the issue in question is settled by reference to the general law on that point.

12. Statutory conditions. A totally open contract is unlikely to occur today, as if the contract is by correspondence the Lord Chancellor's Statutory Form of Conditions of Sale (SR&O 1925, No. 779) will apply. There is no statutory definition of correspondence. In *Stearn* v. *Twitchell* (1985) it was held by the Court of Appeal that a single letter evidencing an oral contract was not correspondence and that a contract by correspondence does not include acceptance by letter of an oral offer to buy or sell land. If the parties exchange letters by post in the form of an offer and an unqualified acceptance, this is clearly a contract by correspondence. The scope of the statutory conditions is not as wide as that of either the Law Society's Conditions of Sale or the National Conditions of Sale so that a contract which is subject to the statutory conditions is open on those matters not covered by them.

13. Special conditions of sale. In so far as there is any difference between the terms of a general condition and those of a special condition, the special condition applies. Special conditions commonly deal with the following.

(*a*) The rate of interest, i.e. that which is payable by the purchaser on the balance of the purchase monies when completion does not take place on the agreed completion date. If not dealt with by the special conditions, then the matter is governed by the general conditions (*see* **25**).

(*b*) The date for completion.

(*c*) The root of title.

(*d*) The capacity in which the vendor is selling, e.g. trustees for sale, beneficial owner.

(e) Any encumbrance affecting the property, e.g. leases.

(f) The commencement of title.

Comparisons between the general conditions of sale in the Law Society's Conditions of Sale and the National Conditions of Sale

14. Introduction. The general conditions of these two standard forms are reproduced in Appendix 6. The differences and similarities are discussed in **15–38** below.

15. Vacant possession. In both cases, this will be dealt with by special conditions. If a contract does not deal with the matter and does not disclose any tenancies subject to which the property is sold, a term that the property is sold with vacant possession is implied into the contract (*Cook* v. *Taylor* (1942)) (*see also* 15:9(f)).

> NOTE: The Matrimonial Homes Act 1983, s. 4 implies into a contract for the sale of a dwelling house, which has been the matrimonial home of the vendor and his/her spouse and which is not held by them as co-trustees, that if the property is sold with vacant possession the vendor will, before completion, have discharged any Class F charge registered by the spouse to protect his/her rights of occupation. This applies even if the vendor did not know that such a charge has been registered (*see Watts* v. *Waller* (1972)) and also if the charge is registered after the contract has been made (*see Wroth* v. *Tyler* (1973)). Section 4 can be excluded by a special condition in the contract. The normal method of discharge is for the vendor to send the purchaser an application for discharge signed by the *spouse* or authorised solicitor (*see Holmes* v. *Kennard & Son* (1984)).

16. Evidence of tenancies. Both sets of conditions oblige the vendor to supply the purchaser with abstracts or copies of any lease or agreement in writing (LS 6 and NC 18(1)). The LS conditions also cover oral agreements while the NC merely state that no objection can be taken if there is no agreement in writing (NC 18(1)). The vendor should always supply details of all tenancies.

17. The deposit. A deposit is only payable if there is a general or special condition to this effect; at common law, such a term will not be implied into a contract (*see Doe d. Gray* v. *Stanion* (1836)). Under NC 2(1) and LS 9 a deposit of 10 per cent of the purchase is to be paid to the vendor's solicitors to be held by them as stakeholders. LS 9 provides that this "normal" deposit may be varied by agreement in writing to accept a lesser sum. NC 2(1) allows variation through the insertion of a special condition conflicting with the general condition. When calculating the purchase price under NC, chattels are included whereas they are excluded under LS.

A stakeholder is the agent of both parties so that the vendor may not apply the deposit towards his purchase without the purchaser's consent. It may be agreed between the parties that the deposit is to be held by the vendor's solicitors as agent for the vendor. As it is then under the sole control of the vendor, he may use it towards his purchase without reference to the purchaser.

If the contract is silent about the capacity in which the vendor's solicitors hold the deposit, they hold it as agents for the vendor.

18. Non-payment of the deposit. At common law, a deposit should be in cash or by banker's draft at the date of the contract (normally the date of exchange of contracts). Often a cheque drawn upon a solicitor's bank account is acceptable but one drawn on the purchaser's bank account is not.

In NC 3 no specific mention is made and NC 2(2) simply refers to a "cheque taken for the deposit" when dealing with the question of non-payment so that presumably a cheque from any source is acceptable.

Non-payment of the deposit due to the dishonouring of a cheque is now specifically mentioned in both sets of decisions. In *Myton Ltd* v. *Schwab-Morris* (1974) it was held that the dishonour of a cheque for the payment of a deposit was either a failure to fulfil a condition precedent or the breach of a fundamental term entitling the vendor to rescind the contract if he wishes. In *Millichamp* v. *Jones* (1982) the correct view was stated that, generally, payment of a deposit was a term of the contract and that failure to pay it would be a fundamental breach entitling the vendor to rescind the contract (this view was followed in *Damon Cia Naviera S.A.* v. *Hapay Lloyd International S.A.* (1983)).

Where any cheque has been dishonoured, the vendor has seven working days within which to notify the purchaser that he is repudiating the contract for breach (LS). The NC state that the vendor has the right to elect to treat the contract as discharged by breach or to enforce payment of the deposit by suing on the cheque (2(2)). The wording in NC 2(2) reflects the fact that it was drafted before *Millichamp* v. *Jones*.

19. Insurance. (*See* in this context the provisions of LPA 1925, s. 47, referred to in 7:7.)

Under LS 11(4) and NC 21(1) the vendor is under no duty to continue to insure the property once he has contracted to sell it, unless (LS) the property is leasehold and he is obliged to insure it under the lease or (NC) he is under an obligation to a third party to insure it, e.g. a lessor or mortgagor.

The LS condition excludes the operation of LPA 1925, s. 47 but provides that where a vendor has maintained a policy and the property is damaged or insured after contract and before completion, the purchaser (who should have also insured the property) will pay an abated sum on completion, the amount of the abatement being the sum the vendor has or should have received under his own insurance policy. If the vendor has not maintained a policy, the common law position will apply, and the purchaser will be required to pay the full purchase price on completion. If he has taken out his own insurance policy, he will claim under that.

NC 21(3) preserves the right of the purchaser under the LPA to have his interest noted on a policy if the vendor has kept one going, though he may be required to pay a part of the premium. But note that the vendor is still under no obligation to maintain a policy. The only safe position for a purchaser is to take out his own insurance after contracts have been exchanged.

20. Abstract of title. The vendor must supply an abstract for unregistered land or the documents mentioned in LRA 1925, s. 110 for registered land upon exchange of contracts under LS 12, whereas

whereas NC 9 states that it must be delivered not later than eleven working days after the date of the contract.

LS 12 requires that office copies of entries are to be supplied for registered land: photocopies of land or charge certificates will not do. Where an abstract is supplied, this must be a marked abstract, i.e. one that is certified as having been compared with the original documents of title. All relevant documents of title must be supplied at the vendor's expense.

Neither office copies or a marked abstract are necessary under NC 9.

21. Requisitions. Different time limits are specified within which requisitions must be raised. LS 15 states that the purchaser must deliver them within six working days of receipt of the abstract or, if this is received before the date of the contract, within six working days of the date of the contract. The vendor must reply within four working days of the delivery of the requisitions and the purchaser has four working days within which to raise observations on these replies. NC 9 requires the purchaser to deliver his requisitions within eleven working days after the delivery of the abstract. No time limit is specified within which the vendor must reply, therefore he must reply within a reasonable time. The purchaser must raise his objections to the vendor's replies within six working days after the delivery of the replies.

Time is of the essence for the purchaser when raising requisitions under both sets of conditions. If he is out of time, the vendor need not reply unless the matter goes to the root of the contract (*see* 11:**6**).

LS 5(5) and NC 9(5) refer to an imperfect or defective abstract: for those parts of the abstract that are delivered promptly, time runs in the normal way; for those parts that are delivered later, the time within which requisitions are to be raised starts from the date of actual delivery.

It should be noted that in an attempt to deal with the results of *Williams & Glyn's Bank* v. *Boland* (1979) NC 9(2) states that the purchaser may raise requisitions concerning persons who are or who may be in occupation so that the purchaser may be satisfied that he will not be prejudiced by such interests. This would not appear to give the purchaser any more protection than he already enjoys.

22. Easements, rights and liabilities. LS 5 and NC 14 both acknowledge the duty of the vendor to disclose all easements and other liabilities of which he is aware and which are not apparent upon inspection. In addition, LS 5 also demands that the vendor discloses liabilities of which he ought to know unless the purchaser is or should as a prudent purchaser have known or discovered its existence at the date of the contract.

23. Identity and boundaries. NC 13 requires the purchaser to accept the property as identified in the abstracted documents and provides that, if required, a statutory declaration showing twelve years' title shall be produced at the purchaser's expense. LS 13 is similar: it states that the vendor shall produce such evidence as may reasonably identify the property but that if the evidence does not do so, the vendor at his expense must produce a statutory declaration showing the relevant facts, the form to be agreed by the purchaser. Both conditions state that the vendor shall not be required to define boundaries, fences, ditches, hedges or walls or separately to identify parts of the property held under different titles. NC 13(3) states that the purchaser shall be deemed to buy with full notice in all respects of the actual state and condition of the property and, except where it is to be constructed or converted by the vendor, to take the property as it is.

24. Occupation before completion. Both sets of conditions allow the purchaser to enter into occupation of the premises before completion with the consent of the vendor. The purchaser does so as a licensee. He must pay or indemnify the vendor for all outgoings and pay interest on the balance at the prescribed rate (*see* 25). In addition, he must insure the property, keep it in a good state of repair and is entitled to receive any rents and profits. The purchaser's licence to occupy terminates either on the contractual date for completion or upon five working days' notice being given by the vendor (LS 19(5)) and on discharge or rescission of the contract or upon seven working days' notice or longer given by the vendor (NC 8(2)). Note that if a domestic purchaser is given access to do repairs, neither NC 8 or LS 18 applies.

25. Interest on purchase money. The rate of interest may be dealt with in either the special or general conditions. LS 1(1) and NC 1(4) state that the rate is that prescribed from time to time under the Land Compensation Act 1961, s. 32. It is payable from the contractual date of completion to the actual date of completion.

26. Date of completion. Under an open contract, completion takes place within a reasonable time of contracts being exchanged. What is reasonable is a question of fact bearing in mind the matters of investigating title and preparation of the necessary conveyancing documents (*see Johnson* v. *Humphrey* (1946)). NC 5 provides that completion shall take place on the day mentioned in the contract or, if no such date is specified, on the twenty-sixth working day after the date of the contract or the delivery of the abstract, whichever is the later. LS 21 similarly provides that if there is no date specifically fixed for completion it is to take place twenty-five working days from the date of the contract.

27. Completion. This subject receives detailed consideration in the general conditions. Payment at completion should be by one of the following methods:

(*a*) legal tender;
(*b*) banker's draft—a common method;
(*c*) an unconditional authority to release any deposit held by a stakeholder (and payment of the balance by one of the other methods);
(*d*) any other method agreed with the vendor.

The National Conditions also mention:

(*e*) telegraphic transfer to a particular bank or branch for the credit of a specified account (if the vendor agrees or requests it) (the vendor will bear in mind whether or not the banks concerned guarantee same day transfers); and
(*f*) a cheque guaranteed by a bank designated under the Building Societies Act 1962.

At common law, completion takes place wherever the vendor wishes and payment is to be made by legal tender. Under the general conditions of sale, completion takes place at the vendor's solicitor's offices or (LS 21(1)) upon giving five working days' notice at the offices of his mortgagees or their solicitors' offices or (NC) at such offices as the vendor may reasonably require, which will include those mentioned in LS 21(1). Completion may be either the common law (face-to-face) method with the purchaser or his agent attending at the offices of the vendor's solicitors etc. or by the increasingly common postal method of exchange. For the Law Society Code of Completion by Post (*see* LS 21(3) (Appendix 6)) provides that if the monies are not received by 2.30 p.m. on the day fixed for completion, the purchaser will be deemed to have completed on the next working day. NC 5(5) imposes a time limit of 2.15 p.m. only if the date fixed for completion is a Friday. Where time limits are imposed, it is to provide the vendor with the opportunity to bank the monies the same day. Individual contracts may impose their own time limits by means of a special condition.

28. Other matters. Also dealt with in LS and NC conditions and discussed in more detail elsewhere are:

- (*a*) notices to complete (*see* **30, 31**);
- (*b*) failure to complete (*see* **29**);
- (*c*) leaseholds (*see* Chap. 19);
- (*d*) misdescription (*see* Chap. 8).

Failure to complete

29. Time not of the essence. Unless there is a special condition to that effect or it is a necessary implication (*see* **35**), time is not of the essence in connection with the date for completion. Therefore, failure to complete by the contractual date does not entitle the innocent party to treat the contract as repudiated by the delay. However, it is still a breach of contract for which the innocent party may recover damages (*see Raineri* v. *Miles & Anor* (1979)). Under LS 22 the innocent party may elect within five working days to receive compensation on the outstanding monies at the prescribed rate as liquidated damages. NC 7 states that a purchaser in default shall pay interest at the prescribed rate. Presumably the vendor may sue for any damages suffered above that sum.

30. Effect of notice to complete. If an aggrieved party wishes to terminate the contract he must ensure that a reasonable time has elapsed between the date for completion and the date on which he serves a notice on the other party indicating that unless they complete by the date stated in the notice, he will treat the contract as discharged. The notice has the effect of making time of the essence, so that failure to complete by the specified date is a repudiatory breach.

31. Service of notice under an open contract. In this situation, the aggrieved party has two problems. (1) How long after the delay in completion does he have to wait before serving the notice? (2) Having served the notice, how long should the period of notice be? The notice can be served only after the delay in completing is such that it would be unfair to require the innocent party to wait any longer. The period of notice within which completion should take place must be a reasonable time, taking into account the steps necessary to complete the transactions (*see Crawford* v. *Toogood* (1879)). In *Nott* v. *Riccard* (1856) a notice of fourteen days was upheld whereas in *Pegg* v. *Wisden* (1852) six weeks' notice was insufficient.

32. Position under LS and NC conditions. The obvious difficulties confronting the innocent party under an open contract do not occur under either of the standard form contracts. NC 22 and LS 23 provide that notice making time of the essence may be served at any time after the date fixed for completion by either party to the contract. They further state that the notice makes time of the essence so that failure to complete within sixteen (NC) or fifteen (LS) working days, excluding the day of service, brings the contract to an end.

33. Position of the party serving the notice. The party serving the notice, at the date of serving it, must be ready, willing and able to complete the transaction or the notice is ineffective.

In *De Medina* v. *Norman* (1842) "ready and willing" was defined as having "not only the disposition but also the capacity to act". Therefore, a vendor, who has not proved a good title to the land, may not seek by this means to force a doubtful title on his purchaser (*Horton* v. *Kurzke* (1971)).

34. Notice should not be served after a decree of specific performance has been granted. (*See Singh* v. *Nazear* (1979).)

35. When time is of the essence. As already stated, prima facie, time is not of the essence with regard to a completion date. By inserting a special condition to this effect, the parties may make time of the essence. In this situation, failure to complete by that date is automatically a repudiatory breach of contract with all the results that flow from it. Another situation where time is automatically of the essence is where it is a necessary implication from the circumstances of the contract. Lord Romilly MR in *Hudson* v. *Temple* (1860) said that the implication was present "where the property sold is required for some immediate purpose, such as trade or manufacture, or where the property is of a determinable character, as an estate for life". This implication cannot stand where the express provisions of the contract are at variance with it. Thus in *Ellis* v. *Lawrence* (1969) premises were being sold in which an ironmongery business was conducted. Following *Hudson* v. *Temple* the contract was such that time was of the essence. However, the conditions of sale provided that notice had to be served to make time of the essence. This contractual provision overrode the presumption.

36. Failure to complete by the stated date when time is of the essence. The innocent party can elect to rescind the contract. NC 22 entitles a vendor to forfeit any deposit paid by the defaulting purchaser and, if the vendor resells within one year of the date fixed for completion incurring a loss, the purchaser must make good that loss. Credit is given for the forfeited deposit. Under LS 23(5) a vendor must notify the purchaser within one month of the re-sale either that he is claiming liquidated damages as outlined in LS 23(5) (similar to NC 22) or that he intends to sue under the common law rules for unliquidated damages as in *Raineri* v. *Miles* (1981). The latter would enable the vendor to sue not only for his loss but also for losses incurred by third parties for which the vendor is being sued.

A purchaser in similar circumstances is entitled under LS 23(4) to a return of any deposit paid upon serving notice to this effect. This is without prejudice to any other claim for damages he may have.

37. Return of a contractually forfeited deposit. LPA 1925, s. 49(2), where a court refuses to grant a decree of specific performance or in any action for the return of the deposit the court may, if it thinks fit, order the repayment of any deposit. In *Universal Corporation* v. *Five Ways Properties Ltd* (1979) the purchaser paid a 10 per cent deposit of £85,000. He was unable to complete even after a completion notice had been served on him under the 1976 NC. Upon expiration of the notice, the vendor rescinded the contract and forfeited the deposit. Subsequently the purchaser sought the return of the deposit. The Court of Appeal held that the purchaser's writ should not be struck out as failing to disclose a cause of action for s. 49(2) was not restricted to cases where a decree of specific performance could be granted. It gave the court an unqualified discretion to order return of a deposit, where this was the fairest course between the parties. The discretion was to be exercised judicially and all pertinent matters, including the terms of the contract, had to be taken into account. The National Conditions provided that the deposit may be forfeited "unless the court otherwise directs". This was thought by two members of the Court of Appeal to demonstrate that the vendor did not have an absolute right to forfeit the deposit. (There is no such phrase in the LS conditions.) The purchaser's claim was remitted for a hearing at first instance.

NOTE: For remedies following breach of contract *see* Chap. 15.

38. Waiver and extension of time. The non-defaulting party may decide to treat the contract as still in existence despite the fundamental breach of contract. This waiver may be express, e.g. a letter to this effect, or it can be implied from any action after the relevant date from which it can be inferred that the contract is still extant. For example, in *Hipwell* v. *Knight* (1835) accepting an abstract of title and raising requisitions on it was evidence that the contract was not regarded as being at an end. Having waived his rights, it is possible for the innocent party to make time of the essence again by serving a fresh notice to complete.

Rather than expressly waiving his rights, an extension of time may be granted to the defaulting party. Here the new completion date is one when time is of the essence. There is no need to serve a fresh completion notice as such. Compare this with LS 23(8) which allows either party to serve a second completion notice, where a first completion notice has been served and the time for completion has been extended *either* by agreement *or* by implication.

Pre-contract deposits paid to estate agents

39. Capacity of estate agents. Pre-contract deposits are those sometimes paid by a purchaser before exchange of contracts as an earnest of good faith. In the majority of cases, these are paid to estate agents. In the past this had given rise to a debate about the capacity in which such persons received the deposit, usually when the agent disappears with such monies or becomes bankrupt having improperly used the money for his own purposes.

In *Burt* v. *Claude Cousins & Co. Ltd* (1971) and *Barrington* v. *Lee* (1972) it was held that the estate agent received the pre-contract deposit as agent for the vendor. Therefore, if the agent defaulted in his duties, his principal (the vendor) was liable to re-imburse the purchaser.

The House of Lords in *Sorrell* v. *Finch* (1976) overruled the previous cases. They pointed out that before contracts are exchanged, the purchaser is entitled to demand the return of his money. The vendor cannot prevent this so that the estate agent cannot be said to be his agent at that time. It follows that if the estate agent acts improperly at any time before exchange, the purchaser's only action is against the estate agent personally. Once a contract of sale is concluded, the question of the pre-contract deposit is to be governed by the terms of the contract. It would seem that the vendor would be liable if the estate agent defaults at this stage. Now he is the vendor's agent.

40. The Estate Agents Act 1979. Since May 1982, pre-contract deposits paid to estate agents are to be held on trust for the person who is entitled to call for it to be paid over to him. Trust monies cannot be seized by the estate agent's trustee-in-bankruptcy. They are held on trust for the appropriate beneficiary.

Progress test 6

1. Define the functions of the particulars of sale and the conditions of sale. (**2**)

2. What estate or interest is assumed to be the subject of the sale unless something to the contrary appears in the particulars of sale? (**5**)

3. What is an "open" contract? (**11**)

4. Can a purchaser assume that the property is sold with vacant possession? (**15**)

5. When is the Matrimonial Homes Act 1983, s. 4 relevant to a contract for the sale of land? (**15**)

6. What difference does it make if the vendor's solicitor holds the deposit as a stakeholder rather than as the agent of the vendor? (**17**)

7. When must the abstract of title be delivered by the vendor to the purchaser? (**20**)

8. What easements and other liabilities must the vendor disclose to the purchaser? (**22**)

9. Is the vendor required to identify exactly the boundaries of the property? (**23**)

10. What is meant by "time being of the essence" and when is this the case? (**29–35**)

11. Are damages available to a purchaser if a vendor fails to complete on the agreed date? (**29, 36**)

7

The position of the parties after exchange of contracts

The vendor

1. The vendor as constructive trustee. Once a valid contract has been concluded between the parties, the vendor holds the property as a trustee for the purchaser who is the beneficial owner. This trusteeship differs from an ordinary trusteeship in several ways:

(a) the vendor is entitled to the rents and profits from the land until the date fixed for completion and must pay the outgoings (e.g. rates, ground rent where applicable) until then;

(b) he has a right to retain possession of the property until the purchase monies or the balance of the purchase monies are paid;

(c) he has a lien over the property in respect of any unpaid part of the purchase monies.

2. The vendor's lien. The lien arises independently of any agreement between the parties and may be enforced by the vendor against the purchaser and his personal representatives after his death. If the vendor parts with the title deeds without receiving all unpaid purchase monies, the lien can be registered as a Class C(III) land charge (*see* 12:6). If registered the lien is enforceable against subsequent purchasers unless they obtain a legal estate for value without actual or constructive notice of the lien. In *Rice* v. *Rice* (1853) the vendor conveyed land to the purchaser without receiving the purchase monies even though the deed contained a receipt stating that they had been paid. In those particular circumstances

Death of vendor. The personal representatives of a deceased vendor are entitled to and can be compelled to convey the property to the purchaser. The purchase monies will be paid to the personal representatives who hold the monies in accordance with the terms of the will if there is one, or in accordance with rules relating to intestacy if there is no will.

Death of purchaser. The personal representatives of a deceased purchaser are also entitled to complete the purchase and can be compelled to do so by the vendor. The beneficiary who is entitled to the property takes it subject to a charge for the unpaid purchase monies (*Re Birmingham, Savage* v. *Stannard* (1959)) but this does not affect the vendor's right to obtain payment from the personal representatives.

Progress test 7

1. The vendor is a constructive trustee of the property. What are the three ways in which this trusteeship differs from the normal trusteeship? **(1)**
2. Why would a vendor register his lien as a Class C(III) land charge? **(2)**
3. How long does the vendor's duty to take reasonable care of the property last? **(3)**
4. How does the purchaser's lien arise? **(6)**
5. When may the purchaser claim the insurance monies payable under a contract of insurance maintained by the vendor? **(7)**
6. What is the effect of the vendor becomes bankrupt after contracts have been exchanged? **(8)**
7. What is the effect if the purchaser becomes bankrupt in similar circumstances? **(9)**
8. What is the effect of the vendor dying after exchange of contracts and before completion? **(10)**
9. What is the effect of the purchaser dying in the same circumstances? **(11)**

the vendor's lien was postponed in favour of an equitable mortgagee who took without notice of the lien.

The lien will be lost automatically if the vendor agrees to take a mortgage of the property in lieu of the outstanding monies and the lien is subject to the limitation period.

Exceptionally the contract of sale itself may prevent any lien arising as being contrary to the nature of the contract, e.g. *Re Brentwood Brick and Coal Co. Ltd* (1876) where the intention of the parties was that the purchaser should resell or mortgage the property and pay off the vendor from the proceeds. If a lien were to arise this would prevent or impede a resale or mortgage and so frustrate the intention of the parties. Similarly a power of resale in the contract of sale will prevent the vendor's lien arising for the same reason (*see Re Birmingham, Savage* v. *Stannard* (1959)). Prima facie, by subrogation, a third-party lender is entitled to the vendor's lien unless this is inconsistent with the contract of sale or would be unjust (*Boodle Hatfield* v. *British Films Ltd* (1985)).

3. The duty to take reasonable care. The vendor is bound to take reasonable care of the property. In *Foster* v. *Deacon* (1818) it was said that this extended to keeping even the garden in good order. If he culpably lets the property fall into disrepair or in any other way fails to prevent loss or damage to the property where reasonable care would have prevented this, he is liable to the purchaser (e.g. *Clarke* v. *Ramuz* (1891)—land damaged by trespasser removing large quantities of soil; *Mohamed Haji Abdullah* v. *Ghela Manet Shah* (1959)—the vendor let the property which created a tenancy protected by statute). The duty lasts as long as the vendor remains in possession, even where this may be delayed as a result of the purchaser failing to complete on the agreed date.

4. Interest. When the time fixed for completion has passed and if the delay is the purchaser's fault, the vendor can charge interest on the balance of the purchase monies. It is sometimes stated in the contract of sale that instead of charging interest the vendor may retain the rents and profits from the land (*see also* 6:25).

The purchaser

5. The purchaser as beneficial owner. After the exchange of contracts, as the purchaser is beneficially entitled to the property, he is entitled to any increase in the value of the land between contract and conveyance (not to the rents and profits, *see* 1) and will have to bear any loss or damage sustained during that period, subject to a right to sue the vendor for damage resulting from breach of his duty of care (*see* 3).

In *Hillingdon Estates Co. Ltd* v. *Stonefield Estates* (1952) it was held that the purchaser would have to complete the sale, despite the fact that a compulsory purchase order had been made, the notice to treat (*see* 23:19) having been served after contracts were exchanged.

6. The purchaser's lien. The purchaser has a right of lien over the property, similar to the vendor's, in respect of any part of the purchase price which he pays before completion, such as the deposit. This right of lien has been likened to the vendor executing a mortgage of the property to the purchaser for the monies which the purchaser has paid to the vendor.

This lien (like the vendor's lien) can be enforced by a court order for the sale of the property, the lien being discharged out of the proceeds of sale.

7. Insuring the property. LPA 1925, s. 47 provides that if, after the date of the contract, monies become payable under any policy of insurance maintained by the vendor in respect of loss or damage to the property, on completion the purchaser will be able to claim the monies from the vendor. This section applies only:

(*a*) if there is no contrary stipulation in the contract of sale (there usually is);

(*b*) the consent of the insurers has been obtained; and

(*c*) the purchaser has paid the proportionate part of the insurance premium from the date of contract.

In practice the purchaser, rather than rely on s. 47, should arrange his own insurance on the property after exchange of contracts (*see also* 6:19).

Bankruptcy and death

8. Bankruptcy of the vendor. The normal princi apply so that the trustee-in-bankruptcy stands i vendor and therefore can compel the purchaser to If a date has been fixed for completion and time is the contract (which is not normally the case), sho commit an act of bankruptcy, the purchaser can resci and recover his deposit if on the completion date ther in-bankruptcy able to complete the sale.

The trustee-in-bankruptcy is obliged to complete purchaser tenders the purchase monies or the balance of completion day (*Pearce* v. *Bastable's Trustee* (1901)).

Should the trustee be unwilling to continue with the can disclaim an onerous contract. However, when he take property from the vendor, he takes it subject to the pu equitable interest in the land (*see* 5). As a result the only wa effectively disclaim the contract is by disclaiming any intere land and so effectively giving it to the purchaser, witho purchaser having to pay the outstanding monies.

9. Bankruptcy of purchaser. When a purchaser is declared bankr all his property vests in his trustee-in-bankruptcy. This trustee c compel the vendor to complete the transaction by paying th outstanding monies on the day fixed for completion.

If the vendor wishes to go ahead with the sale and the trustee is the reluctant party, the trustee has the right to disclaim onerous contracts. It must be borne in mind that in those circumstances the vendor is entitled to keep any deposit that has been paid to him (*see ex. p. Barrell* (1875)).

Where the vendor knows that the purchaser has committed an act of bankruptcy but has not been formally declared bankrupt, he should not complete the contract as it will not be valid or binding on a trustee-in-bankruptcy appointed under a petition for bankruptcy presented within three months of the act of bankruptcy. In appropriate circumstances, the vendor may present a petition for the bankruptcy of the purchaser.

8

Misdescription, misrepresentation and non-disclosure

Misdescription

1. Definition. It will be recalled that the function of the particulars of sale in the contract is to describe the property being sold (*see* 6:3–9), and this description must be correct. To be a misdescription there must be a misstatement of fact.

In *Watson* v. *Burton* (1957) it was said that words such as "valuable", "extensive" and "suitable for development" when used to describe property were typical auctioneer's "puff" and were not to be regarded as part of the contract. In this case, the contract stated that the area of the property was 3,920 square yards, but the actual area was 2,360 square yards, so there was an actionable misdescription. In *Brewer* v. *Brown* (1884) the property was said to be enclosed by a rustic wall with a tradesmen's side entrance. The wall was not part of the property being sold and the tradesmen's entrance was used not as of right but on sufferance. Again, there was an actionable misdescription.

2. Examples of misdescriptions. The following are some further examples of misdescription.

(*a*) Describing leasehold land as freehold land (*Re Russ and Brown's Contract* (1934)).

(*b*) Calling an underlease a lease (*Re Thompson and Cottrell's Contract* (1943)). In *Becker* v. *Partridge* (1966) it was held in the circumstances that to describe a sub-underlease as an underlease was not an actionable misdescription.

(*c*) In the case of *Ridley* v. *Oster* (1939) four freehold houses were said to be freehold decontrolled properties, but in one house two rooms were let on tenancies protected by the Rent Act so that it was not accurate to say the properties were decontrolled and thus it was a misdescription.

(*d*) A description can be inaccurate because it leaves out something, e.g. in *Re Brine and Davies's Contract* (1935), the land was said to be registered which implied that the title to the land was absolute, whereas it was only a possessory title. To be an accurate description the land should have been said to be registered with a possessory title. In *Re Englefield Holdings and Sinclair's Contract* (1962) the property was sold subject to a protected tenancy the rent of which was correctly stated as at the date of the contract to sell but it was not mentioned that a certificate of disrepair had been served which reduced the rent until the specified repairs had been carried out. Cf. *Mustafa* v. *Baptist Union Corporation Ltd* (1983)—a technically accurate description may be a misdescription if it would mislead an ordinary reasonable person, e.g. by detailing the accommodation but not mentioning a room—the house excluded from the sale.

Remedies for misdescription

3. Material misdescription. If the misdescription is substantial or material, the purchaser is entitled to rescind the contract. In *Flight* v. *Booth* (1834) it was stated that to be material the misdescription must affect the subject-matter of the contract so that it may reasonably be supposed that, but for such misdescription, the purchaser might never have entered into the contract at all. Whether the misdescription is material is a question of fact to be decided in the light of the individual circumstances of each case.

The above comments equally apply where the misdescription is an inaccurately drawn plan or map.

4. Immaterial misdescription. Where the misdescription is immaterial (and assuming that it is not also a misrepresentation, *see* **8**), the purchaser has no right to rescind the contract and in the absence of fraud he must complete the contract but subject to an abatement of the purchase price if the misdescription affects the value of the property (*see Jacobs* v. *Revell* (1900)). This procedure is justified on the basis that where the misdescription is immaterial, although the purchaser is not getting exactly what he contracted for, he is getting substantially what he expected.

The purchaser should claim this compensation before completion takes place because if a conveyance is taken by the purchaser without making this claim he is deemed to waive it (*Joliffe* v. *Baker* (1883)) unless the purchaser could not have discovered the truth before completion (*Clayton* v. *Leech* (1889)).

5. The right of election. Instead of rescinding the contract in the case of material misdescription, the purchaser may elect to go on with the transaction subject to a reduction in the purchase price for the inaccuracy.

The right to compensation may be barred (as mentioned in **4**) if the purchaser does not make his claim before completion. In addition, if the misdescription cannot be quantified in monetary terms (*Rudd* v. *Lascelles* (1900)—property subject to an undisclosed restrictive covenant) it will be lost, as in the case where a purchaser knew of the inaccuracy at the date of the contract.

If the misdescription is embodied in the conveyance, however, the purchaser may have an action against the vendor for breach of the implied covenants of title (*Re Wallis and Barnard's Contract* (1899), and *see* Chap. 14).

Where compensation is payable it is assessed by the method appropriate to the case in hand, which could be by actuarial calculation or by an enquiry (*see Aspinalls to Powell and Schulefield* (1889)).

6. Misdescription in purchaser's favour. The vendor has no right to rescind the contract where the misdescription is in the purchaser's favour as where the contract gives the purchaser a greater area of land than he bargained for. Neither can the vendor compel the purchaser to pay an increased purchase price. In *Lloyd* v. *Stanbury* (1971), Brightman J said that "it lay entirely within the power of the (vendors) to define with precision what land they wished to retain and what land they wished to sell. If they failed to do that accurately in the contract they have only themselves to blame".

In cases where the misdescription is substantial the courts can refuse an application by the purchaser for a decree of specific performance on the grounds of hardship to the vendor, thus leaving the purchaser with his claim for damages for breach of contract (*see* *Lloyd* v. *Stanbury* (1971)).

7. Conditions of sale and misdescription. If a clause is inserted into the contract which purports to deprive the purchaser of his right to rescind the contract or to claim compensation because of a misdescription that clause will not prevent the purchaser from resisting an application for specific performance by the vendor where the misdescription is material. However, such a clause will be effective in denying the purchaser a reduction in the purchase price if he wishes to complete the purchase. In a situation where the vendor is seeking to compel the completion of the contract against the wishes of the purchaser then such a condition will not prevent the court ordering a reduction in the purchase price.

LS 7 (*see* Appendix 2) provides that no error, omission or misstatement in the contract or in any plan or statement made in the course of negotiations shall annul the sale, but either party is entitled to compensation if the misdescription materially affects the property. The clause also states that the vendor cannot compel the purchaser to accept or the purchaser to compel the vendor to convey with or without compensation property which differs substantially from that which was contracted to be sold, if this would prejudice the purchaser or vendor respectively. Neither does it affect the right of the purchaser to rescind the contract for a material misdescription where compensation cannot be assessed. Immaterial misdescription will not give rise to a claim for damages.

In *Walker* v. *Boyle* (1982) the court considered the effect of NC 17 (old edition) which is similar to LS 7 above. In this case the purchaser was entitled to rescind a contract because of an innocent misrepresentation made by the vendor, when the true facts were within his knowledge and the purchaser could reasonably have refused to exchange contracts if he had known about the boundary dispute.

The vendor was not entitled to reply on NC 17 in those circumstances and even if he could NC 17 did not satisfy the test of reasonableness in s. 11 of the Unfair Contract Terms Act which applied, as it was an exclusion clause within s. 3 of the Misrepresentation Act 1967.

NC 17 has been redrawn following this decision. It states that no error, misstatement or omission in any preliminary answer shall annul the sale or give rise to compensation unless it materially affects the property, in which case compensation will be paid. However, these provisions do not apply if the error or omission is made recklessly or fraudulently or if it would prevent the purchaser from getting substantially what he contracted to buy.

Misrepresentation

8. Definition. Misrepresentation is an untrue statement of fact made by one party or his agent which induces the other party to enter into the contract. An opinion and a statement of intention must be distinguished from a statement of fact. In *Bissett* v. *Wilkinson* (1927) the vendor was selling a farm which he had not used for sheep rearing and said that it would take 2,000 sheep which turned out to be untrue. It was held that this was a statement of opinion and not a misrepresentation. An opinion must be honestly and actually held by the representor or it will constitute a statement of fact not of opinion. In *Smith* v. *Land & House Property Corporation* (1884) it was said that a tenant who was in arrears with his rent could not honestly be said to be a desirable tenant and this was therefore a misrepresentation.

The misrepresentation must have been one reason (though not the only one) why the innocent party entered into the contract. The innocent party must also have relied on this statement. In *Attwood* v. *Small* (1838) the respondents failed in their action even though there had been a misrepresentation about the capacity of a mine, because the respondents had obtained a report from their own surveyor (which was also inaccurate) and were assumed to have relied on this, to the exclusion of the appellants' misrepresentation.

The effect of an actionable misrepresentation is to make the contract voidable, *not* void.

There are three types of misrepresentation:

(*a*) fraudulent misrepresentation;
(*b*) negligent misrepresentation;
(*c*) innocent misrepresentation.

These are discussed in detail in **9–12** below.

9. Fraudulent misrepresentation. Fraudulent misrepresentation has been defined as a false statement made knowingly or without belief in its truth, or recklessly, careless whether it be true or false (*Derry* v. *Peek* (1889)). The innocent party may sue for damages in the tort of deceit and rescind the contract before or after completion.

10. Negligent misrepresentation. Here although there is no fraud, the representor cannot prove that he had reasonable grounds to believe and did so believe in the truth of the statement up to the time that the contract was made (Misrepresentation Act 1967, s. 2). The remedies available are rescission of the contract or damages.

11. The rule in *Hedley Byrne & Co.* v. *Heller & Partners*. It should be remembered that the innocent victim of a negligent misrepresentation may be able to obtain damages under the principle laid down in the case of *Hedley Byrne & Co.* v. *Heller & Partners* (1964), where it can be shown that:

(*a*) the representor owed a duty of care to the representee, arising from a special relationship, i.e. where the representor had some special skill or knowledge and knew or reasonably should have known that the representee would rely on that statement;

(*b*) the representation was a breach of that duty; and

(*c*) as a result of that breach, loss has been suffered by the representee.

In *Esso Petroleum* v. *Mardon* (1976) the court held that statements made in pre-contractual negotiations, where there was a special relationship, came within the *Hedley Byrne* principle. In this case the estimate of petrol sales was negligent. (The facts occurred before the Misrepresentation Act 1967 came into force.)

Despite the passing of the Misrepresentation Act, this remedy is still important because it covers statements of intent and opinions which are excluded by the Act, as well as statements by third parties.

In a situation where it is possible to sue under the Act and under the tortious rule, it should be noted that s. 2(1) of the Act places the onus of disproving negligence on the defendant, whereas in *Hedley Byrne* v. *Heller* the plaintiff had to prove a special relationship and negligence.

12. Innocent misrepresentation. Where the misrepresentation is made neither fraudulently nor negligently but is still an untrue statement, it is an innocent misrepresentation. The importance of this distinction is that the only remedy available is rescission. If the right to rescind has been lost, even through no fault of the plaintiff, he is left without a remedy. Where rescission is available, under the Misrepresentation Act 1967, s. 2(2) the courts may award damages instead of rescission. (For misrepresentation and the rule in *Bain* v. *Fothergill, see* 15:**8**.)

13. Exclusion clauses. The Unfair Contract Terms Act 1977, s. 8 has amended the Misrepresentation Act 1967, s. 3. The amended section is as follows:

"3. If a contract contains a term which would exclude or restrict

(*a*) any liability to which a party to a contract may be subject by reason of any misrepresentation made by him before the contract was made, or

(*b*) any remedy available to another party to the contract by reason of such a misrepresentation

then the term shall be of no effect except in so far as it satisfies the requirements of reasonableness as stated in s. 11(1) of the Unfair Contract Terms Act 1977 and it is for those claiming that the term satisfies the requirement to show that it does."

Section 11(1) of the Unfair Contract Terms Act states:

"In relation to a contract term the requirement of reasonableness for the purposes of s. 3 of the Misrepresentation Act 1967 is that the term shall have been a fair and reasonable one to be included having regard to the circumstances which were, or ought reasonably to have been, known or in the contemplation of the parties when the contract was made."

NOTE: The Unfair Contract Terms Act 1977 came into force on 1st February 1978 and only applies to contracts made on or after that date. It should be remembered that ss. 2–4 of the Act dealing with exclusion clauses purporting to restrict or exclude liability for death, personal injury and other loss or damage due to negligence *do not apply* to contracts relating to the creation or transfer of an interest in land or to the termination of such an interest, whether by extinction, merger, surrender, forfeiture or otherwise (1st Schedule to the Act). However, while not applying to contracts for the sale of land, the sections will apply to other contracts that the purchaser enters into, e.g. employing his own surveyor, searches with the local authority, etc.

It will be noted that *Overbrooke Estates Ltd* v. *Glencombe Properties Ltd* (1974) held that s. 3 of the 1967 Act does not apply to a term restricting an agent's authority to make any representation.

Non-disclosure

14. Obligation on vendor to disclose latent defects. Non-disclosure arises when there is a duty to disclose which is not fulfilled. Generally in the law of contract the principle is that of *caveat emptor*, "let the buyer beware". In other words it is up to the purchaser to make sure that what he is buying is worth the money he is paying for it. This principle is modified in contracts for the sale of land to the extent that the vendor is obliged to disclose any latent defects in his title. These are matters affecting the vendor's title which would not be discoverable by the purchaser if he inspected the property with reasonable care, e.g. restrictive covenants.

15. Patent defects. Patent defects do not have to be disclosed as they are apparent on inspection, so that even if the purchaser fails to inspect the property he is deemed to have constructive notice if a reasonably careful inspection would have disclosed them.

In *Yandle & Sons* v. *Sutton* (1922) it was said that the purchaser takes the property subject to those defects which are patent to the eye, including those defects which are a necessary consequence of something which is patent to the eye.

Rights of way can be patent defects, as in *Bowles* v. *Round* (1800), but the mere existence of a path or track across the land is not sufficient, for it may be just a path used by the vendor or may indicate a private rather than a public right of way.

In *Re Leyland and Taylor's Contract* (1900) a notice to carry out private street works was held to be a patent defect and therefore did not have to be disclosed, because an inspection of the property would have shown that such a notice was likely to be served at any time. A party wall notice in *Carlish* v. *Salt* (1906) was held to be a defect in title which was latent.

Where there is a representation in the contract as to a patent defect, the purchaser is entitled to rely on the vendor's representation even if it conflicts with the evidence available from an inspection of the land. In *Dykes* v. *Blake* (1838) a plan of the land did not disclose a right of way over the land, which was apparent upon inspection. The purchaser was able to show that there was an actionable misrepresentation.

16. Occupiers other than the vendor. If the vendor is not in occupation of the land, the purchaser takes it subject to rights of those in occupation, e.g. tenants, as the reasonable purchaser would have inspected the property and enquired of them what their interests were. Occupation by a tenant does not give notice of the lessor's rights (*see Hunt* v. *Luck* (1902)).

Following the decision in *Caunce* v. *Caunce* (1969) it was said that if the vendor is in occupation, the purchaser is not affected with notice of the equitable interests of any person who may be resident there and whose occupation is consistent with the title offered by the vendor. Therefore, the mortgagee did not have notice of the wife's equitable interest in the property simply because she was residing there at the date of the mortgage, the mortgage being in the husband's name alone.

In the later case of *Hodgson* v. *Marks* (1971) it was doubted if the purchaser was entitled to refrain from enquiring about the rights of other occupiers simply because the vendor was in possession and the title offered was consistent with occupation by others, although it was accepted that this was the case where the occupier was the spouse of the vendor.

These principles were reconsidered by the House of Lords in *Williams & Glyn's Bank Ltd* v. *Boland* (1980) and *Williams & Glyn's Bank Ltd* v. *Brown* (1980). The facts were similar and the appeals consolidated. In each case the husband was sole registered proprietor, the wife having an equitable interest by reason of a contribution towards the purchase price. Subsequently the husband charged the property to the bank, without informing the wife. The wife had not taken any steps to protect her equitable interest by registration of a restriction, caution or notice. The bank, aware that the wife was in occupation, failed to enquire if she had any interest in the house. It failed in its claim for possession against the wife. It was stated that lenders (and by analogy purchasers) should realise that many wives have equitable interests in the matrimonial home and it should have made enquiries.

This case (and *Hodgson* v. *Marks*) concerned registered land and held that the wife had an overriding interest within LRA 1925, s. 70(i) *(g)*—the rights of every person in actual occupation bind all who subsequently obtain interests in the land. *Caunce* v. *Caunce* (1969) was severely criticised but not overruled as it concerned unregistered land.

The authority of *Caunce* v. *Caunce* (1960) is now doubtful, but two subsequent Court of Appeal decisions in *Midland Bank Ltd* v. *Farmpride Hatcheries* (1981) and *Bristol & West Building Society* v. *Henning* (1985) have not clarified the position. In the first a managing director, with a right to occupy a company house, arranged a mortgage of company land including the house. It was held that the bank was not bound by his occupation rights under an undisclosed service agreement either because the bank had constructive notice but the managing director was estopped by his non-disclosure or that the bank had no notice as a reasonable mortgagee/purchaser would not have made enquiries about the occupation of the managing director. The facts of this case are somewhat unusual but the second case deals with a common set of facts. The house was vested in a man's name alone and bought with the help of a building society mortgage in his name alone. The woman maintained that she had an equitable interest in the property and resisted a claim for possession. The Court of Appeal decided that if she had an interest it arose under a trust based on the imputed intention of the parties and that the intention must have contemplated that her interest was subject to that of the society for without the society's charge the house could not have been bought at all. Therefore the building society's claim for possession succeeded.

It is submitted that even if the Court of Appeal appears to have attempted to confine Boland to subsequent and not contemporaneous mortgages, this should be treated with extreme caution until the House of Lords reviews the position.

17. Latent defects in title which do not have to be disclosed. Latent defects which have ceased to be enforceable do not have to be disclosed. For example, in *Wilkes* v. *Spooner* (1911) the vendor was not obliged to reveal a restrictive covenant as he was a bona fide purchaser for value without notice of it, and as it was not enforceable against him, neither would it be enforceable against a purchaser from him. In *Hepworth* v. *Pickles* (1900) a restrictive covenant had been breached for the past twenty years. It was held to have been waived or released as the breach had been quite open and no disclosure was necessary.

18. Physical defects in the land. The *caveat emptor* rule has the effect that the vendor is not required to disclose physical defects in the land, whether these are latent or patent defects. (This will not prevent a misrepresentation about the quality of the land being actionable, if all the other necessary conditions are fulfilled, *see* **8**.)

In *Hill* v. *Harris* (1965) the Court of Appeal approved the statement of Devlin J (as he then was) in *Edler* v. *Auerbach* (1950) that it is the purchaser's concern to satisfy himself that the premises are fit for the purposes for which he wants them, whether the fitness depends on the state of their structure or the state of the law and any other relevant circumstances. (In this context it should be noted that the purchaser must ascertain that the present use of the property is one authorised by the Town and Country Planning Acts—*see Mitchell* v. *Beacon Estates (Finsbury Park) Ltd* (1949).)

However, the vendor may not rely on the principle of non-disclosure where the effect of non-disclosure is to negative a statement in the contract about the physical quality of the land, as in *Re Puckett and Smith's Contract* (1902) where the land was described as suitable for building purposes and later the purchaser discovered an underground culvert which meant that the land could not be used for building purposes. The purchaser was entitled to relief.

A defect in the physical quality of the land may also be a defect in title and if it is a latent defect must be revealed to the purchaser (*see*, for example, *Re Belcham and Gawley's Contract* (1930)).

Progress test 8

1. What remedies are available for misdescription? (**3–7**)

2. Can the vendor rescind the contract where the misdescription is in the purchaser's favour? (**6**)

3. What is a misrepresentation? (**8**)

4. Define fraudulent misrepresentation. (**9**)

5. What is negligent misrepresentation? (**10**)

6. What conditions must be satisfied before a victim of a negligent misrepresentation can also sue under the principle laid down in the case of *Hedley Byrne & Co.* v. *Heller & Partners* (1964)? (**11**)

7. Are rights of way patent or latent defects? (**15**)

8. Does the vendor have to disclose physical defects in the land? (**18**)

9

The abstract of title

Function and nature of the abstract

1. The duty of the vendor to prove his title. The vendor is under an obligation to prove that he does own the estate or interest in the land which he has contracted to sell or that he can compel the transfer of that interest to the purchaser. In other words the vendor must show a good title to the land. The problems of deducing title in particular circumstances are discussed in Chap. 10. Deducing title in leasehold transactions is discussed in Chap. 19.

2. Power to compel transfer. It is not sufficient to show that someone else *can* convey the estate or interest, even if that person is willing to do so. *See Re Bryant and Barningham's Contract* (1890): trustees contracted to sell land, but they had no power to do so; the tenant for life under the settlement, who was empowered to convey it, offered to do so. The purchaser refused this offer and the court turned down an application for a decree of specific performance as the tenant for life could not be compelled to transfer the land, and to force the purchaser to carry on with the contract would have the effect of creating a new contract between the purchaser and the tenant for life.

In *Re Baker and Selmon's Contract* (1907) the beneficiaries of a trust had agreed that the trustee should sell the land and he could in pursuance of that agreement compel them to sell, so that the purchaser was not entitled to object to any lack of title on the part of the vendor/trustee.

The case of *Elliott* v. *Pierson* (1948) demonstrates that the same principle can apply to a company. Here the vendor contracted to sell land which was vested in a company in which he had a substantial controlling interest. Through the use of his voting rights the vendor would be able to force the company to convey the land to the purchaser, so no objection could be taken to his title. In a situation where the vendor does not have a controlling shareholding, the objection would be sustainable.

3. What is a good title? In the recent case of *MEPC Ltd* v. *Christian-Edwards and Others* (1979) the House of Lords considered what constituted a good title. The purchasers claimed that the vendors had not shown a good title to the property in accordance with the contract. Their objection to the title was based on the fact that in 1912 the vendors/trustees had agreed to sell the property to M. A deed in 1930 recited that the purchase to M had not been completed and by the consent of all interested parties the performance of it had been suspended. M died in 1942. Documents executed between 1930 and 1942 contained no further reference to the contract.

Although there was no clear evidence of the abandonment of the contract, the court felt that it had been abandoned and that no representative of M could, at the time of the contract of sale to the purchasers (1973), have established a case for specific performance against them. Concluding that, on the facts, *it was beyond reasonable doubt* that the purchasers were not at risk of the encumbrance being successfully asserted against them, the court decided that it should declare in favour of a good title shown by the vendors.

4. Vendor's duty to deliver proper abstract. The abstract is an epitome of the various documents and events which together demonstrate that the vendor has a good title to the land. The vendor must, at his own expense, produce and deliver a proper abstract of title to the purchaser, unless there is an agreement to the contrary. The vendor is not excused from this obligation simply because some of the title deeds are not in his possession. He is bound to pay for the costs, if any, which he incurs for obtaining sight of these deeds so that he can draw up the abstract in proper form.

5. Form of the abstract. The traditional form of the abstract is to write or type it out on so-called brief paper, giving the date, stamp duty paid, parties, covenants, powers, recitals, parcels, habendum and execution together with the certificate of value. A peculiar form of "shorthand" is used; for example, conveyance becomes convy. In preference to this rather cumbersome method of abstraction it is permissible, and today is usual, to supply photocopies of the original documents provided that they are accompanied by an epitome or list giving in chronological order the date, parties and nature of each document in respect of which a photocopy is supplied. (*See* the specimen epitomes in the Sixth Schedule to LPA 1925.)

6. General statutory restrictions on title under an open contract.
LPA 1925, s. 45 prevents a purchaser from requiring the production, a copy or an abstract of any deed, will or other document which forms part of the pre-root title. Neither can he raise any requisition or objection on such documents. Where within the statutory chain of title he comes across a recital referring to a pre-root document, he must assume, unless the contrary appears, that the recitals are correct and give all material contents of the documents and that each document was duly executed (LPA 1925, s. 45(1)(*b*)).

The section goes on to state that the purchaser *is* entitled to require the production of an abstract or copy of:

(*a*) a power of attorney under which any abstracted document was executed;

(*b*) any document creating or disposing of an interest, power or obligation which is not shown to have ceased or expired and subject to which any part of the property is disposed of by an abstracted document; and

(*c*) any document creating any limitation or trust by reference to which any part of the property is disposed of by an abstracted document.

If a purchaser should discover a defect in the pre-root title, his power to rescind the contract will depend on whether the defect makes the title merely doubtful or positively bad. If it is merely doubtful, e.g. if the root has been lost, but there are subsequent documents, then he is bound to take the title, because with the passing of time it will have become at least a good holding title (*see Re Scott and Alvarez's Contract* (1895)). If it is a bad title, e.g. a trustee has sold in breach of trust and the purchaser knew it, he is entitled to rescind the contract but will remain liable for damages and to lose his deposit unless the court exercises its discretionary power under LPA 1925, s. 49(2) and orders its repayment (*see* 15:2).

The student might care to compare the statutory rule.

7. Criminal liability. LPA 1925, s. 183 makes it a criminal offence if, with the intention of defrauding a purchaser, any person who is disposing of property for money or money's worth conceals a material document or encumbrance or falsifies any pedigree to induce the purchaser to accept the title offered. As well as the vendor, his solicitor and other agents may also incur criminal liability. In addition to these sanctions, the vendor, his solicitor and other agents may face a civil action instituted by the purchaser and those deriving title under him for loss by reason of the concealment of an instrument or encumbrance or the falsification of the pedigree.

8. The contents of the abstract. The abstract starts with the root of title and as a general principle every deed which dealt with the property subsequently should be abstracted. The exceptions to this rule are:

(*a*) those deeds affecting equitable interests which will be over-reached by the conveyance (LPA 1925, s. 10);

(*b*) wills where the testator died after 1925;

(*c*) expired leases.

NOTE: Equitable mortgages, even though they have been discharged or will be paid off on completion, should be abstracted. In practice this is not done, unless the mortgage is referred to in another abstracted document or is registered as a land charge. Legal mortgages and charges should always be abstracted; this includes those that have been discharged, in which case the receipt is also abstracted.

Root of title

9. Introduction. This is the document with which the abstract begins. To be a good root of title the document, without the help of any extrinsic evidence (i.e. evidence which is external to the document), must deal with or prove the ownership of both the legal and the equitable estate in the property which is being sold. It must also contain a sufficient description of the property so that it can be identified and it must not cast any doubt on the vendor's title. In *Re Duce and Boots Cash Chemists (Southern) Ltd's Contract* (1937) a son who was his father's executor assented to the vesting of the father's property in himself, even though his sister had a right to occupy a house making that settled property. The son sold the house and when the purchaser in turn wished to sell the house, his purchaser successfully objected to the title on the basis that the recitals showed that it was settled property.

10. Examples of good roots of title. A conveyance for value of the freehold estate is the best possible root of title. A mortgage deed, a voluntary conveyance, a specific devise in a will of a testator who died before 1926 and an assent drawn up after 1925 are all good roots of title. It can be argued that a mortgage created by way of legal charge after 1925 is not a good root of title because it does not deal with the whole legal and equitable estate, but in practice it often is.

The following are *not* good roots of title: a lease, an equitable mortgage, a general devise in a pre-1926 will, a post-1925 will, and a post-1925 disentailing deed.

11. Possessory titles and adverse possession. Under an open contract, if the vendor's title is possessory he must start the chain of title with a good root, proving the title of a former owner which is older than the statutory period of title, at present fifteen years (*see* **12**). The abstract must go on to show that the vendor has extinguished that title and all other interests. The Limitation Act 1980, s. 15 states that twelve years' undisputed possession of land is sufficient to bar almost all claims to the land except the most unusual, e.g. claims by the Crown.

As the root of title under an open contract must be a good root, it cannot be a statutory declaration, though this may be the form in which the evidence that the previous owner's title has been extinguished is presented.

In *Re Atkinson and Horsell's Contract* (1912) it was agreed that the root would be a particular document which was abstracted. The chain from that root was incomplete for it did not show that the vendor's title was lawfully from that root. The root was dated 1842, and in 1874 the vendor's predecessors in title had entered into possession of the property illegally. The vendor's title, derived from this action, was possessory based on the adverse entry into possession in 1874. The purchaser was obliged to carry on with the purchase even though he objected to the title, the court holding that it was still a good marketable title.

This can be compared with the decision in *George Wimpey* v. *Sohn* (1967) where the contract specifically stated that a statutory declaration showing twenty years' undisputed possession would be produced. The declaration produced proved only twelve years' adverse possession. In this case, as the special condition relating to the title had not been fulfilled, the purchaser was entitled to rescind the contract.

12. Length of title. LPA 1969, s. 23 sets the statutory minimum period for the investigation of title to unregistered land at fifteen years. Previously, the period was thirty years. Therefore, under an open contract the vendor must deduce his title for a period which is at least fifteen years from the date of the contract. As the abstract must start with a good root, he must go back to the first good root which took place at least fifteen years ago. This means that in practice, title is deduced for a period of more than fifteen years. For example, vendor and purchaser enter into a contract on 31st December 1978. The vendor bought the house on 6th March 1968 from X. X bought the house on 23rd May 1960 from Y. Thus the root of title is the conveyance dated 23rd May 1960, deducing title over an eighteen-year period.

13. A title of less than the statutory period. In the contract, unless it is an open contract, it will be stated which document is to be the root of title. The purchaser may be offered a title of less than fifteen years. Should he accept such a title? The main risk that the purchaser runs if he accepts a shorter period is that of being bound by any equitable interest of which he would have had notice had he obtained and investigated a fifteen-year title. This is because of the effect of LPA 1925, s. 199(1)(*ii*)(*a*) which states that a purchaser has constructive notice of any fact or thing which would have come to his knowledge if such enquiries and inspections had been as ought reasonably to have been made by him. He is not deemed to have constructive notice of anything which is void for non-registration.

A purchaser should be very cautious of accepting anything less than a fifteen-year title.

14. Undisclosed land charges. LCA 1972, s. 3(1) which re-enacts LCA 1925, s. 10(2) provides that land charges are to be registered against the name of the estate owner for the time being. There is, therefore, a possibility that when the purchaser receives the abstract which complies with the fifteen-year rule but does not go back to 1925, he runs the risk of being bound by a land charge he knew nothing about and was not disclosed by his search as he did not know which names to search against.

A remedy is given to the purchaser in these circumstances by LPA 1969, s. 25, which states that as long as the purchaser can prove that:

(*a*) he had no actual or imputed notice of the charge;
(*b*) it was not registered against the name of an estate owner comprised in the abstract of title; and
(*c*) the date of completion was after 1969.

then he is entitled to be compensated for his loss by the Chief Land Registrar, so long as he has investigated the relevant title. Under an open contract this means that if the title did not begin with a good root, there is no right to compensation.

Lost documents

15. Lost title deeds. Where the vendor has lost some or all of the title deeds or they have been destroyed, it is not necessary to disclose this fact in the contract (*see Re Stuart and Olivant and Seadon's Contract* (1896)). In practice it is better to insert a special condition in the contract stating what secondary evidence will be produced to prove title owing to the non-production of the title deeds. This evidence may take the form of a counterpart lease, draft, copy or abstract and must demonstrate the contents of the lost document(s) and their due execution. It will also be necessary for the vendor to swear a statutory declaration explaining how the loss or destruction occurred and setting out the available secondary evidence. This may be supplemented by a statutory declaration from the solicitor who acted for the vendor on the purchase of the property, stating that:

 (*a*) a good and marketable title was deduced;

 (*b*) the documents of title were examined;

 (*c*) the conveyance or assignment to the vendor was duly executed and stamped; and

 (*d*) the title deeds were sent to the vendor or his mortgagee, as appropriate.

In addition an insurance policy may be obtainable from one of the larger insurance companies which will indemnify the purchaser and those deriving title from him should the title deeds be found and prove that the vendor does not own the property.

16. Voluntary registration for lost title deeds. Should all or some of the title deeds have been destroyed by enemy action, natural disaster or fire or lost or destroyed by theft or be in the custody of a solicitor, building society or bank, application may be made to the Land Registry for voluntary registration of title (*see* 26:**19**).

17. Lost Land or Charge Certificates. Where a Land or Charge Certificate (*see* 25:**15–22**) has been lost, application for a copy certificate may be made to the Registrar of the Land Registry.

Delivery and examination of abstract

18. Delivery of the abstract. (*See also* 6:**20**). Under an open contract the abstract must be delivered within a reasonable time of the exchange of contracts (but *see* **22** below). In *Compton* v. *Bagley* (1892) it was stated that fourteen days in most cases would be the relevant period. Otherwise the conditions of sale will specify the date for delivery. The National Conditions of Sale specify a period of eleven working days after the date of the contract, i.e. exchange, and the Law Society's Conditions of Sale state that it shall be delivered upon exchange.

The cost of production and delivery is borne by the vendor, and includes the cost of obtaining documents not in his possession unless this has been varied by agreement, e.g. by inserting a special condition to the contrary (*see* 6:**13**).

19. Delay in delivering the abstract. As time is not of the essence in respect of the delivery of the abstract (unless there is a special condition to this effect), the general principles of law apply. Therefore, following non-delivery within the specified time where there is one under the conditions of sale or within a reasonable time under an open contract, the purchaser should serve notice on the vendor that unless the abstract is delivered within the time stated in the notice, which must be a reasonable time, the purchaser will repudiate the contract at the expiration of the specified period. The purchaser is entitled to repudiate the contract even though at that date the completion date has not yet arrived and even if the vendor should deliver the abstract outside the specified period.

The purchaser must send such a notice as otherwise delay does not entitle the purchaser to repudiate the contract (*see Compton* v. *Bagley* (1892)).

20. Examining the abstract. Once the vendor has delivered the abstract, the purchaser must examine the abstract against the original documents. The purpose of this examination or verification is to:

(*a*) ensure that what has been abstracted has been properly and correctly abstracted;

(*b*) ensure that what has not been abstracted is immaterial;

(*c*) ensure that each document has been properly executed, attested and stamped;

(*d*) ensure that no memoranda have been endorsed on the title deeds or documents, nor anything else relating to execution or attestation which warrants further enquiry.

In the absence of suspicious circumstances, deeds are presumed duly executed if they are produced from proper custody, i.e. from a place from which they may reasonably be expected to be found, e.g. the vendor's solicitor's office or the mortgagee's solicitor's office.

21. The statutory presumption. LPA 1925, s. 45(6) states that recitals, statements and descriptions of facts, matters and parties contained in deeds, instruments or statutory declarations, twenty years old at the date of the contract, shall, unless and except as they may be proved to be inaccurate, be taken to be sufficient evidence of the truth of such facts, matters and descriptions. Therefore if it is stated in a deed that the street name has been changed and the deed is twenty years old or more, it is not necessary to produce a certified copy of the order made by the local authority changing the name, which would otherwise be required.

22. Title deduced before exchange. In practice the purchaser may request that the title be deduced before contracts are exchanged. For example, where the purchaser's solicitor is not acting for the purchaser's mortgagee the latter's solicitor may require sight of the title before committing the mortgagee to advancing the purchase monies. The purchaser will have to negotiate this matter with the vendor.

Progress test 9

1. What is a good root of title? (**9, 10**)

2. What is the statutory minimum period for the investigation of title as set out in LPA 1969, s. 23? (**12**)

3. X is buying land and has received an abstract of title which deduces title for sixteen years. Twenty years ago a land charge was created and registered by the then owner. His name was not known to X and so the charge was not revealed by X's search at the Land Charges Department of the Land Registry. Is he bound by the charge and has he any remedy? (**14**)

4. Y informs you that he has lost all the title deeds to his house, which he is about to sell. How can he prove his title? (**15**)

5. What difference would it make if Y's title deeds had been lost

while in the possession of his solicitor? (**16**)

6. P is buying a house from V. V has not supplied an abstract of title within the time specified in the contract. What can P do about this? (**19**)

7. What is the purpose of examining the abstract of title? (**20**)

10
Deducing title in particular cases

Joint tenants and tenants for life as vendors

1. Joint tenants as vendors. Where two or more people are beneficially entitled to the legal estate, it is vested in them as joint tenants upon a trust for sale (unless the land is subject to an SLA settlement), the beneficial interests being held either as joint tenants or as tenants in common, according to the terms of the deed vesting the property in them. The purchaser will have to obtain a receipt for the purchase monies from at least two trustees or a trust corporation (LPA 1925, s. 27). This receipt is incorporated into the conveyance (*see* 13:**11**).

2. Survivor of joint tenants. If the property is vested in two persons who are joint tenants in law and equity and one dies without severing the tenancy, the survivor is solely and beneficially entitled to the property and can deal with the legal estate as though it were not held upon trust for sale (LPA 1925, s. 36 as amended by the Law of Property (Amendment) Act 1926, s. 7).

3. Statutory presumption. The difficulty that the survivor faced in the past was of proving that there had been no severance of the beneficial joint tenancy. To sever the tenancy it is necessary that a notice in writing be given by the tenant who desires to sever the tenancy to the other tenants. (It should be remembered that it is not possible to sever the joint tenancy of the legal estate, only that of the equitable interest.) The Law of Property (Joint Tenants) Act 1964 was passed to help overcome this evidential problem. Section 1 of this Act states that the survivor of two or more joint tenants shall, in favour of a purchaser of a legal estate, be deemed to be solely and beneficially interested if he conveys as beneficial owner or the conveyance states that he is a beneficial owner. This statutory presumption will not apply:

(*a*) if a memorandum of severance has been endorsed on the conveyance vesting the land in the joint tenants; or

(*b*) if a receiving order in bankruptcy or a petition against any joint tenant has been registered under LCA 1972, the purchaser, by such registration, having notice of it at the date of the conveyance between the survivor and the purchaser.

The presumption does not apply to registered land.

4. A tenant for life as vendor. If the property is settled within the meaning of SLA 1925, s. 1, the legal estate is vested in the person who is the tenant for life for the purposes of the Act as defined by s. 19. If there is no such person or that person lacks the capacity to hold a legal estate, e.g. he is a minor, the legal estate is held by the statutory owners, who are usually the trustees of the settlement.

A conveyance of settled land by the tenant for life or, where appropriate, the statutory owners, will overreach:

(*a*) limitations, powers and provisions of the settlement;

(*b*) estates, interests or charges subsisting or to arise within the settlement; and

(*c*) all annuities, limited owner's charges and general equitable charges even if registered as land charges (SLA 1925, s. 72).

The provisions of SLA 1925, s. 18 should be noted. Where the land is subject to a vesting instrument and the trustees of the settlement have not been discharged under the Act, any disposition of the legal estate by the tenant for life or the statutory owners will be void unless it is a disposition authorised by the Act and the capital monies are paid to the trustees of the settlement, being either a trust corporation or at least two in number. As an alternative the money may be paid into court.

The power of the tenant for life to sell the settled land is found in

s. 38; the regulations respecting sales, e.g. that they must be for the best consideration in money that can reasonably be obtained, in s. 39; the power to lease the land whether for ordinary building, mining or forestry purposes in s. 41; the regulations for leasing in ss. 42–48. These should be studied by the student.

Trustees for sale as vendors

5. **Creation of trusts for sale.** An immediate binding trust for sale may be created expressly or implied by statute in the following circumstances.

(*a*) When trustees have lent money on a mortgage of land and the mortgagor's equity of redemption has been extinguished (LPA 1925, s. 31), e.g. by an order of foreclosure.

(*b*) Where a settlement of either personal property or of land held on a trust for sale contains a power to invest in land and the trustees exercise this power, the land so bought is vested in them upon trust for sale.

(*c*) Where the owner of land dies intestate, his personal representatives hold the land upon trust for sale, as they do the rest of his estate (AEA 1925, s. 33).

(*d*) Where land is held by beneficial co-owners (*see* 1). Where the land is settled and several people constitute the tenant for life, the trust for sale does not arise.

6. **Protection given to a purchaser when buying from trustees for sale.**

(*a*) LPA 1925, s. 23 protects the purchaser by holding that where land is subject to an express or statutory trust for sale, the trust, as regards the safety and protection of the purchaser, shall be deemed to be subsisting until the land has been conveyed to or under the direction of the persons interested in the proceeds of sale.

Therefore, even though the purchaser knows that the proceeds of sale have become vested in persons of full age, who between them are entitled to the whole of the trust property and who can under the rule in *Saunders* v. *Vautier* (1841) bring the trust to an end, he may rely on s. 23 until the land is actually conveyed to them or under their directions. If, as in *Re Cook* (1948), the legal and equitable interests have vested in one person, then the trust for sale has come to an end.

(*b*) A trust for sale imposes a duty on the trustees to sell the property with a power to postpone sale. LPA 1925, s. 25(2) states that a purchaser is not concerned with any directions respecting the postponement of sale.

(*c*) A trust for sale may provide that the trustees have to obtain the consent of named persons, no more than four, before they sell the trust assets. Under LPA 1925, s. 26(1) a purchaser need only be concerned to see that two persons have agreed to the sale going through. If one of the persons required to consent to the sale is under age or subject to some other disability, his consent is not necessary anyway.

(*d*) LPA 1925, s. 24 states that the persons having the power to appoint new trustees of a conveyance of land on trust for sale shall be bound to appoint the same persons, if any, who are for the time being trustees of the settlement of the proceeds of sale, but a purchaser shall not be concerned to see if the proper persons have been appointed trustees of the conveyance of the land.

(*e*) Neither is a purchaser of a legal estate from the trustees of sale concerned with the trusts affecting the proceeds of sale, even if the trusts are declared by the same instrument by which the trust for sale is created so that he has express notice of the trusts (LPA 1925, s. 27(1)), provided that the purchaser pays the purchase monies to at least two trustees or a trust corporation (LPA 1925, s. 27(2)).

7. Overreaching. A conveyance by trustees for sale to a purchaser of a legal estate in land shall overreach any equitable interest or power affecting that estate, whether or not the purchaser has notice of it, provided that:

(*a*) the statutory requirements respecting the payment of capital money arising under a disposition upon trust for sale are complied with (*see* **6**); and

(*b*) the interest is one which is capable of being overreached (*see* **8**).

A purchaser who does not pay the money in accordance with the statutory requirements does not obtain a good title and takes subject to the rights of the beneficiaries. A sole trustee for sale can validly grant a lease and so pass a good title, provided no capital monies are involved in the transaction.

In the recent (highly controversial) Court of Appeal decision in *City of London B.S.* v. *Flegg* (1985) it was held that the interest of a beneficiary behind a trust for sale who is in occupation of the property will not be overreached, even where s. 27(2) is complied with, as s. 14 preserves the interest of a person in occupation or possession, where his interest entitles him to be in occupation or possession.

8. Matters not overreached. LPA 1925, s. 2(2) states that equitable interests and powers will be overreached where the sale fulfils the conditions mentioned in **7.** However, s. 2(3) states that the following are not overreached by such a sale:

(*a*) an equitable interest protected by the deposit of title deeds which relate to the legal estate;

(*b*) the benefit of any covenant or agreement which restricts the user of land;

(*c*) an equitable easement affecting the land;

(*d*) a contract to convey a legal estate in the land, whether this estate contract is an option to purchase or a right of pre-emption;

(*e*) any equitable interest protected by registration under LCA 1972 other than:

(*i*) an annuity as defined by that Act; or

(*ii*) a limited owner's charge or a general equitable charge (*see* 12:**6**).

Personal representatives as vendors

9. Powers of personal representatives. The term "personal representatives" covers executors and administrators of a deceased person's estate. Only they are permitted to deal with the estate. AEA 1925, s. 39 defines their powers, which include all the powers of trustees for sale during the administration of the estate.

A purchaser is not concerned to see if the sale is a proper one for the trustees to make and is not affected by a subsequent revocation of the personal representatives' grant (AEA 1925, s. 37). A sale by the personal representatives overreaches the beneficial interests under a will or those arising on an intestacy which relate to the property.

One important difference between the position of a personal representative and that of a trustee is that a single personal representative can give a good receipt for capital monies, even though the land is held upon a trust for sale, e.g. because the land is subject to an intestacy. However, where two or more personal representatives have been appointed, they must all join in the conveyance on sale (AEA 1925, s. 2(2)).

10. Assents by personal representatives. Personal representatives can pass a legal estate to a purchaser or to the person(s) entitled on intestacy or under the will (AEA 1925, s. 36(1)). This applies only if the estate has devolved on them.

In *Re Stirrup's Contract* (1961) a beneficiary under a will survived the testator but died before the personal representatives vested it in him. Therefore they assented to the property vesting in the deceased beneficiary's personal representatives who assented under seal to it vesting in X. X's purchaser, P, asked the court to rectify the defect in title which had arisen because technically when the property passed to X, this should have been carried out by way of a conveyance not an assent. This was because the property had not devolved on this second group of personal representatives—it had been vested in them by the personal representatives of the testator. It was held that although this was technically quite correct, the assent had passed the legal estate to X and P was not entitled to rectification of the document. In this case the assent to X was under seal. It has been suggested that the court would not have held that the estate was vested in X if the assent in his favour had been under hand (*see* note below).

11. Form of assents. AEA 1925, s. 36(4) provides that to be effective an assent must:

(*a*) be in writing;
(*b*) be signed by the personal representatives; and
(*c*) name the persons in whose favour it is given.

It can only be used to vest the legal estate in a person who is entitled to it under the terms of a will or under the intestacy rules. It cannot be used to pass title to a purchaser. In the latter case the normal rule applies that to pass a legal estate in land a deed is necessary (LPA 1925, s. 52(1)).

NOTE: Assents may be "under hand", i.e. simply in writing, or "under seal", i.e. in writing and also in the form of a deed (*see* 13:**29**).

12. The decision in Re King's Will Trusts (1964). This case exploded the idea that it was not necessary for the personal representatives to assent to the vesting of the property in themselves when they are entitled to it in some other capacity, e.g. as a beneficiary or as a trustee.

The facts of this case were that a surviving executor who was also a trustee executed a deed appointing another person as a trustee. It was held that as the executor/trustee had never assented to the vesting in himself of the trust property as a trustee, he could not appoint a new trustee and automatically vest the legal estate in him. It was also said in this case that the same principle applied where the personal representative is the beneficiary entitled to the property. When the personal representative has finished the administration of the estate, he should then assent to the vesting in himself of the legal estate, which he formerly held as personal representative.

There has never been any doubt that the assent was needed where the trustees or beneficiaries were not also the personal representatives (this case was not doubted in *Re Edward's Will Trusts* (1981)).

13. Protection given to those dealing with the personal representatives.

(*a*) AEA 1925, s. 36(5) gives a person in whose favour an assent or conveyance is made (purchaser or beneficiary) a right to insist that a memorandum of the assent or conveyance be endorsed on the grant of representation at the cost of the estate and that the grant of representation be produced, again at the cost of the estate, to prove that the notice has been endorsed on it. This right should always be taken advantage of. It is normal practice to do so on a sale but it is even more important for a beneficiary. He may lose his property to a subsequent purchaser where the personal representatives have stated in writing that they have not given or made any previous assent (though this is untrue), unless there is an endorsement to the contrary on the grant (AEA 1925, s. 36(6)).

(*b*) Section 36(6) states that in favour of a purchaser a statement in writing by personal representatives that they have not made a previous assent or conveyance of the legal estate is sufficient evidence that this is so and will protect the purchaser unless a memorandum of a previous assent or conveyance is endorsed on the grant (*see* (*a*)) or there has been a previous disposition for value.

(*c*) Section 36(7) provides that in favour of a purchaser an assent by a personal representative is sufficient evidence that the person in whose favour it is made is entitled to have the estate vested in him unless there is a note on the grant of a previous assent or conveyance. The subsection says "sufficient", not "conclusive". Where a purchaser discovers a defect in title on examination, he cannot rely on s. 36(7), but must not accept the title unless the defect is removed (*see Re Duce and Boots Cash Chemists (Southern) Ltd's Contract* (1937)).

Sales by mortgagees

14. Statutory power of sale by legal mortgagee. LPA 1925, s. 101(1) states that every legal mortgagee has a statutory power of sale when the legal date for redemption has passed. This is normally six months from the date of the mortgage. (*See also* 18:**6–13**.)

This power of sale cannot be exercised until one of the following conditions laid down in s. 103 has been fulfilled:

(*a*) notice has been served on the mortgagor requiring the repayment of all the mortgage monies and he has not paid the total sum within three months of the service of the notice;

(*b*) some interest due on the mortgage has not been paid and two months have elapsed since the date for payment;

(*c*) the mortgagor has breached some provision of the statute or of the mortgage deed, not being a covenant for the payment of the mortgage sum or interest, e.g. the mortgagor has let the mortgaged premises without the knowledge and consent of the mortgagee.

This statutory power of sale may be extended by the mortgage reserving a power of sale if the mortgagee commits an available act of bankruptcy.

15. Mortgagee's duty to obtain good price. A building society is obliged by the Building Societies Act 1962, s. 36 to sell the mortgaged premises at the best price reasonably obtainable.

Other mortgagees must take reasonable care to obtain the correct market value of the property at the date of sale. In *Cuckmere Brick Co. Ltd* v. *Mutual Finance Ltd* (1971), failure by the mortgagees to advertise the property as having planning permission for flats led to a sale at a reduced price and a breach of the mortgagee's duty.

16. Protection given to purchasers. (LPA 1925, s. 104.) A purchaser buying from a mortgagee selling under a statutory power of sale does not have to enquire if any case has arisen to authorise a sale under the Act or to see that appropriate notice has been given or that the power of sale has otherwise been properly and regularly exercised. A conveyance on sale by a mortgagee shall be deemed to be made in exercise of the statutory power unless a contrary intention appears.

If there has been some irregularity under s. 104(2), the purchaser's title cannot be overturned. His remedy is in damages against the mortgagee.

17. Effect of the sale by the mortgagee. (LPA 1925, ss. 88 and 89.) The effect of a conveyance or assignment by a mortgagee (whether by way of legal mortgage or charge) is to vest the fee simple in the purchaser in fee simple or the residue of the term of years absolute. The conveyance or assignment will overreach all interests over which the mortgagee has priority but is subject to all prior encumbrances.

For example, X mortgages his freehold property by legal charge to A; two years later there is a second mortgage to B, followed three years later by a third mortgage to C. B exercises his power of sale when interest payments remain outstanding for six months. He sells the property to J, who takes the fee simple subject to A's legal charge but free from B and C's legal charge and free from X's equity of redemption.

18. Equitable mortgages. The statutory power of sale applies to equitable mortgages if they are made by deed, as well as to legal mortgages (LPA 1925, s. 101). "By deed" includes a memorandum under seal of the deposit of title deeds as well as the more usual equitable charge by way of mortgage contained in a deed.

19. Lack of power to convey legal estate. The major difficulty that an equitable mortgagee suffers from was demonstrated by *Re Hudson and Howe's Contract* (1887) where it was pointed out that he may have a power of sale but this does not confer on him a right to convey the legal estate in the property. The matter is not free from doubt and for a contrary view *see Re White Rose Cottage* (1965). The general opinion, however, is that an equitable mortgagee is not entitled to convey the legal estate.

In order to overcome this problem a declaration of trust may be inserted in the mortgage deed whereby the mortgagor holds the property on trust for the mortgagee and gives the mortgagee power to remove the mortgagor as trustee and appoint a new trustee. As the legal estate would be vested in the new trustee, when the power of sale was exercised he would pass a legal estate to the purchaser. Another way of achieving this end is by requiring the mortgagor to execute a power of attorney, so that the attorney/mortgagee can then transfer the legal estate to the purchaser when the statutory power of sale has been exercised. He must make it clear that he conveys the property as a mortgagee in order for the legal estate to vest in the purchaser.

20. Court order. If the mortgage is not made by deed, unless the mortgagor agrees to the sale going ahead, the mortgagee's only recourse is to ask the court to order a sale under LPA 1925, s. 91. The court may vest the property in the purchaser, appoint a person to convey the land to the purchaser, or in the case of an equitable mortgage create and vest in the equitable mortgagee a mortgage term so that he can carry out the sale as if the mortgage had been created under seal by way of legal mortgage.

Minors and persons of unsound mind

21. Minors and legal estates in land. A minor (someone under the age of 18) under the provisions of LPA 1925, s. 1(6) cannot hold a legal estate in land. A purported conveyance of a legal estate to a minor does not vest the legal estate in him but operates as an agreement for valuable consideration to execute a settlement in his favour by means of a principal vesting deed and trust instrument, and in the meantime to hold the land on trust for the minor (SLA 1925, s. 27(1)).

A conveyance of a legal estate to a minor jointly with a person of full age vests the legal estate in the person of full age on the statutory trusts (LPA 1925, s. 19(2)). (The statutory trusts are defined by LPA 1925, s. 35 and take the form of an express trust for sale.)

As a result of this disability, which includes under SLA 1925, s. 19(1) being a tenant for life under a settlement, a minor cannot be a trustee (LPA 1925, s. 20), a personal representative (Supreme Court of Judicature (Consolidation) Act 1925, s. 165), or a mortgagee of land (LPA 1925, s. 19(6)).

22. Minors and equitable interests in land. There is nothing which prevents a minor holding an equitable interest in land. Thus where a legal estate in land devolves on a minor through a gift in a will or the operation of the intestacy rules (e.g. "I leave Blackacre to A", and A is a minor at the death of the testator), the land automatically becomes settled land (SLA 1925, s. 27(1)). The legal estate is vested by the personal representatives of the deceased in the trustees of the settlement, and the minor is vested with the equitable interest in the land (LPA 1925, s. 26(6)).

As already noted, a conveyance or lease of land to a minor, *inter vivos*, while ineffective to vest the legal estate in him, will pass the equitable interest to the minor. Again the legal estate becomes the subject of a settlement (SLA 1925, s. 27(1)).

If a minor enters into a contract to buy a legal estate, this contract does not operate to vest the equitable interest in him (*McFarland* v. *Brumby* (1966)). This is because the purchaser is said to obtain an equitable interest in the property, since after contracts have been exchanged, he may ask the court to enforce the contract through the remedy of a decree of specific performance. A minor is not in a position to ask for a decree as this would have the effect of vesting the legal estate in him contrary to statute. Therefore, at this stage the minor does not possess an equitable interest in the land.

23. Voidable contracts. Where a minor buys an equitable interest in land, either through an ineffective attempt to purchase a legal estate or because that was the subject-matter of the contract, the contract is voidable. It can be repudiated by the minor at any time during his minority or within a reasonable time of his attaining his majority.

What is a reasonable time is a question of fact. In *Edwards* v. *Carter* (1893) four years after majority was said to be too long, even though for most of that period, the ex-minor had been ignorant of his right to repudiate the contract. Failure to repudiate within the correct time affirms the contract, which renders it unassailable.

If repudiation takes place, it destroys any future liability under the contract, e.g. to pay rent, but it is unclear whether it will extinguish past liabilities, e.g. rent due prior to the date of repudiation but unpaid.

The minor may recover monies paid under the contract only if there has been a total failure of consideration. In *Holmes* v. *Blogg* (1818) the minor repudiated a lease after he had taken possession of the premises. He was not able to recover the premium which he had paid. A purchase price paid under similar circumstances would not be repaid. However, in *Corpe* v. *Overton* (1833) the minor avoided the contract for the sale before he had moved into the premises. The court held that there had been a total failure of consideration, so the minor recovered the deposit which he had paid.

Normally, only the minor has a right to avoid the contract, but the other party has a right to do so if the minor has committed fraud, e.g. by falsely stating that he was an adult (*see Lempriere* v. *Lange* (1879)—the lessor avoided the contract; the lessee, a minor, had stated he was an adult).

24. Sales by minors. Such a contract is voidable at the instance of the minor during his minority and for a reasonable time after he has attained his majority. If he does avoid the contract, his property returns to him without the need for any conveyance and he is not obliged to refund monies paid to him unless he has committed fraud in the course of the contract.

A conveyance by a minor of a legal interest has no effect other than to transfer the minor's equitable interest subject to his right to avoid the contract. The land remains settled land, though it appears that the purchaser may require the legal estate to be vested in him by means of a vesting deed (SLA 1925, ss. 1 and 20).

25. Mortgages. A mortgage to a minor to secure repayment of money lent to him is void under the Infants Relief Act 1874, s. 1. As a result the mortgagee cannot sue for repayment of the monies advanced to the minor but if the mortgage monies were used to pay the vendor, then to that extent the mortgagee is entitled to an equitable charge on the property as against the mortgagor.

26. Persons of unsound mind.

(a) *Where a receiver has been appointed under the Mental Health Act 1983.* In this situation the person of unsound mind no longer possesses the capacity to enter into any contract. Any attempt to do so is null and void. The receiver is entitled to enter into contracts for the purchase and sale of land on behalf of persons suffering from this disability.

(b) *Where no receiver has been appointed.* A contract entered into by a person of unsound mind is binding on him, if the other party to the contract is unaware of that infirmity at the date of the contract (*see Hart* v. *O'Connor* (1985)). If the other party was aware of it, the contract is voidable at the instance of the person suffering from mental infirmity, his receiver or his personal representative. In *Broughton* v. *Snook* (1938) it was stated that it is for the party alleging that there was incapacity to prove it. Not only are contracts for the sale of land voidable but also conveyances for valuable consideration (*Selby* v. *Jackson* (1844)). This may be contrasted with a voluntary conveyance of land which is void if one of the parties is of unsound mind (*Elliott* v. *Ince* (1857)).

Charities, companies and unincorporated associations as vendors

27. Sales by charities. If a charity wishes to sell, lease or otherwise dispose of land forming part of the permanent endowment of the charity, then in accordance with the Charities Act 1960, s. 29 an order of the court or the Charity Commissioners is required before the disposition takes place. This requirement also applies where the land is to be charged or mortgaged.

A lease of up to twenty-one years does not fall within s. 29. A charity may apply to the court for exemption from the provisions of s. 29 and some charities are exempt from s. 29 by statute.

There are no restrictions on sales to charities.

28. Sales by companies. A company registered under the Companies Act 1985 only has the power to carry out those actions which are specified (or reasonably incidental to those purposes) in its memorandum of association. A contract which is *ultra vires* the company is void. However, the European Communities Act 1972, s. 9 provides that in favour of a person acting in good faith and the transaction has been agreed to by the board of directors, the contract shall be as valid as if they had that power. If the purchaser knows that the company has not the power to enter into the contract, then he cannot take advantage of s. 9.

Where s. 9 is not available the only remedy the purchaser has is to trace his money or other property which has been transferred to the company. The same principle applies when the company is buying land.

29. Unincorporated associations. These hold their property and make their contracts through their agents, e.g. partners are agents for each other in business transactions and the committee members of a club may be agents for the other members. Alternatively some members of the unincorporated association may be appointed trustees of the property for the benefit of the other members.

Voluntary conveyances and bankruptcy

30. Requirements of Bankruptcy Act 1914, s. 42. A voluntary conveyance can be a good root of title and a good link in the chain of title (*see* 9:**9–10**). However, the purchaser when presented with a title which contains such a deed should bear in mind the Bankruptcy Act 1914, s. 42 which provides that a voluntary conveyance is voidable by the trustee-in-bankruptcy of the donor, if the donor becomes bankrupt within two years of the date of the conveyance. If he becomes bankrupt after two years but within ten years of the date of the conveyance, it is voidable, but if it can be proved that:

(a) at the date of the conveyance the donor could pay all his debts without using the property comprised in the conveyance; and

(b) the donor's interest passed to the donee(s) or trustees immediately on execution of the conveyance,

then the conveyance cannot be avoided by the trustee-in-bankruptcy.

NOTE: The statute states that the conveyance is void not voidable, but in *Re Carter and Kenderdine's Contract* (1897) it was held that void meant voidable.

31. Bona fide purchaser for value without notice of bankruptcy.
It should be noted that once the land passes to a bona fide purchaser for value without notice of an act of bankruptcy, the voluntary conveyance, even if within the ten-year period, cannot then be overturned by the trustee-in-bankruptcy. For example, X voluntarily conveys property to Y in 1966. X becomes bankrupt in 1970. The conveyance is voidable by the trustee-in-bankruptcy. Y sells the property to C, a bona fide purchaser for value without notice. The 1966 conveyance can no longer be avoided by the trustee-in-bankruptcy and C has a good title.

It may be difficult in practice to prove that the purchaser for value is without notice, for a bankruptcy petition or receiving order will invariably be registered as a land charge in the register of pending actions or the register of writs and orders (*see* 12:**2, 4**). Registration of such a charge constitutes notice to the purchaser whether he searches the register or not (*see* 12:**7** and Preface).

32. Conveyance to defraud creditors. A purchaser must have regard also to LPA 1925, s. 172 which states that a conveyance made with the intention of defrauding creditors is voidable at the instance of the person(s) thereby prejudiced. There is no time limit on this section. However, s. 172(3) gives a good title to a purchaser for value or for good consideration who takes in good faith without notice of the intention to defraud creditors at the date of the conveyance.

Powers of attorney

33. Formalities required to execute a power of attorney. The

Powers of Attorney Act 1971, s. 1 provides that a power of attorney must be signed and sealed by, or by the direction and in the presence of, the donor of the power. In other words the power must be executed as a deed either personally by the donor or by someone else acting in accordance with the instructions of the donor, who must be present when that person executes the deed.

When a trustee executes a power of attorney, as well as the above formalities, the deed must be witnessed by at least one person. Written notice of the delegation must be given before or within seven days of its execution to his fellow trustees and the person(s), if any, who has power to appoint new trustees. Failure to give the notice does not invalidate the power of attorney. The trustee cannot appoint as his attorney his sole co-trustee, unless that sole co-trustee is a trust corporation (Powers of Attorney Act 1971, s. 9).

34. Abstracted documents executed under a power of attorney. If one of the abstracted documents has been executed under a power of attorney, the purchaser will wish to satisfy himself that the power has not been revoked before its purported exercise. Statutory protection is given to purchasers by the Powers of Attorney Act 1971, ss. 4 and 5.

35. Power expressed to be irrevocable. The Powers of Attorney Act 1971, s. 4 states that where a power of attorney is expressed to be irrevocable and is expressed to be given to secure either a proprietary interest or the performance of an obligation owed to the donee, the power cannot be discharged by the donor without the consent of the donee (the attorney), as long as the obligation remains unperformed or the donee retains that interest. Neither will the power be revoked in such circumstances by the death, incapacity or bankruptcy of the donor.

The purchaser from such an attorney obtains a good title. He can assume that the power has not been revoked unless he knows that it has been revoked with the concurrence of the attorney.

A good title will also be obtained by the purchaser if the grant of the power was expressed to be irrevocable and by way of security of a proprietary interest, but where it is not in fact given for such a purpose. Then the revocation without the concurrence of the attorney or the death, incapacity or bankruptcy of the donor will not affect the purchaser, provided that he was unaware that the power was not given to secure a proprietary interest even though it was expressed to be so.

An example of an irrevocable power given to secure a proprietary interest is an equitable mortgage given to a bank with a power of attorney against the mortgagor defaulting on the repayments.

36. Where power of attorney has been revoked. The Powers of Attorney Act 1971, s. 5(2) provides that where a power of attorney has been revoked and a person without knowledge of the revocation deals with the attorney, then the transaction shall, in favour of that person, be as valid as if the power had been in existence. "Person" includes a purchaser. Knowledge in this context includes knowledge of an event, such as the death of the donor of the power, which revokes the power (unless it is covered by s. 4, *see* **10**), even if the person was not aware that death has the effect of revoking the power. For example, X gives a power of attorney to Y. Y sells land to Z exercising the power, after X has died. Z knows X is dead but does not realise its effect. Z cannot take advantage of s. 5(2).

37. Purchaser from a third party. The effect of s. 5(2) is that the validity of the title of a third party who has dealt with an attorney depends on the third party's absence of knowledge that the power of attorney has been revoked before the dealing took place. A purchaser from the third party will be greatly concerned with this matter. Section 5(4) provides that it is to be conclusively presumed in favour of a purchaser from a third party that the third party did not know of the revocation of the power:

(*a*) if the transaction between the attorney and the third party was completed within one year of the power coming into being (this is normally the date of the power); or

(*b*) if outside that period, the third party makes a statutory declaration before or within three months of the completion of the purchase that he did not know of the revocation at the date of his transaction with the attorney.

Thus:

A executes a power of attorney in favour of B (January 1977);
A revokes the power of attorney (September 1977);
B gives the property to Q (November 1977);
Q sells the property to P (February 1978).

P gets a good title, as it is conclusively presumed in his favour that Q did not know of the revocation since the transaction between B and Q took place within one year of January 1977.

Or:

A executes a power of attorney in favour of B (January 1977);
A revokes the power (September 1977);
B gives the property to Q (March 1978);
Q sells the property to P (August 1978).

A statutory declaration by Q any time before August 1978 or up to November 1978 allows s. 5(4) to operate in P's favour.

Enduring powers of attorney

38. Enduring powers of attorney. One important drawback as far as the ordinary power of attorney is concerned is that the power is automatically revoked by the mental incapacity of the donor. The Enduring Powers of Attorney Act 1985 provides for the creation of a power of attorney which is not revoked by such incapacity. An enduring power is defined by EPA, s. 2(1) as one being in the prescribed form and executed by donor and attorney and incorporating the prescribed explanatory information. This is to the effect that the power is intended to continue in spite of the supervening incapacity of the donor.

39. Duty to register the power (s. 4). Once the attorney has reason to believe that the donor is or is becoming mentally incapable, he must apply to the court for registration of the power. Section 1(1)(*b*) provides that attorney may not act under the authority of a power when the donor is mentally incapable unless the court orders him to do so or the instrument has been registered under s. 6 or he is exercising his powers under s. 1(2) (**41** below).

40. Protection given to third parties. If the donor has become mentally incapable and no application has been made for registration, the Power of Attorney Act 1971, s. 5 has been extended to protect a person who without knowledge of the incapacity deals with the attorney (s. 1(1)(c)). It is as though the power had been revoked (*see* Powers of Attorney Act 1971, s. 5).

41. Protection between application for registration and registration. During this period the attorney may only act under the power to the extent that it is necessary to maintain the donor as to prevent loss to his estate or to maintain himself or other persons subject to EPA, s. 1(2). However, a person dealing with an attorney during this period who is unaware that the attorney is acting outside s. 1(2) is protected as the transaction is as valid as if it were one within s. 1(2).

42. Effect of registration (s. 7). Once the power is registered under s. 6 the donor cannot validly revoke it unless the court confirms the revocation, the attorney cannot validly disclaim the power until the court is given notice of disclaimer, and the donor cannot extend or restrict the scope of the authority. These restrictions apply for as long as an instrument is registered under the Act even though the donor may no longer be mentally impaired.

43. Protection given to attorneys and third parties when power is invalid or revoked (s. 9). Where a registered power did not create a valid enduring power or where the instrument had been a valid enduring power it would have been revoked, or where it would have expired then by s. 9(3) the transaction between the attorney and another person shall, in favour of that person, be as valid as if the power had been in existence unless that person knew that (*a*) the instrument did not create a valid enduring power *or* (*b*) an event has occurred which would have revoked a valid enduring power *or* (*c*) the power would have expired before that date, if it was a valid enduring power.

In favour of a purchaser from a third party who dealt with the attorney, there is a conclusive presumption that the third party did not know of any of the above matters. If either the transaction between the attorney and the third party took place within twelve months of the date of registration of the power *or* the third party makes a statutory declaration, before or within three months of the completion of the transaction that, at the time, he has no reason to doubt that the attorney had the authority to carry out the transaction.

Progress test 10

1. When will the statutory presumption contained in the Law of Property (Joint Tenants) Act 1964, s. 1 not apply? (**1**)

2. What will be overreached by a conveyance on sale of settled land by the tenant for life? (**4**)

3. What interests will not be overreached by a conveyance on sale by trustees for sale? (**8**)

4. What form must an assent be in to be effective? (**11**)

5. What is the significance of the decision in *Re King's Will Trusts* (1964)? (**12**)

6. Explain the statutory protection given to a purchaser from a mortgagee selling under his statutory power of sale. (**16**)

7. In what ways may an equitable mortgagee ensure that if he is obliged to exercise his power of sale he will be able to convey a legal estate to his purchaser? (**19**)

8. What is the effect of a minor entering into a contract to buy land? (**22**)

9. What is the effect of a person of unsound mind entering into a contract to buy land, where no receiver has been appointed? (**26**)

10. M has been offered a ten-year lease on land which forms part of the permanent endowment of a charity. Must an order of the court or of the Charity Commissioners be obtained before the lease is granted? (**27**)

11. In the context of a voluntary conveyance when the donor of the property has become bankrupt, what is the significance of (*a*) a period of two years, and (*b*) a period of ten years from the date of the conveyance? (**30**)

12. When can a power of attorney not be discharged without the consent of the attorney? (**35**)

13. In what circumstances can a purchaser from a third party feel confident that the third party was unaware that the attorney's power had been revoked before his dealing with the attorney? (**37**)

11

Requisitions on title

Nature of requisitions

1. Introduction. After receiving the abstract of title, the purchaser's solicitor examines it to see that it demonstrates that the vendor possesses the title which he has contracted to sell. Any doubt or objection to the title is raised by the purchaser's solicitor sending a written requisition on the matter to the vendor's solicitor. This is not just a question, but requires the vendor to remove the alleged defect from his title.

2. Subject-matter of requisitions. Subject to the provisions of LPA 1925, s. 45(1)(*b*) which prevents the purchaser raising requisitions on pre-root documents, the purchaser is entitled to raise requisitions on any part of the abstract which is unsatisfactory, e.g. if it discloses a mortgage or restrictive covenant which was not disclosed by the contract or if it appears that the purchaser's title to the land may be doubtful because of a lost deed in the chain of title. The purchaser will raise a requisition on the matter, which has the effect of requiring the vendor either to remedy the defect or to give a satisfactory explanation to the purchaser showing why it is not a defect or why it is a matter on which it is improper to raise a requisition (*see* **4**). The nature of the requisitions raised depends entirely on the abstract in any particular case.

3. Matters other than the title. Although requisitions should refer only to queries and defects in the title, in practice other matters are also covered, e.g. asking how the vendor requires the purchase monies to be paid and where and whether a receipt for rates will be produced on completion (*see* 17:5).

Often printed requisition forms are used and it is customary to ask for confirmation that if the preliminary enquiries were repeated as requisitions, the replies would be the same. This particular question has been criticised as letting in improper requisitions (*see* **4**) and duplicating work, although it was approved in *Goody* v. *Baring* (1956).

4. Improper requisitions. The purchaser should not raise requisitions which infer that relevant matters might have been suppressed from the abstract (*see Re Ford and Hill* (1879)). The purchaser does not need to raise requisitions on matters of conveyance (*Bain* v. *Fothergill* (1874)), as these are defects which the vendor can remove independently of the concurrence of another, e.g. the discharge of a mortgage affecting the property (*Jackson and Oakshott, Re* (1880)) or the appointment of trustees for the purpose of giving a receipt for capital monies arising on the sale of settled land (*Hatten* v. *Russell* (1888)).

Time limits

5. Time within which requisitions are to be raised. When the contract is open on this point, requisitions should be raised within a reasonable time (*see* for the time limits under the Law Society and the National Conditions of Sale).

In *Upperton* v. *Nickelson* (1871) it was held that if the vendor failed to deliver the abstract by the specified date, the purchaser was released from his obligation to deliver his requisitions within a specified time. But NC 9(4) requires the purchaser to raise his requisitions within the normal time period even though the abstract was not delivered in due time.

As already mentioned (*see* 6:21) if an abstract is imperfect the time within which requisitions should be raised is postponed until the missing documents are delivered *but* only as regards matters disclosed by those documents. Matters apparent from the imperfect abstract must be taken up within the ordinary time period.

Time is of the essence when raising requisitions, and if the purchaser does not keep to these times he has no right to expect the vendor to answer his query unless it is a matter to which the time periods do not apply (*see* **6**).

6. Requisitions to which the time period does not apply.

(*a*) *A defect going to the root of the title.* This type of requisition may be raised at any time before completion, for if the vendor has broken or has no means of performing his contract, this is a fundamental objection. In *Want* v. *Stallibrass* (1873) the purchaser, out of time, objected that the vendor/trustees had no power of sale. The court upheld this as a requisition going to the root of the title.

(*b*) *Defects not revealed by the abstract.* These are defects which the purchaser discovers through his own endeavours, e.g. land charge searches and enquiries of local authorities.

(*c*) *Matters of conveyance* (*see* **4**). If these are raised they are not subject to any time limit (*Re Scott and Eave's Contract* (1902)).

Vendor's replies to the requisitions

7. Omissions from the abstract. An omission from the abstract may be remedied by an answer to a requisition, with the result that the expense of verification is cast on the purchaser.

8. Time limits. The vendor must reply to the requisitions within a reasonable time. The purchaser may make time of the essence for an unanswered requisition by serving a notice on the vendor requiring him to give his answer by a specified date. Failure to reply by this date (provided it is a reasonable date) entitles the purchaser to rescind the contract. In *Re Stone and Saville's Contract* (1963) it was held that a notice to complete (*see* 6:30) served by the vendor on the purchaser, when requisitions going to the root of the title were unanswered, entitled the purchaser to rescind the contract at once. It was not necessary for the purchaser to serve a notice making time of the essence for the replies to the requisitions. A new provision in LS 15(2) not only imposes a time limit of four working days on the vendor but also makes time of the essence.

9. Replies to out-of-time requisitions. When replying to out-of-time requisitions, the vendor's solicitor should state that he does so "without prejudice", so that he preserves his right to object that these requisitions were sent out of time. If he does not do this, his reply will be deemed to have waived any objection he may have had to their late delivery.

10. Purchaser's observations on the vendor's replies. The purchaser, having received the vendor's replies, may still not be satisfied with the situation. In that case he can send observations on the vendor's replies. These must be sent within four (LS) or six (NC) working days of receiving the replies or he will be considered to have been satisfied on this matter as time is of the essence, according to LS 15(5) and NC 9.

As already stated, a purchaser who discovers a defect going to the root of the title may rescind the contract before the date for completion has arrived. Where this occurs, the purchaser must take care that he does not waive his right to rescind by asking for an explanation or demanding the getting in of outstanding interests (*see Elliott and H. Elliott (Builders)* v. *Pierson* (1948)).

11. The vendor's right to rescind. LS 16 and NC 10 give the vendor the right to rescind the contract if the purchaser persists in any requisition which the vendor is unable or unwilling *on reasonable grounds* to remove. Before he rescinds, he must serve notice on the purchaser that unless the requisition is withdrawn within seven working days (LS) or ten working days (NC) he will rescind the contract. If the purchaser still refuses to withdraw he may rescind the contract. Where the right to rescind is properly exercised the vendor is obliged to return the deposit to the purchaser, who must return the abstract to the vendor.

This condition is construed restrictively by the courts and only an honest vendor who has acted promptly and reasonably may rely on it. It cannot be used by a vendor who was reckless in contracting to sell what he did not own or as an excuse to avoid a legitimate expense. In *Greaves* v. *Wilson* (1858) the mortgagee of the land refused to agree to the sale. The vendor purported to rescind the contract on the grounds that to force him to obtain the consent of the mortgagee was unreasonable. The court held the vendor had no right to rescind the contract and awarded the purchaser damages for breach of contract.

In *Baines* v. *Tweddle* (1959) the type of recklessness which will prevent a vendor from exercising his right of rescission was described as "an unacceptable indifference to the situation of a purchaser who is allowed to enter into a contract with the expectation of obtaining a title which the vendor has no reasonable expectation of being able to deliver". As in *Greaves* v. *Wilson* (1858), this case concerned a vendor who contracted to sell the land free from encumbrances, without ensuring that his mortgagees would join in the sale to discharge the existing mortgage. The earlier case of *Re Des Reaux and Setchfield's Contract* (1926) makes the same point in relation to the recklessness of the vendor. The vendor will not be able to exercise his contractual right of rescission in relation to a matter of conveyance, as this cannot be the subject of a requisition (*see Leominster Properties Ltd* v. *Broadway Finance Ltd* (1981)).

If the vendor has no title at all to the property he has no right to rescind the contract. LS 16 and NC 10 have no application to this type of situation (*see Bowman* v. *Hyland* (1878)). It is a straightforward breach of contract.

12. Purchaser's contractual right of rescission. An important addition to both sets of conditions, to be found in LS 4 and NC 3 but which only apply to a contract if there is a special condition allowing it to operate, is the purchaser's right of rescission. By giving notice to the vendor either within the period mentioned in the special conditions or, if none, within (LS 4(2)) twenty working days of the date of the contract or (NC 3(3)) before the expiration of sixteen working days from the date of the contract, he may bring the contract to an end.

The notice must say on what basis the right of rescission is being exercised; the grounds of rescission are:

(*a*) a financial charge which the vendor cannot or will not discharge before completion;

(*b*) statutory restrictions on a particular use of the use of the premises, where the purchaser is buying the premises for that purpose; and (*c*) a matter likely to materially affect the purchase; (LS) NC any matter materially affecting the value of the premises, this would include the matters mentioned in LS (a) and (b).

The matter complained of must be in existence at the date of the contract. If the purchaser knew of the problem before the date of the contract, excluding all knowledge imputed to him by statute, he cannot use that problem as the basis of rescission.

Time is of the essence when giving notice.

Progress test 11

1. What is a requisition? (**1**)
2. What sort of matter should not be the subject of a requisition? (**4**)
3. What is the time period within which the purchaser must raise his requisitions? (**5**)
4. What sorts of requisitions are not bound by the normal time limits? (**6**)
5. What is the time limit for sending observations on the vendor's replies to requisitions? (**8**)
6. What remedy is given to a vendor where the purchaser persists in an unreasonable requisition? (**11**)

12
Pre-completion searches

This chapter examines the searches that should be made by the purchaser's solicitor immediately before completion in order to ascertain whether there are certain encumbrances affecting the vendor's title.

The Land Charges Department of the Land Registry

1. The five registers. LCA 1972, s. 1(1) lists the five registers that are kept by the department, the last being by far the most important. They are:

- (a) the register of pending actions (*see* **2**);
- (b) the register of annuities (*see* **3**);
- (c) the register of writs and orders (*see* **4**);
- (d) the register of deeds of arrangement (*see* **5**);
- (e) the register of land charges (*see* **6**).

In each register the entry is made against the name of the estate owner or other person whose land is affected.

2. The register of pending actions. (LCA 1972, s. 5.) In this is entered any action, information or proceeding pending in court relating to any interest in the land. A petition in bankruptcy, filed after 1925, is a pending action.

If the pending action is not registered, it will not bind a purchaser (for definition *see* LCA 1972, s. 17(1)) unless he has express notice of it. It should be noted that in relation to a petition in bankruptcy, it is only a purchaser of a legal estate for money or money's worth, acting in good faith and without notice of an available act of bankruptcy, who will not be bound by the petition if it is not registered.

3. The register of annuities. (LCA 1972, Sched. 1.) An annuity is a rentcharge or an annuity for a life or lives or for an estate determinable on a life or lives, provided it was not created by a marriage settlement or by will. It must have been created after 1855 and before 1926. The register will be closed when the existing entries are redundant. Annuities created since 1925 can be registered as Class C(III) charges (*see* **6**), if they do not arise under a settlement or a trust for sale.

4. The register of writs and orders affecting land. (LCA 1972, s. 6.) These entries are concerned with the enforcement of court orders and judgments. They include:

(*a*) writs or orders affecting land issued by the court for the purpose of enforcing a judgment, statute or recognisance;

(*b*) orders appointing a receiver or sequestrator of land;

(*c*) receiving orders in bankruptcy made after 1925.

If not registered, the writ or order will be void as against a purchaser of the land. However, a receiving order in bankruptcy, if not registered, will be void only against a purchaser of a legal estate for money or money's worth, acting in good faith, and without notice of an available act of bankruptcy.

5. The register of deeds of arrangement. (LCA 1972, s. 7.) A deed of arrangement, as defined by s. 1 of the Deeds of Arrangement Act 1914, may be registered by a trustee or by a creditor assenting to the deed or one who takes a benefit under it. Failure to register renders it void in relation to a purchaser of any land comprised in or affected by the deed.

6. The land charges register. (LCA 1972, s. 2.) In this, the most important register, the charges are classified as follows.

(*a*) *Class A* (s. 2(2)). These are charges upon land, created by statute, which only come into existence after the appropriate person has made an application under the particular statute. Once created they may be registered against the estate owner.

(b) *Class B* (s. 2(3)). These are similar charges to those in Class A, except that they are created by the particular statute and *not* by application thereunder.

(c) *Class C* (s. 2(4)). This class is subdivided as follows.

(i) *C(I): a puisne mortgage*, i.e. a legal mortgage not being protected by the deposit of documents relating to the legal estate affected.

(ii) *C(II): a limited owner's charge*, an equitable charge acquired by a tenant for life or by a statutory owner by statute because he has paid the capital transfer taxes or some other liability related to the estate, such liability being given special priority by statute.

(iii) *C(III): a general equitable charge*. This is a "sweeping-up" charge and under it comes any equitable charge which is not protected by the deposit of title deeds, is not included in any other class of land charge and does not arise or affect an interest arising under a trust for sale or settlement, e.g. liens.

(iv) *C(IV): an estate contract*, i.e. a contract by an estate owner, or someone who is entitled at the date of the contract to have the legal estate conveyed to him, to convey or create a legal estate. An option to purchase, a right of pre-emption (but see the doubts expressed in *Pritchard* v. *Briggs* (1980)), an option to renew a lease, even if contained in a lease (*Beesly* v. *Hallwood Estates* (1961) are examples falling within this class).

(d) *Class D* (s. 2(5)). There are three kinds of charge in this class:

(i) D(I), a charge on land acquired by the Commissioners of Inland Revenue for unpaid capital transfer taxes;

(ii) D(II), a restrictive covenant or agreement created after 1925 and not being one made between lessor and lessee (restrictive covenants in leases are never registrable);

(iii) D(III), an equitable easement, right or privilege, being merely equitable and created after 1925, e.g. equitable *profits à prendre*.

(e) *Class E* (s. 2(6)). This class covers annuities (*see* 3) not registrable in the register of annuities and created before 1926.

(*f*) *Class F* (s. 2(7)). This class covers charges affecting the matrimonial home by virtue of a spouse's right of occupation under the Matrimonial Homes Act 1983. In *Gurasz* v. *Gurasz* (1970) it was stated that this section only applies to give a right of occupation to a spouse who has no proprietary, contractual or statutory right. Therefore, if the house is vested jointly as to the legal estate, no charge is registrable. If the spouse has only an equitable interest, then a charge is registrable.

If the spouse is out of occupation, then a charge may be registered without the leave of the court, but the right of occupation is conditional and not enforceable without the leave of the court (see *Watts* v. *Waller* (1972)).

7. The effect of registration and non-registration. (LCA 1972, s. 4.) LPA 1925, s. 198 states that registration of a registrable matter shall be deemed to be actual notice of the interest registered to all persons and for all purposes connected with the land affected. There are three exceptions to the rule, as follows.

(*a*) Where a prior mortgage expressly states that it is to be security for any further advances, if made, then registration of a later mortgage is not deemed to be actual notice and will not prevent "tacking".

(*b*) When a mortgagor has discharged his first mortgage, the first mortgagee is not deemed to have notice of any subsequent mortgagees (to whom the title deeds should now be delivered) simply because the later mortgages were registered (LPA 1925, s. 96(2)).

(*c*) Whether a purchaser knew of a registered land charge when he entered into the contract is to be decided by reference to his actual knowledge (LPA 1969, s. 24).

The effect of non-registration as regards a registrable land charge is that, for Class C(IV) and Class D charges it is void against a purchaser of a legal estate for money or money's worth, and for any other charge it is void against a purchaser for value of any interest in the land affected. In *Midland Bank Trust Co Ltd* v. *Green* (1981) the House of Lords confirmed that the words "money or money's worth" were to be read literally.

Failure to register a charge does not affect its validity in relation to the person who created it. Thus, if a lessee has been granted an option to purchase by the lessor, he can sue for damages, even though he has not registered a Class C(IV) charge (*Wright* v. *Dean* (1948)).

Method of making a land charges search

8. **Mode of search.** A search may be made in person, by post, by telex or by telephone. Personal searches are unsound in practice as only an effective official certificate of the search can give a purchaser priority (*see* **11**).

In order to be effective to gain priority the search must provide no reasonable scope for misunderstanding (*see Du Sautoy* v. *Symes* (1967)).

9. **Postal search.** A postal search effective for all registers is made on Form K15. (A search of the Bankruptcy Only register may be made on Form K17, the only information required being the name of the person searched against.)

The information required for a postal search is as follows.

(*a*) *Name of estate owner*. The forename and surname should be on separate lines. The full correct name must be used (*see Oak Co-operative Building Society* v. *Blackburn* (1968)—a search against an incorrect name is invalid even where registration is against another incorrect name).

(*b*) *Period of years searched against*. The form provides for the period of years during which the estate owner has owned the property to be stated. To avoid error one may state "1926 to the current year" in all cases. This effects a valid search for the relevant period (but causes the Registry extra work).

(*c*) *County and former county*. These should be accurately stated.

(*d*) *Description of property*. If one is given it must be accurate and any relevant former description should be given. No description is necessary, nor should one be given unless the extensive land holdings of the estate owner would cause unacceptable delay in the search, in which case the Land Registry will edit the search to exclude those entries obviously not relevant to the description given.

10. The pre-completion search. (*a*) Searches (except where the estate owner has extensive land holdings) are generally returned by first-class post on the day following delivery of the search form. With this in mind searches should be made so that a large part of the priority period falls after completion in case it is delayed by a few days (*see* **11**).

(*b*) If the search reveals an adverse entry then the purchaser should take steps to ensure either that it does not concern the property purchased or that it is removed before completion or an acceptable undertaking as to its removal is given. An important step to take is to send off to the Registry for an office copy of the entry which will reveal further details of the interest protected. It is a common practice if the entry is referrable to a person other than the vendor (or his predecessor in title) or to land not the subject of the conveyance for the vendor's solicitor to certify the search to that effect. Although a common courtesy a purchaser cannot insist on this.

11. The priority period. The search protects a purchaser against any registration made before completion within fifteen days (i.e. working days—week-ends and bank holidays are not included) from the date of the search certificate.

12. Priority Notices. The need for a Priority Notice arises where there are two successive purchases of the same land (P1 and P2) and the first purchaser (P1) creates a registrable interest. The person with the benefit of that interest might find he loses priority against the second purchaser because he has not registered his interest before P2 takes place.

If the benefitted person registers a Priority Notice at the Land Charges Registry (at least fifteen working days before registration if his land charge is to be effective) and then after his purchase registers the land charge within thirty working days of registering the Priority Notice then his land charge is effective as if registered at the date the charge was created.

For example, A sells land to B reserving a restrictive covenant for his retained neighbouring land. Completion date of sale is 1st June. On that date B will mortgage the land to C to finance the purchase.

Thus, the restrictive covenant cannot effectively be registered in time to take priority over the mortgage. A must register a Priority Notice on, say, 10th May. On 1st June the restrictive covenant is created and when shortly thereafter A registers the covenant pursuant to his Priority Notice it takes effect as if made on 1st June and the mortgagee C therefore takes subject thereto.

Other searches

13. **Company search.** In the case of a purchase from a company vendor, a search should be made through company agents to ascertain the following.

(a) Whether a winding up has been commenced in respect of the company, in which case any disposition by the company would be void unless the court ordered to the contrary (Companies Act 1948, s. 227).

(b) Whether there are any specific charges affecting the property created before 1st January 1970. (Specific charges created on or after that date must be registered at the Land Registry (if appropriate). See LCA 1972, s. 3(7).)

(c) Whether there are any floating charges affecting the company's assets.

14. **Effect of charges against company vendor.** If there is a floating charge the purchaser requires evidence that this has not crystallised (i.e. become a fixed charge on the property in question; see Oliver, Company Law). Evidence of non-crystallisation is adequately provided by a letter to that effect signed by the company secretary or more satisfactorily (though not always insisted upon) by the chargee.

If there is a fixed charge on the property or the floating charge has crystallised the vendor must provide the chargee's release of the property from the charge in question.

15. **Land in Yorkshire.** By virtue of the relevant provisions of LPA 1969, ss. 16–17, the three Yorkshire Deeds Registries are now closed and no special searches are required or necessary in this area. If any query should arise the records are held by the Archivists of the three county councils replacing the former County of Yorkshire.

16. Local search. The question of whether to repeat this before completion should be considered if the search was carried out some time before completion.

Progress test 12

1. When does a purchaser of land take free from the effect of a bankruptcy petition against the estate owner from whom he purchases? (**2**)

2. What is a Class C(IV) land charge? (**6**)

3. What is a Class D(II) land charge? (**6**)

4. When does a purchaser take free from an unregistered Class C(IV) land charge? (**7**)

5. What information must be included in a postal search? (**9**)

6. Explain how the Priority Notice is used. (**12**)

7. When should a company search be made? (**13**)

8. What is meant by evidence of non-crystallisation? (**14**)

13
The conveyance

Preparation of the deed

1. Procedures. The rather elaborate procedure followed in unregistered conveyancing when preparing the conveyance deed is a characteristic part of the "to-and-fro" ritual which is such a feature of each transaction. First the purchaser's solicitor prepares a draft conveyance in duplicate and submits it to the vendor's solicitor. This is done either within the time so stipulated in the contract, if there is one, or in an open contract after a good title has been deduced by the vendor. The vendor's solicitor has the task of approving, or not, the draft conveyance. He returns the top copy with any amendments which he thinks it proper to make made on it in red. The form of the conveyance is for the purchaser to determine and the vendor must refrain from making purely formal alterations. When the form of the deed is so settled, the purchaser's solicitor has it engrossed (i.e. fair-copied). If the purchaser's execution is necessary (i.e. when the purchaser enters into a covenant or makes a grant to the vendor) this is added and then the deed is returned to the vendor's solicitor to be retained until completion.

2. Legal requirement for a deed. LPA 1925, s. 51 provides that land lies in grant, i.e. the legal title can be transferred by a deed of grant. The ancient forms of conveyance such as livery and seisin, feoffment, bargain and sale are declared to be abolished. Section 52 of that Act provides that a conveyance of the legal estate in land must be by a deed. There are certain exceptions set out in s. 52(2). These are:

(*a*) assents by personal representatives (*see* 10:**10–11**);

(*b*) disclaimers made in accordance with the Bankruptcy Act 1914, s. 54 (i.e. a disclaimer of an onerous contract) or not required to be evidenced in writing;

(*c*) surrenders by operation of law;

(*d*) leases for three years or less complying with LPA 1925, s. 54(2);

(*e*) receipts not required by law to be under seal;

(*f*) vesting orders of the court or other competent authority;

(*g*) conveyances taking effect by operation of law.

Layout and contents of a typical conveyance

3. Introduction. Problems arising in the contents of conveyances are discussed in **4–28** below. It should be noted that when drafting in the office recourse must be made to the books of precedents to find the proper form of conveyance that may be adapted to fit each transaction. The forms of conveyance vary according to the type of parties to the transaction, the interest sold, the incidents to which the land is made subject and so on. The student should gain added comprehension of this dimension of practice by examining an authoritative book of precedents, e.g. Volume 19 of the *Encyclopaedia of Forms and Precedents* together with the practical notes printed therein.

A specimen conveyance is illustrated in Fig. 1 to which reference should be made when reading the following paragraphs.

4. Commencement. The commencement in a modern conveyance will state the type of deed which follows, e.g. "THIS CONVEYANCE . . .", "THIS DEED OF GIFT . . .", etc.

5. Date. The date of the deed then follows (*see also* **35–37**). The effective date of the deed is not altered by inserting some other date (*see Goddard's Case* (1584)), but remains the date on which it is unconditionally delivered as a deed. Thus, if a land charges search has expired before the day of completion, protection is not obtained by inserting an earlier date. In fact LCA 1972, s. 11 gives protection only if the transaction is completed within the priority period (*see also* 12:**10–11**).

6. The parties. The full names and addresses of the parties are given. Occasionally a description is added (e.g. their occupation or "gentleman") but this is unnecessary verbiage. The parties will ordinarily be the vendor and the purchaser. In certain circumstances, other parties may be included, as follows.

(*a*) If there is a subsisting mortgage the mortgagee may join in to release the property conveyed (*see also* 18:**18**).

(*b*) In the case of settled land the trustees must be parties to give a receipt for the purchase money (*see* 10:**4**).

(*c*) Where the vendors are trustees for sale a beneficiary or other person may join in to give his consent if such is required (*see* 10:**6**).

(*d*) If the purchaser transfers to a nominee or has negotiated a subsale before completion the nominee or subpurchaser will also be a party and there may be other cases where a further party joins in to take or release some interest in the land.

7. Recital. This is the part of a deed which traditionally begins "WHEREAS . . .". Recitals are a descriptive and not an operative part of a deed. They are introduced to explain any necessary history of the transaction or of the vendor's title or to explain the purpose of the deed. Recitals are unnecessary; this was held as long ago as 1663 in the *Earl of Bath and Earl of Montague's Case*. Some modern precedents dispense with recitals for this reason. Certainly it can be hazardous to introduce a superfluous recital as is illustrated by the case of *Re Duce and Boots Cash Chemists (Southern) Ltd's Contract* (1937). In that case an unnecessary recital in an assent revealed that at the time in question the land was settled land and had been incorrectly vested (*see* 9:**9**).

8. Effect of a recital. There are a number of ways in which a recital may take effect despite the fact that it is not the operative part of the deed.

(*a*) A clear recital may control an ambiguous operative part of the deed. Thus, in *Jenner* v. *Jenner* (1866) the operative part of the deed

This Conveyance

is made the

First day   day of May

One thousand nine hundred and eighty B E T W E E N FRED BLANK of 1

Green Street Blanktown Glamorganshire (hereinafter called "the Vendor")

of the one part and JOHN GAP of 1 Blue Street Blanktown Glamorganshire

(hereinafter called "the Purchaser") of the other part_____

W H E R E A S

(1)   The Vendor is seised of the property hereinafter described for

an estate in fee simple in possession free from encumbrances save as

hereinafter mentioned and has agreed with the Purchaser for the sale to

him of the said property for a like estate at the price of twenty

thousand pounds_____ _____

NOW THIS DEED WITNESSETH

1.   In pursuance of the said agreement and in consideration of the

sum of TWENTY THOUSAND POUNDS now paid by the Purchaser to the Vendor

(the receipt of which sum the Vendor hereby acknowledges) the Vendor as

beneficial owner hereby conveys unto the Purchaser ALL THAT land and

property known as 1 Red Street Blanktown Glamorganshire as was conveyed

to the Vendor by William Hole by a conveyance of Second of May Nineteen

Hundred and Fifty and as is further therein more particularly described

and subject to the covenant therein contained but otherwise free from

encumbrances TO HOLD the same unto the Purchaser in fee simple_____

2.   WITH the object and intent of affording to the Vendor a full

and sufficient indemnity but not further or otherwise the Purchaser

hereby covenants with the Vendor to observe and perform the above

mentioned covenant and to indemnify the Vendor against all actions

claims demands and liability in respect thereof _____

Figure 1 *A specimen conveyance.*

3.   IT IS HEREBY CERTIFIED that the transaction hereby effected
does not form part of a larger transaction or of a series of transactions in respect of which the amount or value or the aggregate
amount or value of the consideration exceeds Twenty thousand pounds

       IN WITNESS whereof the parties hereto have hereunto set their
respective hands and seals the day and year first before written ____

SIGNED SEALED AND DELIVERED   ) *Fred Blank*   **LS**
by the aforementioned   )
FRED BLANK in the presence of)

R. Stone

End Cottage
Chapel Lane
Blanktown

Teacher

SIGNED **SEALED** AND DELIVERED) *John Gap*   **LS**
by the aforementioned   )
JOHN GAP in the presence of   )

M.G. Rush
16 Manor Road
Blanktown

Driver

Figure 1   (*contd.*).

was ambiguous as to which land was intended to pass but the recitals made this clear.

(b) A statement in a recital may operate as an estoppel against the person making the statement. This is illustrated by *Cumberland Court (Brighton)* v. *Taylor* (1964): M had mortgaged the property to D. M then conveyed the property to P. That conveyance to P contained a recital in common form that the vendor was seised in possession free from encumbrances. The receipt which D gave to discharge the mortgage was dated after the conveyance to P and thus by virtue of LPA 1925, s. 115(2) would operate not as a receipt but as a transfer of the mortgage to M. However, the court held that the effect of the recital of seisin free from encumbrances would estop M claiming that the receipt operated as a transfer.

(c) A recital may also have a statutory effect, as follows.

(i) LPA 1925, s. 45(6) provides that recitals, statements and descriptions of facts, matters and parties contained in instruments twenty years old are sufficient evidence of their truth unless proved to be inaccurate. This provision loses some of its importance when it is remembered that ordinarily only a fifteen-year title need be deduced (*see* 9:**12**).

(ii) AEA 1925, s. 36(6) provides that a statement in writing by a personal representative that he has made no assent or conveyance of the relevant land may in favour of a purchaser be sufficient evidence that no assent or conveyance has been made (*see* 10:**13**).

(iii) For the effect of a recital that a sole surviving joint tenant is beneficially entitled, *see* Law of Property (Joint Tenants) Act 1964, s. 1 and 10:**2–3**.

9. Omitting the recital. As a golden rule in drafting a modern conveyance one might be advised to omit recitals wherever possible. Nevertheless solicitors are loathe to discard even a time-wasting habit and, for example, it is still customary to recite the seisin of the vendor although this is quite unnecessary. Farrand (*Contract and Conveyance*) suggests: "for reasons of estoppel . . . it is submitted that recitals should not be omitted altogether . . .". However, a conveyancer does not seek to rely on the speculative effect of an estoppel and the sounder principle might be to omit all unnecessary, non-operative words where the alleged benefit is hypothetical and potentially hazardous.

10. The testatum. The operative part of the deed is still sometimes referred to as "the premises". It begins with the part of the deed called the "testatum" which is introductory and purely formal, viz. "NOW THIS DEED WITNESSETH".

11. Consideration and receipt. The formal words of the testatum are followed by a statement of the consideration for the transaction and a receipt by the vendor for the purchase money. In the case of settled land or land held on trust for sale or other cases where some party joins in to receive all or part of the purchase money, the receipt clause is varied appropriately. The receipt clause has three important effects, as follows.

(*a*) The receipt clause is a sufficient discharge for the purchase money and no other receipt is required by endorsement on the deed or otherwise (LPA 1925, s. 67). It may be noted that s. 67 does not prevent a vendor proving that part or all of the purchase money has not been paid (*Wilson* v. *Keating* (1859)). Neither does the presence of a receipt clause prevent the vendor having an unpaid vendor's lien (*Mackreth* v. *Symmons* (1808); *see also* 7:2).

(*b*) LPA 1925, s. 68 provides that the existence of this clause is, in favour of a subsequent purchaser who does not have notice of non-payment, sufficient evidence of the payment stated therein.

(*c*) A vendor's solicitor who produces the executed deed with the receipt clause need produce no other authority to receive the purchase money. The purchaser may thus safely pay the vendor's solicitor (LPA 1925, s. 69). Doubt has been expressed as to whether this provision protects the purchaser who pays the vendor's solicitor's clerk or his agent or London agent instead of the vendor's solicitor (*see* Law Society's *Digest Opinions*, Nos. 163 and 164). Although the wording of the section suggests that this doubt is justified no notice is taken of that in practice.

12. The words of grant. These are the words which pass the vendor's legal estate to the purchaser. Formerly verbose and technical words of grant were used. LPA 1925, s. 60 abolished the need for technical words of limitation (*see also* **19**). In addition, s. 51(2) of the Act provided that "the use of the word grant is not necessary to convey land or create any interest therein". Now any words showing the vendor's intention to pass the legal estate are sufficient for that purpose (*see Re Stirrup's Contract* (1961), 10:**10**). The usual words are "The vendor as beneficial owner [or as appropriate, *see* 14:**2–6**] hereby conveys . . ."

13. The parcels clause. This is the description of the property comprised in the conveyance. Although contemporary draftsmen have tended towards greater brevity in the description of the property, *utmost care* must still be exercised in this area and particular care taken to avoid the meaningless or erroneous transcription of previous descriptions of the land conveyed. There is a great deal of case law on the construction of particular parcels clauses, and the guiding principles and rules are discussed in **14–18** below.

14. Construction of a description where there is a verbal description and a plan. The draftsman in such cases (as in any case where there are two descriptions of the same subject-matter) must make it clear which is to prevail. Thus, it should be clear whether the plan is merely illustrative or whether it contains the operative description.

(*a*) The words "more clearly described in the plan" would indicate that the plan is meant to prevail over any deficiencies in the verbal description (*Eastwood* v. *Ashton* (1915)).

(*b*) The words "for the purposes of identification only" would clearly indicate that the verbal description is paramount and the plan only illustrative.

(*c*) In *Wiggington and Milner* v. *Winster Engineering* (1978) the Court of Appeal held that although a plan annexed to the conveyance and referred to as "for identification only" could not override an unambiguous verbal description, such a plan could be referred to where the description was unclear in order to determine the extent of the land conveyed.

15. Falsa demonstratio non nocet cum de corpore constat.

Where there is more than one description (whether including a plan or not) the court will apply this maxim to reject any description which is manifestly inaccurate. Thus, in *Maxted* v. *Plymouth Corporation* (1957) the Court of Appeal was able to reject a plan which, clearly inaccurately, excluded from the conveyance a strip of land adjoining a road included in the contract for sale. In contrast in *Truckell* v. *Stock* (1957) the court found that a verbal description (which included the whole of a dwelling house and thus the footings and eaves) and a plan (which appeared to exclude the footings and eaves) were not in conflict. Neither was erroneous: the plan was merely a plan view at ground level and the footings and eaves were thus included in the conveyance. There was no need to apply the maxim.

16. Presumptions. There are certain presumptions that the courts call in aid in the construction of parcels clauses, such as the following.

(*a*) Where the boundary is delimited by a hedge and a ditch there is a presumption that the boundary is on the other side of the ditch from the hedge (*see Vowles* v. *Miller* (1810)). This is supposedly because a landowner in building a hedge would stand on his boundary line and dig along it a ditch, the soil from which would form the bank for his hedge.

(*b*) Where land adjoins a road the presumption is that the adjoining landowner owns up to the mid-point of the road and thus a conveyance of that land includes that part of the road (*see LNWR* v. *Mayor of Westminster* (1902)).

(*c*) Where land adjoins a non-tidal river the land under the river up to the mid-point of the river is presumed to belong thereto (*see Blount* v. *Layard* (1891)).

17. Grants by the vendor. After the physical description in the parcels clause there follows any further grant by the vendor of easements or similar rights. These are commonly introduced by the words "TOGETHER WITH . . ."

When drafting grants the following points should be noted.

(*a*) The perpetuity rule applies to fresh rights which may arise at some future date but not rights over a road or through drains which already exist (*see Dunn* v. *Blackdown Properties Ltd* (1961)). Thus, where the rule does apply, if no perpetuity period is expressed the grant will be invalid if the right is not exercised during the "wait and see" period (*see* Perpetuities and Accumulations Act 1964, s. 3).

(*b*) Detailed drafting cannot be considered but the areas of concern are:

(*i*) the land to have the benefit of the right;

(*ii*) the parties to have the benefit;

(*iii*) the exact user to be allowed and the time for which the right may be exercised.

18. Exceptions and reservations. These will usually form part of the parcels clause and they put a limit on what the purchaser takes. An "exception" is the retaining by the vendor of some existing right or interest, e.g. an exception to the vendor of mining and mineral rights under the transferred property. A "reservation" is the description of some new right which the vendor is thenceforth to enjoy, e.g. the reservation of a new right of way over the land sold.

19. The habendum. This clause describes the estate which is transferred. We have seen the effect of LPA 1925, s. 60 (*see* 12). Nevertheless, even in freehold sales it is still the practice to include a formal habendum, the common form being "TO HOLD unto the purchaser in fee simple". In any event s. 60 provides that "a conveyance of freehold land . . . without words of limitation . . . shall pass to the grantee the fee simple or other the whole interest which the grantor had power to convey in such land, unless a contrary intention appears in the conveyance". Farrand (*Contract and Conveyance*) provides a salutary warning against failing to use the traditional words of limitation, as "the (statutory) provision is insufficiently certain in that a contrary intention may always inconveniently appear".

20. The reddendum. In a lease this is the next following clause which specifies the rent and rent days.

21. Covenants. Next the conveyance may include covenants either negative or positive on the part of either party. In modern conveyancing particularly on large building estates these covenants on the part of the purchaser may be very lengthy and are frequently contained in a schedule to the conveyance or transfer.

22. Indemnity covenants. Where the vendor remains liable on a covenant after the sale he should ensure that the purchaser enters into a covenant to indemnify the vendor in respect of any liability arising from a future breach of such a covenant (*see* clause 2 in the specimen conveyance in Fig. 1). Both the standard forms of conditions of sale (*see* Appendix 2) give the vendor a right to have such a covenant inserted in the conveyance (NC 19(5) and LS 11(2)). In the case of leasehold land conveyed for a valuable consideration such an indemnity covenant is implied by LPA 1925, s. 77—*see* 14:**13** (or in the case of registered land by LRA 1925, s. 24, although here the covenant is implied whether the transfer is for value or not).

The effect of the covenant is to indemnify the vendor against any liability under the covenant and for any costs and expenses in respect thereof. In his turn the purchaser should take such a covenant from his purchaser so that if he is liable under the indemnity covenant he can in his turn recover from his purchaser. The indemnity covenants should form an unbroken chain from purchaser to purchaser.

23. Express assignment of a covenant. An express assignment of a covenant is required if:

(*a*) the covenant is not annexed to the land intended to be benefited;

(*b*) the covenant is to pay a rentcharge, because the benefit of a covenant to pay a rentcharge does not run with the land (*Grant* v. *Edmondson* (1931)).

24. Declaration of trust. In drafting the conveyance a solicitor who is acting for co-owners of property (most commonly a husband and wife) must give some thought and take instructions as to the capacity in which they wish to hold the property—whether as joint tenants or as tenants in common. If their shares are unequal then thought must be given to preparation of a separate declaration of trust setting out their respective interests and then the property will be conveyed to them jointly "on the trusts declared by a declaration of trust made between the purchasers and dated ...th day of ...".

25. Joint tenants. Where the property is conveyed to joint tenants a clause is very often included declaring that they hold as joint tenants in equity and then conferring on the co-owners extended powers of dealing with the land. The part of the clause conferring additional powers is in the following form:

> "until the expiration of twenty-one years from the death of the survivor of the purchasers the trustees for the time being of this deed shall have power to sell, mortgage, charge or lease or otherwise dispose of all or any part of the said property with all the powers in that behalf of an absolute owner".

The practical advantages of this clause are rather remote from the ordinary purchaser. So far as the original owners are concerned they in any event have all the powers of an absolute owner while they themselves own the entire beneficial interest. The purchaser, of course, cannot assume that they do own the whole beneficial interest and ought not to enquire into the beneficial ownership. Thus, so far as a purchaser is concerned, the joint tenants have the powers of dealing with the land conferred on trustees for sale by LPA 1925, s. 28 and SLA 1925, Part II. These powers may be unduly restrictive in the areas of mortgaging and leasing and the clause quoted above removes these restrictions. (A further detailed analysis of the effect and need for such a clause in a conveyance to joint tenants is found in Farrand, *Contract and Conveyance*.)

26. The acknowledgment for production. If appropriate, this will follow (*see* **16:7**).

27. The certificate for value. This is invariably the final clause (*see* the specimen conveyance on pp. 137–8) and certifies which band of ad valorem stamp duty, if any, the transaction falls within (*see* **17:1**).

28. The testimonium. This is the formal clause which precedes the parties' execution of the deed and is in some such form as: "IN

WITNESS whereof the parties hereto have hereunto set their respective hands and seals the day and year first before written''.

Execution and attestation of the deed

29. Manner of execution. LPA 1925, s. 73(1) provides that "where an individual executes a deed, he shall either sign or place his mark upon the same and sealing alone shall not be deemed sufficient". Although this elusively worded provision is not explicit there are three formal requirements for a deed, namely it must be signed, sealed and delivered. The effective date of the deed is the time of delivery (*see* 5 and 35–37, and *Goddard's Case* (1584)).

30. The signature. This may be a signature or a mark. There is a lack of case law, but there is no reason to expect a narrower construction than under the Wills Act 1837 where the courts have given an extensive meaning to the requirement for a "signature" (*see*, for example, *Jenkins* v. *Gaisford and Thring* (1863) where the "signature" was effected by means of an engraved stamp and this was held valid).

31. The seal. A small paper-wax seal is now commonly used. The courts have leant in favour of upholding the validity of documents in this regard rather than insisting on an over-technical compliance with the requirement for sealing. Thus, in *Stromdale and Ball* v. *Burden* (1952) it did not matter that the seal was not affixed by the signatory; his signature was sufficient recognition of the seal. Similarly, in *Re Smith* (1892) where the document was expressed to be "sealed with my seal" but no seal was apparent, the deed was held valid without further evidence of the sealing. In *First National Securities* v. *Jones* (1978) CA a mortgage deed was signed by the mortgagor. The signature was across a printed circle at the end of the deed and in that circle were printed the letters LS (standing for the Latin phrase *locus sigilli* meaning the place of the seal). This mortgage was held to be validly executed.

32. Delivery of the deed. Delivery is the act which makes the document an effective deed. Delivery may be by express formal words, i.e. "I deliver this as my solemn deed and covenant", or, as is invariably the case today, implied from any words or acts showing that the document is intended to be finally executed (*see Xenos* v. *Wickham* (1866)).

33. Attestation. At common law the validity of a deed is not affected by the fact that the signature is not witnessed (but for registered transfers, *see* 28:7). However, it is the invariable custom for all conveyancing deeds to be witnessed by some person not a party thereto who adds his signature and customarily his address and description.

34. Execution of instruments by corporations. The relevant provisions are contained in LPA 1925, s. 74. Where the corporate seal has been fixed to the deed and attested by two witnesses purporting to be "his clerk, secretary or other permanent officer or his deputy, and a member of the board of directors, council or other governing body of the corporation", then the deed is deemed to be executed properly. A purchaser is not prejudiced by some internal irregularity in the company: *D'Silva* v. *Lister House Development* (1971).

Escrow

35. Definitions. The term "escrow" need cause no confusion. An escrow is simply a deed that has been delivered conditionally. It is not an effective deed of the party so delivering it until the condition is fulfilled. On fulfilment of the condition the deed is an effective deed from the original date of delivery (*see* e.g. *Alan Estates Ltd* v. *W. G. Stores Ltd* (1981)). The effect of this rule is that the legal estate is said to have passed at the time of the original conditional delivery. This does not affect the vendor's right to rents and profits pending completion (*see* 7:1). (Nor does the rule affect the validity of searches where this depends on the date of "completion", *see* 12:11.)

36. Examples. It will readily be appreciated that in the routine conveyancing situation the vendor's solicitor may obtain his client's execution some days before the business of completion actually takes place. Such circumstances will readily give rise to the inference that the deed was delivered as an escrow. The following cases have discussed the question of what, in such a case, is the condition of the escrow.

(a) *Kingston* v. *Ambrian Investment Co. Ltd* (1975). Where a vendor executes a conveyance in advance of completion he ordinarily does so subject to a condition thereafter to be fulfilled. In the Court of Appeal Buckley and Scarman LJJ said this condition was that completion should take place "in due course". Lord Denning MR in the same case amplified this as "simply that the purchaser should pay the purchase price and costs within a reasonable time".

(b) *Glissing* v. *Green* (1975) CA. In this case where the vendor executed the conveyance in advance of completion the court explained further the nature of the implied condition. There was "an implied condition that (the transaction) would be completed in due course in accordance with normal conveyancing practice". Once a completion notice had been validly served and expired then it was impossible for the purchaser to satisfy the condition by tendering the purchase money and offering to complete.

37. Companies. In *Beesly* v. *Hallwood Estates* (1961) the Court of Appeal held that a company could deliver a deed as an escrow.

Progress test 13

1. How may recitals in a deed take effect? (**8**)
2. What are the three effects of the receipt in the body of a conveyance? (**11**)
3. Explain what is meant by the "habendum". (**19**)
4. When is express assignment of the benefit of a covenant necessary? (**23**)
5. What is the value of the usual clause extending the powers of disposition of joint tenants? (**25**)
6. What is required for a deed to be validly sealed? (**31**)
7. What is meant by delivery of a deed? (**32**)
8. What are the requirements for execution of a deed on behalf of a corporation? (**34**)
9. Explain what is meant by "delivery in escrow". (**35**)

14
Implied covenants

Covenants for title

1. Nature of the covenants for title. The covenants for title are the various promises made by the vendor to the purchaser as to the title which is transferred. These promises are made in the conveyance. The doctrine of merger is discussed in 17:**6–7**. It will be seen that after completion the vendor's contractual promises will have merged in the conveyance and the purchaser must rely on the covenants for title in the conveyance.

2. Nature of the implied covenants. In the past the vendor's covenants for title were set out at great length in the conveyance. These days covenants for title are implied by virtue of LPA 1925, s. 76 and additional covenants are implied in leasehold transactions by LPA 1925, s. 77. The covenants implied in each case depend upon the capacity in which the vendor conveys the property. It must be noted that the parties may in their contract introduce different covenants or vary the statutory covenants. In freehold conveyancing this is uncommon. In leasehold conveyancing the usual covenants may be varied where there is an existing breach of the covenants in the lease.

3. Implied covenants in conveyance as beneficial owner. Where a person conveys *and* is expressed to convey as beneficial owner, the following are implied:

    (*a*) good right to convey;

    (*b*) covenant for quiet enjoyment;
    (*c*) freedom from encumbrances;
    (*d*) covenant for further assurance.

These covenants are set out in LPA 1925, Sched. 2, Part I and should be carefully examined in full. It will be seen that in the Act they are actually described as a single covenant and set out in one block. However, for convenience of discussion, the textbooks invariably classify them as if there were four covenants as above.

These covenants are implied only if the conveyance is for valuable consideration. This does not include marriage consideration.

4. Implied covenants in conveyance as "settlor". (LPA 1925, s. 76(1)(E); Sched. 2, Part V.) Where a person conveys and is expressed to convey as settlor then a covenant for further assurance is the only covenant implied. A conveyance may be made as settlor in the case of a conveyance of land into a settlement or of an outright gift.

5. Implied covenants in conveyance by a fiduciary owner. Where a person conveys and is expressed to convey as "mortgagee", ' trustee" or "personal representative" or "under an order of the court", only one covenant is implied by LPA 1925, s. 76(1)(F); Sched. 2, Part VI, namely a covenant that the person conveying has not encumbered the title. This covenant may be implied in an assent whether it is by deed or under hand (*see* 10:**11**).

6. Implied covenants on a mortgage of land. Where freehold land is mortgaged by a mortgagor who charges the land as "beneficial owner" then the usual beneficial-owner covenants set out in **3** are implied by virtue of LPA 1925, s. 76(1)(D). This covenant is set out in Sched. 2, Part IV. In the case of leasehold land it includes, as well as the beneficial-owner covenants, a covenant with the mortgagee to pay the rent and perform the covenants in the lease so long as any money remains owing on the security. (The effect of the mortgagor's covenant is further discussed in **7**.)

7. Liability of the vendor. In the case of a mortgagor his implied covenants as beneficial owner are absolute and he is liable for any breach thereof. In other cases the beneficial-owner covenants are qualified. In these cases the vendor is liable for any breach caused by an act or omission of himself or any person through whom he claims otherwise than for value.

For example, S sells Redhouse to V. V sells Redhouse to P. Before selling the land S had mortgaged it to H Ltd who now wish to enforce their mortgage. P has no action against V on the implied covenants for title unless he took from S other than for value, i.e. if the conveyance to V was other than a conveyance on sale.

The vendor is also liable for the acts or omissions of any person claiming through him. This is illustrated by *David* v. *Sabin* (1893), in which the facts were as follows.

V leased a parcel of land to T. T mortgaged this land to M. T subsequently surrendered his lease to V but the mortgage remained undischarged. V did not know of the existence of the mortgage. V then sold the property to P conveying as beneficial owner. The existence of the unredeemed mortgage was a breach of the implied covenant for title for which V was liable although it was created by T and V had no knowledge of it.

In *David* v. *Sabin* an *obiter* of Lindley LJ suggested that the vendor is liable in respect of an act or omission affecting the title by anyone claiming in trust for the vendor.

8. Benefit of the covenant. The benefit of the covenant once given runs with the land (LPA 1925, s. 76). Thus, it has been seen in the example in **7** that, where the conveyance to V was a conveyance on sale, P could not sue V in respect of the mortgage which S had made to the company H Ltd. However, the benefit of the covenant which S gave V is annexed to the land. P is thus able to sue S for breach of the covenant as the benefit has passed to him.

9. Onus of proof in actions for breach. The person endeavouring to bring an action for breach of an implied covenant for title has the onus of proving that the person through whom he claims is liable for the breach (*see Stoney* v. *Eastbourne Rural District Council* (1927)). There may also be a practical difficulty in such a case of finding the previous owner whom he wishes to sue.

Implied covenants in leasehold transactions

10. Assignment of a lease by a beneficial owner. In an assignment of a lease by and expressed as by a beneficial owner s. 76 implies the same covenants as in the case of a freehold conveyance. In addition (except in the case of a mortgage) s. 76(1)(B) implies a further covenant to the effect that the lease was validly granted and is still subsisting and that the covenants and other obligations on the part of the lessee have been complied with up to the date of the conveyance (Sched. 2, Part II). As is the case with freehold conveyances, marriage is not regarded as valuable consideration in this context. It has been queried whether the lessee's obligations under the lease amount to valuable consideration (where there is no premium), but there can be no real doubt particularly if one of the obligations is to pay rent.

11. Assignment of lease as settlor or fiduciary owner. In an assignment of a lease as and expressed to be in any of these categories, the same covenants are implied as in the case of a freehold conveyance (*see* **4** and **5** above) and the further covenant in s. 76(1)(B) is not implied.

12. Grant of a lease. It must be carefully noted that there are no implied covenants for title on the grant of a lease or an under-lease.

13. Covenants by the assignee to perform the lease. The original lessee will always be bound in contract to pay the rent and perform the other obligations of the lease unless he is released by the landlord from his obligations. The lessee will, therefore, try to ensure that when he assigns the lease, his assignee covenants with him to perform the obligations under the lease and to indemnify the assignor in respect of his liability thereunder.

(*a*) In the case of an assignment for valuable consideration (other than a mortgage) of *all the land* comprised in a lease for the entire residue of the term, then LPA 1925, s. 77(1)(C) implies on the part of the assignee the covenant set out in Sched. 2, Part IX of the Act. That is a covenant with the assignor to pay the rent, perform the covenants and other obligations under the lease, and indemnify the assignor in respect of his liability under the lease.

(*b*) LPA 1925, s. 77(1)(D)(i) implies a covenant by the assignee with the assignor in a conveyance for valuable consideration (other than a mortgage) of *part of the land* comprised in a lease. The covenant (set out in Sched. 2, Part X(i) of the Act) is to pay the apportioned rent, perform the covenants and obligations in the lease, and indemnify the assignor in respect of any liability therefor.

14. Covenant by conveying party. In the situation covered by **13**(*b*), s. 77(1)(D)(ii) implies a covenant by the conveying party with the assignee. This covenant (set out in Sched. 2, Part X(ii) of the Act) is that the conveying party will pay the balance of the rent (that is the apportioned rent on the unsold part), perform the covenants under the lease, and indemnify the assignee against the consequences of the assignor's breach or non-performance.

15. Rent legally apportioned. Where in a conveyance of part of the land in a lease the rent is legally apportioned (i.e. apportioned with the consent of the lessor) then the covenants in s. 77(1)(D) by the assignor and the assignee respectively are not implied. The reason for this is that in such a case each party will have entered into an express covenant with the lessor to pay his apportioned part of the rent and perform the covenants in the lease.

16. Assignment other than for valuable consideration. On an assignment other than for valuable consideration an express indemnity covenant should be taken by the assignor.

17. Covenant with landlord. Many leases provide that on an assignment the assignee must enter into a deed of covenant directly with the landlord to pay the rent and perform the covenants and obligations under the lease.

NOTE: Proof of performance of covenants and breach of covenants in leasehold transactions are discussed in 19:**13–15**.

Progress test 14

1. What are the four covenants for title implied in a sale for value by the expression "as beneficial owner"? (**3**)

2. What covenant is implied by the expression "as mortgagee"? (**5**)

3. What covenants are implied on the mortgage of land by a beneficial owner? (**6**)

4. Suppose A purchases a house from B in ignorance of a lease which B has granted to X and then sells the house to C who is also ignorant of the lease. Is A liable to C under the implied covenant for title? (**7**)

5. Is B liable to C under the implied covenant for title? (**8**)

6. Does C have the onus of proving who granted the lease or do A and B have the onus of disproving that they granted it? (**9**)

7. What covenants for title are implied on the assignment of a lease by a beneficial owner? (**10**)

8. What covenant to perform the lease is contained in an assignment for valuable consideration? (**13**)

9. How are the covenants in question 8 varied on the assignment of part of the land if the rent is legally apportioned? (**15**)

15

Remedies for disputes and breach of contract

Vendor and purchaser summons

1. Availability of remedy. LPA 1925, s. 49(1) makes available to either the purchaser or the vendor a summary remedy for any dispute: "in respect of any requisitions or objections, or any claim for compensation or any other question arising out of or connected with the contract (not being a question affecting the existence or validity of the contract)".

2. Return of deposit. Section 49(2) provides that "where the court refuses to grant specific performance of a contract, or in any action for the return of a deposit, the court may if it thinks fit, order the return of any deposit".

It was not clear in the past whether this subsection gave the court jurisdiction in a vendor and purchaser summons to order return of the deposit on an application by the purchaser in a case where the vendor would have been awarded specific performance if he had claimed this instead of rescinding and forfeiting the deposit. That point arose before the Court of Appeal in *Universal Corporation* v. *Five Ways Properties Ltd* (1979). The purchaser had paid a deposit of £88,500 but failed to complete and the vendor had in due course rescinded and forfeited the deposit. The purchaser applied to the court for a return of his deposit. The judge struck out his claim. The Court of Appeal declared that the judge was wrong. Section 49(2) gave the court an unfettered discretion to award a return of a deposit where justice so required. The judge's order striking out the purchaser's claim was accordingly reversed and the issue of whether the deposit ought to be returned remained to be tried (*see also* 6:**37**).

3. Use of remedy. Other situations where a vendor and purchaser summons might be used are:

(*a*) a dispute as to whether the vendor has shown a good title;

(*b*) a dispute as to whether the purchaser has raised a valid requisition;

(*c*) a dispute as to whether either party has validly withdrawn from the contract;

(*d*) a dispute as to whether a completion notice (*see* 6:**30–33**) served by either party was valid.

Remedies for breach of contract

4. Availability of remedies. Either party may bring an action for breach of contract before completion has taken place. The remedies available are:

(*a*) damages (*see* **6–10**);

(*b*) specific performance (*see* **11–15**);

(*c*) rescission (*see* **16–20**).

5. Remedies after completion. Once the transaction has been completed these remedies are usually not available. The extent to which they are, the doctrine of merger and the post-completion remedies are discussed in 17:**6–12**.

Damages

6. Introduction. Either party to a contract for the sale of land may recover damages in respect of the other party's breach. The ordinary contractual principles as to measure of damages apply, except as discussed below (*see* **7–9**). In the same way the ordinary rules of remoteness of damage illustrated by *Hadley* v. *Baxendale* (1854) as explained in *Koufos* v. *Czarnikow* (1969) apply.

7. Operation of principles. The operation of these principles is illustrated by the following.

(a) *Beard* v. *Porter* (1948). The vendor in breach of contract could not give the purchaser vacant possession of the property. The purchaser purchased another property instead and could recover as damages the difference between the contractual purchase price and the market value of the property at the time of the breach (for the interesting question of the time of assessment of damages *see* **10**), together with the expenses of his lodgings while finding another property and his legal costs on that other purchase.

(b) *Diamond* v. *Campbell-Jones* (1961). The vendor failed to complete. The purchaser sought as damages his loss of profit on a subsale. The vendor was unaware that there was a subsale in view and the purchaser could not recover in respect of this head of damages.

(c) *Cottrill* v. *Steyning & Littlehampton Building Society* (1966). In contrast the purchaser in this case could recover as part of his damages loss of his expected profit where the vendor was aware of his intention to redevelop the property.

8. The rule in *Bain* v. *Fothergill* (1874). This rule states that if the vendor is in breach of contract through an inability to make a good title the purchaser cannot recover damages for loss of bargain. He can only recover:

(a) his deposit together with interest thereon and interest on the balance of the purchase money if it has been lying idle awaiting completion and the vendor is aware of that fact;

(b) the expenses of investigating title.

The rule arose when conveyancing was a more hazardous business and deducing title a more contentious operation than today. The idea behind the rule was to protect the vendor from the hazards of this game which might unfairly fall to his lot. In modern practice the rule would more often operate to allow a vendor repenting of his bargain to escape from his contract relatively scot free. Accordingly the courts have restricted the rule, regarding its operation as anomalous and not to be extended (*see* **9**).

9. Application of *Bain* v. *Fothergill*. The extent of application of the rule is illustrated as follows:

(*a*) In *J. W. Cafes Ltd* v. *Brownlow Trust Ltd* (1950) the rule was held to apply to defects of title arising following a contract to grant a leasehold interest—in that case the existence of a restrictive covenant affecting the use to which the land might be put.

(*b*) The rule does not apply to a breach brought about by the vendor's refusal to make a good title, e.g. in *Day* v. *Singleton* (1899) where the vendor encouraged the lessor to refuse his consent; or in *Malhotra* v. *Choudhury* (1979) where one of two joint tenants contracted to sell but refused to make any attempt to obtain the other's concurrence and was guilty of bad faith.

(*c*) The rule did not apply where the vendor was financially unable to obtain the release of the property from a mortgage (*Re Daniel* v. *Vassall* (1917)). This is so even if the purchaser is aware of the mortgage when making the contract (*Thomas* v. *Kensington* (1942)).

(*d*) Judicial opinion has been expressed that in modern conditions the rule is unfair and anomalous and will not be extended. Thus, in *Wroth* v. *Tyler* (1973) the vendor was in breach of contract because his wife registered a charge under the Matrimonial Homes Act 1967 before completion. Megarry J held that this breach did not come within the rule and the purchaser obtained full damages calculated as the difference between the contract price and the value of the house at the time of the hearing.

(*e*) In *Watts* v. *Spence* (1976) it was held that the rule did not apply to an action for damages for misrepresentation under the Misrepresentation Act 1967, s. 2(1). (*Bain* v. *Fothergill* had never applied to an action for damages for fraudulent misrepresentation.)

(*f*) In *Sharneyford* v. *Edge* (1985) the High Court held that the rule did apply where a vendor could not give vacant possession because an occupier claimed a business tenancy under it. The court also held that damages could be recovered for non-fraudulent misrepresentation under the 1967 Act (not following, however, *Watts* v. *Spence* (which had been followed in *Errington* v. *Martell-Wilson* (1980) as to the measure of damages); the 1976 case allowing the contractual measure of damages, the 1985 case the tortious measure).

(g) In *Ray* v. *Druce* (1985) a vendor had already conveyed part of the property he contracted to sell the purchaser. Although this was the result of lax conveyancing, it was held *Bain* v. *Fothergill* did apply—that the previous conveyance was a while ago (1976) and the extent of the purchaser's knowledge of the difficulty were relevant.

10. Time at which damages are assessed.

(a) In ordinary cases damages are assessed as at the date of the breach (*Johnson* v. *Agnew* (1979) HL).

(b) Where the ordinary rule might cause injustice the court has power to fix some other date. For example, in *Johnson* v. *Agnew*, where one party had refused to comply with an order of specific performance, the date fixed was the date when the possibility of performance of the contract was "lost" as a result of the vendor's mortgagee entering into a binding contract for the sale of the property.

Specific performance

11. Nature of the remedy. Specific performance is an equitable remedy. It is readily available in respect of a breach of contract by either the vendor or the purchaser in a contract for the sale of land. The order of the court is an order to the party in breach compelling performance of the contract. It may be noted that a writ for specific performance may be issued before the contractual completion date (*Hasham* v. *Zenab* (1960)). In such a case damages can be claimed on a cause of action giving rise to such a claim before the trial (*Oakacre Ltd* v. *Claire Cleaners (Holidays) Ltd* (1981)) even though, because the completion date had not been reached, the cause of action had not existed when the writ was issued.

12. Refusal of the remedy. Specific performance may be refused by the court if the contract is illegal or if there is no mutuality between the parties (i.e. the remedy is not available to both parties; see *Flight* v. *Bolland* (1828) where specific performance was held not to be available in favour of a minor since it could not be ordered against him). Specific performance may also be refused where the contract is affected by fraud, mistake, misrepresentation, inequitable conduct, hardship to the other party or delay in pursuing the remedy.

13. Delay. Where the purchaser has taken possession and then seeks to obtain an order for specific performance for the vendor to convey the legal title, the vendor cannot claim "laches" (i.e. delay) as a bar to the remedy. This was held in *Williams* v. *Greatrex* (1956) because the purchaser should not be prejudiced as he had relied on his equitable title and the vendor's acquiescence in his possession. Recently in *Lazard Bros & Co* v. *Fairfield Properties* (1977) Megarry J held that even in the absence of possession delay in itself is not enough to bar the remedy. The delay must have been such as to prejudice the other party.

14. Specific performance plus indemnity. In *Grant* v. *Dawkins* (1973) Mr Justice Goff awarded the purchaser an indemnity in addition to specific performance. The property sold was subject to mortgages. The mortgage debts were more than the purchase price. The purchaser could abate the price and that being insufficient was able to recover as damages or indemnity the excess required to redeem the mortgages.

15. Specific performance and damages. In *Johnson* v. *Agnew* (1979) the court dealt with the following points.

(*a*) The fact that one party had obtained an order of specific performance did not prevent him applying to the court for damages (e.g. if he could not enforce the order). On this point the decision in *Capital and Suburban Properties Ltd* v. *Swycher* (1976) was wrong.

(*b*) In such a case the court could award common law damages. Accordingly, in so far as *Biggin* v. *Minton* (1977) had held that in such a case any damages in lieu of specific performance under the Chancery Amendment Act 1858, s. 2 could be awarded, that case was wrong.

(*c*) In such a case the court would order damages if it was equitable to do so because once the matter was in the hands of a court of equity it should thereafter be dealt with on equitable principles.

Thus, in this case the vendor was awarded damages because it was the purchaser's fault that the decree of specific performance had not been complied with.

It should be noted that in the circumstances discussed above the plaintiff will ordinarily have to make an election whether to pursue the remedy of specific performance when the action is commenced.

Rescission

16. Nature of the remedy. Rescission is the remedy whereby the contracting parties are restored to their original position. The contract is "undone" *ab initio* and the property or money which has passed thereunder is returned.

17. Availability. Rescission may take place:

(*a*) by agreement between the parties;

(*b*) where a contractual provision entitles one party to rescind the contract on specified terms in certain circumstances (*see*, for example, the contractual provisions discussed in 6:**36–38**);

(*c*) where a breach of contract by one party entitles the other to treat the contract as at an end; (A recent example is *Pips (Leisure Productions) Ltd* v. *Walton* (1981), where on a contract for the sale of a lease forfeiture proceedings had been commenced against the vendor, the purchaser was able to rescind even before the contractual completion date.)

(*d*) where one party applies to the court for the remedy of rescission to be awarded.

An action for rescission may be brought following a breach of contract by the other party or on the grounds of misrepresentation, mistake, fraud, equitable fraud or any other ground on which a court of equity is prepared to set the contract aside.

18. Rescission and damages. In *Horsler* v. *Zorro* (1975) Megarry J held that a plaintiff could not seek rescission and damages as alternatives. This statement of principle was much criticised. The principles have been restated disapproving *Horsler* v. *Zorro* in

Buckland v. *Farmar and Moody* (1979) by Goff LJ and on this point Lord Justice Goff's judgment was approved by the House of Lords in *Johnson* v. *Agnew* (1979). These principles are as follows.

(*a*) Where rescission is sought as a remedy in itself, e.g. for mistake, then damages cannot also be sought at the same time. The effect of rescission in such a case is to annul the contract *ab initio*, which means that the plaintiff loses the right to damages. (In the case of a misrepresentation, however, it may be that as a result of the Misrepresentation Act 1967 a plaintiff is able both to sue for damages under s. 2(1) and to claim rescission.)

(*b*) Where the contract has been rescinded by the plaintiff because of the other's breach or where rescission is sought as an affirmation that the contract has been repudiated by the other's breach, then damages may be sought.

Thus, in *Buckland* v. *Farmar and Moody* the vendor had written to the purchaser to say that the contract was rescinded following the purchaser's failure to complete. The vendor was still entitled to maintain an action for damages.

19. Examples. The following two examples further illustrate these principles.

(*a*) V contracts to sell Blackacre to P. He then conveys the land to X. This is a fundamental breach of contract by V which terminates the contract. P may treat the contract as rescinded and sue V for damages.

(*b*) V contracts to sell Blackacre to P and refuses to complete on time. P serves a valid notice to complete and when this expires he may rescind the contract and sue for damages.

20. Effect of rescission. Each party is required to return any benefit he has received under the contract (but *see* **2** for discussion of LPA 1925, s. 49 and the court's discretion to return the deposit). In an action for rescission the plaintiff may not also claim damages (*see* **18** above). He may, however, claim an indemnity in respect of any loss he has incurred as a result of some obligation under the contract (*Whittington* v. *Seale-Hayne* (1900)). For example, L leases office premises to T. T covenants to rebuild the office partitions. T rescinds because of L's misrepresentation. T can in his action for misrepresentation recover as an indemnity the loss he has incurred in complying with his contractual obligation under this covenant.

Progress test 15

1. When does the court have jurisdiction to order return of the purchaser's deposit? (**2**)

2. Give examples of the rules for remoteness of damages applied to conveyancing contracts. (**7**)

3. Explain the rule in *Bain* v. *Fothergill* (1874). (**8**)

4. How has the operation of the rule in *Bain* v. *Fothergill* been restricted? (**9**)

5. When will the court refuse specific performance? (**12**)

6. When can a party obtain damages having already been awarded an order of specific performance? (**15**)

7. What is the relationship between the remedy of rescission and the availability of damages? (**18**)

8. What is the effect of rescission? (**20**)

16
Completion of the transaction

Introduction

1. Time and place. The date for completion should be stated in the contract (*see* 6:**26**). Ordinarily completion will take place at the office of the vendor's solicitor (*see* 6:**27**). If there is an outstanding mortgage on the property and the mortgagee will not release the deeds to the vendor's solicitor until after it is discharged then completion will take place at the mortgagee's solicitor's premises.

2. Meaning of completion. Completion is the occasion for the following rituals:

(*a*) settling of the financial account between the vendor and the purchaser;

(*b*) completion of the legal work and handing over of the executed deed and the title deeds to the purchaser's solicitor.

In unregistered conveyancing the legal estate is vested in the purchaser (for the position in registered conveyancing *see* 26:**4**). The purchaser is also entitled to possession of the property and although the solicitor obviously cannot oversee the transfer of possession he should ensure that satisfactory arrangements have been made to that end.

The mechanics of completion

3. The purchase money. The purchaser's solicitor must attend on completion with the balance of the purchase money. Nowadays informal completions where the completion money is sent by telegraphic transfer or post are common in practice. The vendor's solicitor is obliged to accept only cash or its equivalent. This means that in practice a banker's draft is the means of payment. If a loss is caused because the purchaser's solicitor accepts a cheque (or any other form of conditional payment) then he is personally liable (*Pape* v. *Westacott* (1894)). The conveyance or transfer provides a receipt for the money and LPA 1925, s. 69 provides that this receipt in the deed is sufficient authority for the vendor's solicitor to receive the money (*see* 13:**11**).

4. Examination of title deeds. On completion the purchaser's solicitor will examine the title deeds and ensure that the abstract of title supplied is an accurate account thereof. Failure to examine the abstract until completion may cause problems in raising requisitions out of time (*see* 11:**5**). It may be negligent to leave the examination until completion (*Emmet on Title*). Nevertheless the practice of leaving examination of the deeds until completion is a universal one. In case of any doubt (e.g. an unclear abstract or illegible photocopies of old deeds) an appointment should be made to examine the original deeds within the time for raising requisitions on title.

5. Marking the abstract. Where the purchaser's solicitor does not on completion obtain the title deeds he instead marks the abstract of title as compared with the original; that is, he compares the abstract with the original and satisfies himself that they correspond and then endorses the abstract as "Examined against the originals at the office of . . ." and dates and signs the endorsement. This examined and endorsed abstract is then utilised in lieu of title deeds when the purchaser in his turn comes to sell the property. In practice the new purchaser accepts the examined abstract at face value (unless there is some defect on the face of it) and does not seek to see the original title deeds. (This practice of accepting marked abstracts is universally accepted although in the opinion of the Law Society it may be negligent, *see* 66 LS Gaz. (1969) 96.)

6. Vendor's right to retain the title deeds. Ordinarily on completion the purchaser is entitled to possession of the title deeds to the property. LPA 1925, s. 45(9) provides that (subject to any stipulation to the contrary, s. 45(10)) the vendor is entitled to retain documents of title in the following circumstances.

(*a*) When he retains any part of the land to which the documents relate. This includes the case where they refer merely to the extinguishment of rights of way over the land retained (*Re Lehmann and Walker's Contract* (1906)), but not where the document is a mortgage of the land sold and also of a life policy. The life policy is not retained "land" (*Re Williams and The Duchess of Newcastle's Contract* (1897)).

(*b*) When the document is a trust instrument, or other instrument creating a subsisting trust or relating to the appointment or discharge of a trustee of a subsisting trust.

7. Acknowledgment for production. Where the purchaser is not entitled to the title deeds they still remain a vital part of his title. The purchase deed will accordingly contain a clause called "an acknowledgment for production". In addition the clause will in many cases contain an undertaking by the vendor in respect of safe custody of the deeds. The effect of an acknowledgment for production is set out in LPA 1925, s. 64. The obligation once given binds the documents and the person into whose possession or control they come to produce them at the cost of the person requesting production unless prevented from doing so by fire or other inevitable accident (s. 64(2)).

The following further points should be noted.

(*a*) The purchase deed will contain an undertaking for safe custody except where the vendor is a personal representative, a trustee, a tenant for life or a mortgagee, or sells under LRef.A 1967 (*see* s. 10(6)).

(*b*) If the vendor does not have the deeds then an acknowledgment will be obtained from the person, e.g. a mortgagee, who does have custody. Such a fiduciary owner will not give an undertaking for safe custody. Commonly the vendor will covenant to give such an undertaking when the deeds come into his possession.

(*c*) The statutory acknowledgment for production under s. 64

must be given "to another". This means that a personal representative who assents to himself cannot give the statutory form of acknowledgment in that assent. He must give the acknowledgment as personal representative when he later sells as beneficial owner.

(d) Where the statutory form of acknowledgment for production is not given, the purchaser will probably have an equitable right to production of the title deeds.

(e) Apparently the purchaser is entitled only to an acknowledgment of the deeds from and including the root of title.

8. Memoranda endorsed on deeds. In the following two circumstances the purchaser should ensure that a memorandum of his purchase (i.e. a short note referring to it) is endorsed on some important document of title retained by the vendor and that the document with the memorandum endorsed is produced on completion.

(a) Where the vendor sells as personal representative a memorandum of the sale should be endorsed on the grant of representation which he retains. The purchaser is entitled to insist on this being done at the cost of the estate (see 10:**13** and AEA 1925, s. 36(5)).

(b) Where part of the land is sold it is customary for a memorandum of the sale to be endorsed on the conveyance of the whole to the vendor. LPA 1925, s. 200 gives the purchaser a right (where practicable) to this (except in the case of registered land, s. 200(3)) where the purchaser is granted rights over or the benefit of covenants affecting the other land retained.

Where the endorsement of a memorandum is impracticable (usually because of the large number of sales off from a large estate) then a memorandum of the transaction should instead be annexed to the document retained. In a case covered by s. 200 the purchaser has a right to annexation of such a note where endorsement of a memorandum is impracticable.

9. Duplicate conveyance for vendor. Where the purchaser enters into covenants for the protection of land retained or is granted rights thereover the vendor requires a more permanent and detailed record of the conveyance to the purchaser. In such cases it is common for the conveyance to be engrossed in duplicate and the counterpart engrossment retained by the vendor.

10. Informal completions. A recent Privy Council case from Hong Kong, *Edward Wong Finance* v. *Johnson Stokes and Master* (1984), threw doubt on some practices in completions. A purchaser paid the purchase price in reliance on an undertaking that the mortgage would be paid off by the vendor's solicitor. Held the purchaser was negligent—he should have taken steps to ensure that the solicitor had the mortgagee's authority to receive the money.

11. The Law Society's code. Partly as a result of the last mentioned case, the Law Society produced in 1984 a new code for completion by post. This is reproduced in Appendix 6. In practice, it should particularly be noted that a vendor cannot adopt this unless he has any mortgagee's authority to receive the money he will receive to discharge that mortgage. It may also be noted that adopting this code does not in itself absolve the purchaser's solicitors from any potentially negligent practices involved in informal completions (e.g. telegraphing the completion money without examining the title deeds, ensuring vacant possession is available, ensuring the vendor solicitor has had the conveyance executed . . .).

Progress test 16

1. Give an account of what is meant by completion. (**2**)

2. Explain what is meant by "marking the abstract". (**5**)

3. When is the vendor entitled to retain the title deeds? (**6**)

4. What is the effect of the statutory acknowledgment for production? (**7**)

5. When does a purchaser have a right to have a memorandum of the transaction endorsed on a document retained by the vendor? (**8**)

6. Explain the effect of the Law Society's code for postal completions. (**11**)

17

Post completion

Matters to attend to after completion

1. Stamping of deeds.

(*i*) On every transfer on sale of a fee simple or lease or underlease for a term of seven years or more, the purchaser must complete a form giving particulars of the transaction to the Inland Revenue (this form is known as "Stamps L(A) 451" or the "Particulars Delivered" or "PD" form) (Finance Act 1951, s. 28, Sched. 2).

(*ii*) If the land is registered or is being registered for the first time after completion, then if there is no stamp duty payable the particulars must be sent to the Land Registry together with the application for registration (*see* Stamp Duty (Exempt Instruments) Regulations 1985 made under the Finance Act 1985, s. 89).

(*iii*) In every other case to which (*i*) above applies, the deed and the particulars delivered form must be produced to the Inland Revenue within thirty days of the date of the deed.

(*iv*) In every case where stamp duty is payable the deed must be produced to the Inland Revenue within thirty days thereof and the correct stamp duty paid. Presently stamp duty is payable at the rate of 1 per cent of the total consideration on any conveyance where the value is not certified as not exceeding £30,000.

(*v*) Leases. Duty is also payable on the rent and the rate depends upon the length of the lease and applies even if the capital consideration does not exceed £30,000. If the rent exceeds £300 p.a. the 1 per cent duty applies to the capital consideration even if under

£30,000. On a shared ownership lease (*see* Chap. 22) the lessee has the option of paying duty on a freehold basis—this exempts from duty later purchases of further shares in the property.

2. Registration of title. The circumstances when this is necessary are discussed in Chap. 25.

3. Land charges. Various matters concerning land charges may arise after completion. In particular the solicitor must be careful to see that any outstanding land charges are cancelled and any necessary registrations effected.

(*a*) A vendor who reserves restrictive covenants for the benefit of land retained must ensure that these are protected by registration as a Class D(II) charge and also that the Priority Notice mechanism is used wherever that is appropriate (*see* 12:**6, 12**).

(*b*) A purchaser should ensure that the vendor's undertaking in respect of outstanding mortgages includes the obligation to cancel and deliver certificates of cancellation of any registered puisne mortgage (Class C(I) land charge) or other charge registered as a Class C(III) general equitable charge.

(*c*) A purchaser whose purchase includes some species of option agreement (e.g. the right to an extended lease or to purchase the freehold reversion of a lease) should ensure that this right is protected by registering it as an estate contract (Class C(IV) land charge).

4. Compliance with undertakings given on completion. This is discussed in 18:2–5.

5. Apportionments and completion statements. In completing the transaction the following steps will be taken to ensure that accounts are settled between the vendor and purchaser and between the solicitor and his client.

(*a*) *Apportionments.* Certain outgoings in respect of the property sold may require apportioning between the vendor and the purchaser to the day of completion. Although both rent and rates fall to be apportioned in this way under an open contract, the two standard forms of conditions of sale make express and detailed provision.

The standard requisitions on title raised will ask the vendor to provide a completion statement showing these apportionments. In practice rents received and ground rents payable are apportioned by the parties' solicitors, but the practice of apportioning rates has become rather uncommon, the parties in domestic conveyancing simply informing the local authority of the date of changed possession and leaving the local authority to apportion the charge.

When conveyancing flats the service charge if any must also be apportioned. The purchaser's solicitor must here take care to enquire into possible future heavy burdens on the service charge or arrears or deficits from earlier periods chargeable, for example, to a management company of which the tenants are members.

(b) *The completion statement.* This is the name for the account which a solicitor supplies to his client following completion and showing how the solicitor has dealt with the money he has handled and what balance is due to the client (or the solicitor).

Where a vendor's solicitor has to redeem his client's mortgage on completion or give his undertaking to do so (*see* 18:2) he will have obtained a statement from the mortgagee of the balance due in ample time. In any event he will have prepared his completion account well before completion to ensure that sufficient funds are available for the transaction to be carried through.

The doctrine of merger

6. Meaning of merger. Upon completion the contract for the sale is said to be extinguished and to merge in the conveyance. The effect of this is that to the extent that merger operates the purchaser is restricted to his remedies for breach of the covenants for title or to have the transaction set aside, but cannot bring an action upon the contract.

7. Effect. The effect of the doctrine of merger is to extinguish the contract *only to the extent that the deed is intended to cover the same ground* (*see Palmer* v. *Johnson* (1884)). This means that if the contract covers some collateral matter then to that extent an action may be brought on the contract to enforce that stipulation notwithstanding completion. The most common example is where the vendor has in the same contract as for the sale of the land also contracted to build a house. Then a stipulation, e.g. that the house be built to a specified standard, may be enforced even after completion (*Lawrence* v. *Cassel* (1930)). In the same way in *Feldman* v. *Mansell* (1962) a term in the contract that the vendor would provide the purchaser with copies of specified leases could be enforced after completion.

Remedies following completion

8. Action on covenants for title. The effect of the doctrine of merger (*see* **7**) means that unless there is an action based on some collateral matter the purchaser's remedy is to bring an action on the implied (or if there are any, the express) covenants for title. The nature and limitations of these has been outlined in Chap. 14.

9. Other remedies. Apart from an action on the covenants for title, either of the following may be available:

(*a*) rectification (*see* **10–11**);
(*b*) rescission (*see* **12**).

10. Rectification. This is an equitable remedy. It means altering the effect of a document to conform to the agreed or expressed intention of the parties or a party thereto. A deed may always be rectified with the concurrence of all parties thereto. Otherwise rectification is available to either party on application to the court. Various aspects of the remedy were considered recently by the Court of Appeal in *Joscelyne* v. *Nissen* (1970). It is now clear that rectification of an instrument may be granted even though there was no prior contract between the parties provided they were agreed as to the intended contents of the instrument.

That case also commented on the standard of proof required. Traditionally this was "irrefragable evidence" of the prior agreement. The Court of Appeal preferred the more modern and less exacting standard of "convincing proof".

11. Availability of rectification. Rectification is available if both parties have made the same mistake (a common mistake). It is also available in the following cases where only one party is mistaken.

(*a*) Where there is only one party to the instrument, e.g. a deed poll.

(*b*) Where the party who is not mistaken is guilty of fraud (*Hoblyn* v. *Hoblyn* (1889); *Lovesy* v. *Smith* (1880)).

(*c*) There is authority that where one party is mistaken and the other party who is not mistaken is aware of that mistake then the non-mistaken party is estopped from resisting the mistaken party's claim to rectification (*Whitely* v. *Delaney* (1914)).

(*d*) Where one party only is mistaken and *restitutio in integrum* is possible, the court has jurisdiction to put the non-mistaken party to his election of accepting either rectification or rescission. (Authority for this is found in *Paget* v. *Marshall* (1884). In that case a lessor mistakenly included the first floor of the property in the lease. He sought rectification. The lessee was put to the election of either accepting the lease as rectified to exclude the first floor or of having the contract rescinded. This rule was doubted in *May* v. *Fry* (1900) but approved by Denning LJ in the Court of Appeal in *Solle* v. *Butcher* (1950).)

12. Rescission. After completion either party may be able to apply to the court for rescission. This is an equitable discretionary remedy (discussed further in 15:**16–20**). It is available on any ground which would in equity justify setting aside the transaction, e.g. fraud, equitable fraud, undue influence, mistake or misrepresentation.

The unpaid vendor's lien

13. Continuation of right after completion. As soon as he enters into a binding contract to sell land the vendor has an equitable lien over the land to the extent that the purchase money is unpaid (*see* 7:**2**). The lien is a charge on the land enforceable by foreclosure or by applying to the court for an order for sale of the property. The right continues even after completion or after the vendor has parted with possession or the title deeds on completion and even though the conveyance contains a receipt for the whole price (*Winter* v. *Lord Anson* (1827)).

14. Position if vendor takes legal mortgage. The vendor does not have his lien if he takes instead a legal mortgage of the property sold (*Capital Finance Co. Ltd* v. *Stokes* (1969)).

15. Registration as land charge. If the vendor does not retain the title deeds as his security then the lien is registrable as a general equitable charge (Class C(III) land charge).

Progress test 17

1. In respect of which transactions must a "particulars delivered" form be completed?   (**1**)

2. What apportionments must be made on completion?   (**5**)

3. What is the effect of merger?   (**7**)

4. When is rectification available at the request of only one party to a deed?   (**11**)

5. Explain what is meant by the unpaid vendor's lien and how it should be protected.   (**13–15**)

Part three

Conveyancing in particular transactions

18
Mortgages in conveyancing

Effect on conveyancing procedure

1. Where the property sold is in mortgage the vendor's solicitor will commonly act for the mortgagee in redeeming the mortgage. However, it is usual in the case of private mortgages and most local authority mortgages that the mortgagee will not part with the deeds until the mortgage is redeemed. In cases where the mortgagee retains possession of the title deeds, since redemption can be effected only out of the purchase price, the mortgagee's own solicitor will act in redemption and completion will take place in his office.

Where the purchase is financed by a simultaneous mortgage the purchaser's solicitor will often act for the new mortgagee, although the mortgagee may require to be separately represented and then both the mortgagee's and the purchaser's solicitors will attend at the vendor's solicitors on completion.

2. **Undertaking to redeem mortgage.** Where the vendor's solicitor acts on redemption of the mortgage, the mortgage is not actually redeemed at completion. The vendor's solicitor receives the purchase money but still has to forward some of this to the mortgagee, redeem the mortgage and obtain a discharge of it. Building societies in particular will not usually receipt the mortgage until after receiving the debt due.

Where redemption is to take place after completion the purchaser does not obtain the unencumbered title for which he has contracted on completion. The practice has become firmly established that the purchaser will complete even so and receive the vendor's solicitor's *undertaking* to redeem the mortgage and forward to the purchaser's solicitor the receipted mortgage deed.

3. Purchaser's refusal of undertaking. In a sale with an unencumbered title the purchaser does not have to accept completion on the basis of such an undertaking but is entitled to insist on the unencumbered title for which he has contracted. Such an attitude would cause considerable inconvenience and the Law Society recommends (at least for building society mortgages) that the purchaser's solicitor should complete on the basis of an undertaking.

If the purchaser wishes to refuse to accept a proffered undertaking and insist on the mortgage being discharged before or on completion he must raise this objection before the period for raising requisitions or objections on title has expired (*see* 11:5) otherwise he will have waived his right so to object (*see Cole* v. *Rose* (1978) where this point was raised).

4. Form of undertaking. In his requisitions the purchaser will request the vendor to state whether the mortgage on the property is to be redeemed before completion or to state the form of his suggested undertaking. The wording of this undertaking has given rise to considerable (often heated) debate in the profession. The wording must be given special care and *no solicitor will sensibly undertake to do what it is not in his own power to perform*.

Many solicitors request an undertaking to return the receipted mortgage within a stipulated time, e.g. fourteen days. This should not be given as the vendor's solicitor has no control over the time it will take the building society to return the mortgage to him or indeed over the vicissitudes of the postal service. Consequently the Law Society's recommended form of undertaking promises to forward to the purchaser's solicitor the receipted mortgage "as soon as it is received from the building society" and not within a stated period (*see* further *A Guide to the Professional Conduct of Solicitors*, p. 70).

5. Enforcement of undertaking. In some cases an undertaking by a solicitor may be enforceable as a contractual obligation. It may also be enforceable by the High Court in exercise of its control over solicitors as officers of the court (Cordery, *Law Relating to Solicitors*). In any event the Law Society may take disciplinary action if the solicitor fails to honour an undertaking given by himself or one of his staff. "This is an example of where the professional conduct obligation is more onerous than the legal requirement" (*A Guide to the Professional Conduct of Solicitors*, p. 68).

Sale by a mortgagee

6. Power of sale in mortgage by deed. LPA 1925, s. 101 implies a power of sale by the mortgagee in any mortgage (whether legal or equitable) made by deed. This power is conferred only if the legal date for redemption is passed ("the mortgage money is due"), *see* s. 101(1). In an instalment mortgage this condition is satisfied if one instalment has been due (*see Payne* v. *Cardiff RDC* (1932)). (*See also* 10:**14–20**.)

7. Conditions for exercise of the statutory power of sale. Before the power of sale can be exercised one of the conditions laid down by LPA 1925, s. 103 must be satisfied. These conditions are that:

(*a*) notice requiring repayment has been served and there has been default for three months after this notice; *or*

(*b*) there are two months' arrears of interest due; *or*

(*c*) there has been some breach of a term of the mortgage (other than of the covenant to repay capital and interest).

8. Form of the sale. The sale may be by private treaty, by auction or by tender. A building society must take reasonable care to obtain the best price reasonably obtainable (Building Societies Act 1962, s. 36). Any other mortgagee must take reasonable care to obtain the proper market value (*Cuckmere Brick Co. Ltd* v. *Mutual Finance Ltd* (1971)). In any event the sale must be a bona fide sale, e.g. the mortgagee may not sell to himself even indirectly (*Downes* v. *Grazebrook* (1817) and *Williams* v. *Wellingborough Council* (1975)). The mortgagee may sell to a company in which he is interested if he acts in good faith and obtains the best price reasonably obtainable (*see Tse Kwong Lam* v. *Wong Chit Sen* (1983)).

9. Application of proceeds of sale. LPA 1925, s. 105 provides that the mortgagee shall apply the proceeds of sale first in discharge of any encumbrances prior to his mortgage. The balance is held by him on trust firstly to pay the costs and expenses of the sale, then to discharge the mortgage debt, then to be paid to the person entitled to the mortgagee's property or to give receipt for the proceeds of sale.

10. Power of sale in other mortgages (i.e. not by deed). LPA 1925, s. 101 does not apply to these mortgages. Accordingly the mortgagee must obtain some other power to transfer the legal estate in pursuance of an express power of sale given in the mortgage. The conveyancing devices used for this purpose are for the mortgage to contain either a power of attorney in the mortgagee's favour or a declaration of trust in his favour, each allowing the mortgagee to convey the legal estate (*see* 10:**19**).

11. No sale before possession. In practice a mortgagee will most commonly not sell the security until he has obtained possession so that he can sell with vacant possession.

12. Courts discretion to defer possession proceedings. A legal mortgage gives the mortgagee the right to possession by virtue of the estate he has in the land. In practice the protection given the mortgagor by the Administration of Justice Act 1970, s. 36 and the Administration of Justice Act 1973, s. 8(1) is important. Before these provisions the court appeared to have no inherent jurisdiction to defer possession proceedings except by a short adjournment (*see*, for example, *Birmingham Citizens' Permanent Building Society* v. *Caunt* (1962)). In the case of mortgages of dwelling houses such jurisdiction is now given to the court.

The court has a discretion, where the mortgagor is likely to be able within a reasonable period to pay any sum due, to postpone or adjourn the order or to adjourn the proceedings. This discretion may be exercised if the mortgagor is likely to be able to pay the amount he would have been expected to pay if there had been no default (s. 8 of the 1973 Act). Thus, in an instalment mortgage where a default has, under a condition in the mortgage, rendered the whole debt due, the court may exercise the discretion if the mortgagor can show his ability to pay the existing arrears and current instalments.

It may be noted that this statutory discretion appears not to apply to common form bank mortgages used to secure a running overdraft (*see Habib Bank Ltd* v. *Tailor* (1982)) but has been applied to an endowment mortgage (*Bank of Scotland* v. *Grimes* (1985)).

13. Effect of sale. When a contract for sale is entered into, the power of sale is exercised and so long as the contract subsists the equity of redemption is lost (*Lord Waring* v. *London & Manchester Assurance Co. Ltd* (1935)). When the sale is completed the entire legal estate (fee simple or term of years) vested in the mortgagor passes to the purchaser (LPA 1925, s. 104; *see also* 10:**17**).

Acting for a mortgagee on the grant of a mortgage

14. Form and terms. Discussion of these areas properly belongs to the precedent books. For practical purposes the mortgagee will insist on the mortgage being by deed in order to enjoy the benefit of the implied powers of sale and of appointing a receiver (LPA 1925, ss. 101–9; for implied covenants for title in a mortgage, *see* 14:**6**).

15. Investigation of title. There will almost invariably be no contract to grant the mortgage and the mortgagee's requirements as to proof of title may therefore be as strict as desired. This point must be carefully noted where a purchaser requires mortgage money to complete a purchase. He should not exchange contracts on the purchase until the mortgagee has accepted the title.

16. Completion.

(*a*) A mortgagee must be careful to avoid being subject to a tenancy granted by the mortgagor before the mortgage is made. Thus, in *Church of England Building Society* v. *Piskor* (1954) P contracted to purchase the land and then let it to T. On completion of the purchase P also then completed a mortgage to the society. The court held that the lease to T became a legal lease on completion of P's purchase and took priority over the mortgage. If the lease to T had instead been an agreement for a lease, then it would have been registrable as an estate contract (Class C(IV) land charge) and void against the mortgagee unless so registered.

(*b*) After completion a first mortgagee retains the title deeds.

(*c*) In acting for a second mortgagee the following two points should be noted.

(*i*) Express notice of the mortgage must be given to all prior mortgagees. This is important if the prior mortgagees seek to tack for further advances (*see* LPA 1925, s. 94(2)).

(*ii*) The mortgage must be protected by registration as a Class C(I) land charge if made by deed or otherwise as a Class C(III) land charge.

17. Advising the borrower. A number of recent cases have highlighted the dangers of a mortgagee being subjected to undue influence or being given inadequate advice as to the effect of the mortgage:

(*a*) In *King's North Trust Ltd* v. *Bell* (1985) following the little noticed case of *Avon Finance Co.* v. *Bridger* (1979) it was held that a lender who leaves it to another (e.g. a relative of a mortgagor) to obtain that mortgagor's execution may be itself affected by any undue influence enforced on the mortgagor and, thus, unable to enforce its mortgage.

(*b*) A bank's duty to a mortgagor was discussed in *National Westminster Bank plc* v. *Morgan* (1985) and in *Cornish* v. *Midland Bank plc*. In the former, a bank was not guilty of undue influence when its manager attended at the home to obtain the wife's signature to a charge. In the latter, the same view was followed that a bank's relationship with a customer was one which did not give rise to a presumption of undue influence, but there the bank was held to have negligently explained the effect of the mortgage. A person commencing any explanation of the effect of such a deed will readily be held to have a duty to give a complete and accurate explanation.

Discharge of mortgage

18. Form. LPA 1925, s. 115 provides that a mortgage may be discharged by a receipt under hand endorsed on or annexed to the mortgage deed. The receipt must state the name of the person who pays the money (s. 115(1)) although it will still be an effective receipt even if it does not, provided it is intended as a receipt (*see Edwards* v. *Marshall-Lee* (1975)). Alternatively the discharge can be effected by a separate deed (e.g. a reassignment, surrender, release or transfer— s. 115(4)).

19. Building societies. A receipt by a building society is given under the seal of the society in accordance with the Building Societies Act 1962, s. 37. Such a receipt does not show the person by whom the money is paid.

20. Debt paid by someone other than mortgagor. LPA 1925, s. 115(2) provides that if the statutory receipt shows the money to have been paid by a person not entitled to the immediate equity of redemption then it will operate as a transfer of the mortgage to that person (*see* discussion of *Cumberland Court (Brighton)* v. *Taylor* (1964) in 13:8).

Progress test 18

1. Does a purchaser have to accept discharge of a mortgage after completion? (**3**)

2. How should an undertaking to redeem a mortgage be framed? (**4**)

3. How is a solicitor's undertaking enforced? (**5**)

4. When may the statutory power of sale be exercised by a mortgagee? (**7**)

5. How is the statutory power of sale exercisable by a mortgagee? (**8**)

6. When may the court adjourn a mortgagee's possession action? (**12**)

7. What is the effect of a mortgagee entering into a contract for sale? (**13**)

8. What is the form of statutory receipt for a mortgage debt? (**18**)

9. What is the effect of a statutory receipt for discharge of a

mortgage which reveals that the debt was paid by someone other than the mortgagor? (**20**)

19
Leaseholds in conveyancing

Procedural differences

1. Contracts for a lease. Very often there is no formal contract prepared for the grant or disposition of a lease. This is generally so in the case of short leases and commercial leases. In the case of long domestic leaseholds (usually 99 or 999 years) there will invariably be the normal process of draft contract proceeding to an exchange of contracts.

2. The draft lease. Whether or not there is a formal contract to grant the lease, the draft lease is prepared by the lessor's solicitor. This is then submitted to the tenant's solicitor either together with the draft contract or alone if there is to be no formal contract stage. The form of the draft is then "negotiated" by the tenant's solicitor returning it with any amendments marked in red. If these are not agreed the lessor's solicitor amends in green and returns the draft lease. This process can theoretically be even further protracted. The more modern practice of stating reasons why a particular clause will or will not be agreed to is to be welcomed. Particularly in the case of domestic conveyancing on building estates the form of the lease is often presented to the tenant's solicitor on a "take it or leave it" basis.

3. The engrossment. It is very common for the engrossment (fair copy) to be prepared by the lessor's solicitor. The lease will be prepared in duplicate. One part is called "the lease" and is executed by the landlord. The other part is called "the counterpart lease" and is executed by the tenant. The stamp duty to be paid is impressed on the lease and a further 50p stamp duty is paid on the counterpart.

4. Costs in leasehold conveyancing. In leasehold conveyancing it is not at all uncommon for the tenant to pay the landlord's solicitor's fees as well as those of his own solicitor on the grant of the lease. In *Grissel* v. *Robinson* (1836) the court accepted that it was a custom of conveyancing for the tenant, on the grant of a lease, to pay the landlord's solicitor's costs. However, The Costs of Leases Act 1958 enacted that a lessee was not bound so to do unless the parties have agreed in writing that he should do so. Frequently, notably in commercial conveyancing, the tenant will find that such an agreement to pay the landlord's costs is a "take it or leave it" part of the bargain.

5. Completion. The main feature of completion is the exchange of the counterpart lease for the lease. In practice for convenience both parts are often retained by one party (normally the landlord) until the stamp duty has been paid on both parts together. The contract may require the lessee to pay the lessor's 50p duty.

Deducing title

6. Deducing title on the grant of a lease. LPA 1925, s. 44(2) deals with the situation under an open contract. In such a case the purchaser is not entitled to have the freehold title deduced. A purchaser of a short lease may accept this position. In the case of a commercial lease the vendor may refuse to give way and deduce title. However, it is the custom for title to be deduced in the ordinary way to the freehold in the case of a long lease of a dwelling house. Wherever a premium is paid for the grant of the lease the purchaser should insist on the freehold or other reversionary title being deduced. In such a case if there is a simultaneous mortgage to facilitate the purchase the mortgagee will most commonly insist on examining the freehold title and the purchaser who has exchanged contracts without stipulating for this will be unable to satisfy his mortgagee.

7. Deducing title on the grant of an underlease. The purchaser under an open contract is not entitled to call for title to the freehold or reversionary title (LPA 1925, s. 44(2)). He can call for the lease and assignments of the lease out of which his term is granted (*Gosling* v. *Woolf* (1893)).

8. Deducing title on the assignment of a lease or underlease. These cases are dealt with by LPA 1925, s. 44(2) and s. 44(3) respectively. Under an open contract the purchaser, whether of an existing head lease or of an underlease, is not entitled to examine the title to the reversionary interest. Thus, on the purchase of a head lease the purchaser cannot insist on examining the freehold reversion; on the purchase of an underlease or sub-underlease the immediate and previous leasehold titles cannot be called for and neither can the freehold reversion. A purchaser must in these cases stipulate for deduction of the reversionary title in the same circumstances as he would on the grant of a lease (*see* **6**).

On the assignment of a lease the lease is thus the root of title. The lease may be more than fifteen years old. In such a case the lease may be called for together only with assignments and other dealings during the fifteen years preceding the date of the contract (*Williams* v. *Spargo* (1893)).

9. Deducing title on the grant of a sub-underlease. In this case LPA 1925, s. 44(4) applies. The purchaser under an open contract is not entitled to call for title to the leasehold reversion. He may call for the underlease out of which his estate is carved and assignments of that underlease.

10. Example. The following is an example of the above rules applied to a series of transactions with the same property.

(*a*) *In 1930* Lord Oakshire granted a 99-year lease of Whitehouse to Dr Smith. The Doctor in the absence of a stipulation to the contrary was not entitled to have any title deduced.

(*b*) *In 1935* Dr Smith sold his lease to Lord Henry. Lord Henry was entitled to see no title except the 1930 lease and any dealings (such as mortgages) which Dr Smith had entered into in respect thereof.

(c) *In 1940* Lord Henry granted a 40-year underlease to Mary. She was entitled to see the 1930 lease and the 1935 assignment.

Deducing title registered land

11. Grant of lease or underlease.

(a) On the grant of a lease out of registered freehold land, the landlord will show only such title as he agrees to show.

(b) On the grant of an underlease out of a registered lease, the strict legal position is unclear. Probably LRA 1925, s. 110 (*see* 28:3) does not apply. In practice, therefore, the purchaser should stipulate for the registered title to be deduced. For pertinent standard conditions *see* 13.

12. Assignment of lease or underlease.

(a) On the assignment of a registered lease, then LRA 1925, s. 110 does apply. The vendor must thus supply office copy entries, a copy of the lease and an authority to inspect the register (*see* 28:3).

(b) On the assignment of a registered underlease, then s. 110 does apply and title is deduced in the same way as on the assignment of a registered lease.

Deducing leasehold title—standard and special conditions

13. Enlarged landlord's obligations. Since in both registered and unregistered land the vendor's obligation to deduce title in the case of leasehold title is limited, it is essential to consider when it is desirable to enlarge this obligation. The standard conditions of sale provide as follows:

(a) LSC 8(2)—if the lease is less than fifteen years old and the term granted exceeded fifteen years, then the freehold and any reversionary leasehold titles will be deduced for the usual fifteen-year period.

(b) NCS—contains no such extension of the vendor's obligation.

14. Dangers of good leasehold title. A good leasehold title (26:12) should not lightly be accepted where a premium is paid. This is because:

(*a*) The freehold title and the right of the freeholder to grant the lease is not guaranteed.

(*b*) For this reason, the title is not likely to be accepted by a prudent mortgagee as it clearly does not provide as guaranteed a security for his loan as title absolute.

(*c*) There may be incumbrances, e.g. restrictive covenants, affecting the freehold reversion which seriously detract from the value of the lease.

Accordingly the purchaser should attempt to insist on the freehold title being deduced so that he can obtain leasehold title absolute (**26**:**9**).

Prejudice by matters not appearing on the title

15. Matters by which purchaser is not affected. Under the old rule in *Patman* v. *Harland* (1881) a purchaser was said to have constructive notice of matters affecting the property which he could have found out by investigating the superior title *even where he had no right to investigate that title*. This rule was abrogated by LPA 1925, s. 44(5) and where under that section a purchaser is *not entitled* to investigate a superior title he is not affected by notice of matters which he could have discovered by such investigation.

16. Matters by which purchaser is affected. A purchaser remains affected by the following matters.

(*a*) He is, of course, still affected by notice of any matters appearing on the title which he is entitled to inspect even if he does not do so.

(*b*) He is affected by notice of any matters apparent from an inspection of the property.

(*c*) He is affected by notice of all land charges which affect the property (LPA 1925, s. 198) *even though registered against a name appearing on a superior title which he is not entitled to investigate*. Thus, he may be affected on the purchase of a lease by a restrictive covenant registered against a freeholder of whose name he can have no knowledge. The reform in LPA 1969 giving a purchaser a right to compensation in respect of undisclosed land charges appearing on an earlier title does not apply to matters appearing on a superior title which the purchaser is not entitled to investigate because of LPA 1925, s. 44 (*see* LPA 1969, s. 29(9) and (10)).

Covenants

17. Proof of performance of covenants. On completion of the sale of leasehold land the vendor should produce the receipt for the last payment of rent due before completion. On production of this the purchaser is required to assume, unless the contrary appears, that all the covenants and provisions of the lease have been duly performed and observed up to the date of actual completion (LPA 1925, s. 45(2)).

A similar provision applies in the sale of an underlease. LPA 1925, s. 45(3) provides that on production of the receipt for the last payment of rent due before completion the purchaser must, unless the contrary appears, assume that the rent due has been paid and the covenants and provisions observed under both the lease and the underlease.

18. Breach of covenants. If there is a breach of a covenant in the lease and the lease is rendered forfeitable then a purchaser of that lease may rescind on account of the vendor's failure to show a good title. This is so notwithstanding the effect of s. 45 (*see*, e.g., *Becker* v. *Partridge* (1966)).

19. Implied covenants in leasehold sales. These are discussed in 14:**10–17**.

Particular covenants in the lease

20. Consent of landlord or revisionary lessee. It is important to note whether such a consent to assignment (or otherwise parting with possession) is required. In such cases the following points must be observed:

(*a*) LSC 8(4) provides that the vendor will use his best endeavours to obtain such consent; the purchaser will supply information and references as reasonably required; if at least five working days before the contractual completion date consent is not granted or is subject to conditions to which the purchaser reasonably objects, then either party may rescind by notice to the other.

(*b*) NCS 11(5) provides that so long as the purchaser supplies such references and information as may reasonably be required of him the vendor will use his best endeavours to obtain the landlord's licence and pay the fee therefor. If it cannot be obtained the vendor may rescind on the same terms as if the purchaser had persisted in a requisition which the vendor was unable to remove.

(*c*) If consent to assignment is required, then it must not be withheld unreasonably (Landlord and Tenant Act 1927, s. 19).

(*d*) Where consent is required, no sum of money is to be paid therefor except for reasonable legal and other expenses (LPA 1925, s. 144).

(*e*) NOTE: If there is an absolute bar on assignment underletting or parting with possession, then this is binding.

(*f*) *Change of use:* A lease may contain a provision (a "user" consent) prescribing the use to which the tenant is permitted to put the premises. If the clause provides that the landlord's consent is required to a change of use, then that consent may be withheld or not as the landlord chooses—there is no equivalent of Landlord and Tenant Act 1927, s. 19(1) applicable to change of use. Section 19(3) does provide, though, that if consent is required by a lease to a change of use then, unless a structural alteration is required, no premium or extra rent may be charged for consent—the landlord may require reasonable payment for any change or any legal expenses.

21. Right of re-entry.

(*a*) A well-drawn lease will contain a right for the landlord to re-enter the premises if there is breach by the tenant of any covenant in the lease. In the absence of such a right of re-entry the landlord will be left with a perhaps valueless remedy of suing for damages for breach of covenant. It should be noted that a lease should contain a right of re-entry in the case of bankruptcy of the tenant or any surety.

(*b*) If the continuance of the lease is made conditional upon performance of covenants, then no right of re-entry need be reserved. Such an approach to drafting the lease is rare in practice.

22. Relief against forfeiture. The courts have various complex powers to grant relief against forfeiture for non-payment of rent and breach of other covenants. The following should be noted:

(*a*) Although the provisions providing relief for forfeiture for non-payment of rent are complex, the result is that the court will generally grant relief where all rent and costs are paid before judgment and will grant relief after judgment unless this would be inequitable, e.g. on account of delay by the tenant. (It will be noted that the Administration of Justice Act 1985, s. 55 amended the County Courts Act 1984, s. 138 in another attempt to assimilate the High Court and County Court powers.)

(*b*) Before entering any right of entry for breach of a covenant or condition, a landlord must serve a notice requiring the tenant to remedy the breach. This must:

(*i*) specify the breach;

(*ii*) if it is capable of remedy, require it to be remedied;

(*iii*) require compensation in money for the breach (LPA 1925, s. 146).

It will be noted that when a breach is incapable of remedy then the notice need not require one (e.g. *Rugby School (Governors)* v. *Tannahill*—use of premises as a brothel; reaffirmed in *British Petroleum Trust Ltd* v. *Behrendt* (1985)).

(*c*) The tenant may apply to the court for relief against forfeiture (s. 146(2)). This will be granted on broad equitable grounds and on such terms and conditions as the court sees fit.

(*d*) Sub-tenants or mortgagees affected by a forfeiture of the lease may apply for relief under s. 146(4). They can obtain relief only while the landlord is proceeding to enforce a forfeiture and thus not when the forfeiture has taken place. (A good recent illustration is found in *Official Custodian for Charities* v. *Mackey* (1984) 3 All ER 684.)

(*e*) If a s. 146 notice relates to internal decorative repair then a tenant may apply for relief under s. 147 and the court has a wide discretion to grant relief for breach of such covenants so long as the breach is not one of a covenant as to putting in repair, keeping in sanitary condition, keeping fit for human habitation or preservation of the structure.

(*f*) If a lease was granted for a term of not less than seven years and at the date of the s. 146 notice three or more years remain unexpired, then the landlord must give notice in the s. 146 notice that the tenant has the right by serving a counter-notice to insist on the landlord applying to the court for leave before enforcing a forfeiture. (This is provided by Leasehold Property (Repairs) Act 1938 and does not apply to a tenancy of an agricultural holding.)

Progress test 19

1. What are the procedures for drafting and engrossing the lease? (**2, 3**)

2. When must the tenant pay his landlord's costs on the grant of a lease? (**4**)

3. In an open contract for the grant of a lease what title must the vendor deduce? (**6**)

4. In an open contract for the assignment of a lease what title must the vendor deduce? (**8**)

5. In an open contract for the grant of a sub-underlease what title must the vendor deduce? (**9**)

6. Is a tenant subject to a restrictive covenant registered against his landlord? (**16**)

7. What is the effect of producing a clear receipt for the last instalment of ground rent on the completion of a leasehold sale? (**17**)

8. What is the purchaser's position if having contracted to purchase a lease he finds that there is a serious breach of covenant which renders the lease forfeitable? (**18**)

9. May a sum of money be charged for a landlord's consent to assignment? (**20**)

20
Business leases

1. **Security of tenure.** The Landlord and Tenant Act 1954, Part II provides the framework for security of tenure where a tenant occupies premises for the purposes of a business or businesses carried on by him. The basic machinery is that at the end of a term of the lease the landlord who wishes to take possession has to take certain procedural steps and the tenant may have the right to a new lease unless the landlord can prove one of the specified grounds for resisting such a claim.

2. **The definition of business.** This is broad. It "includes a trade, profession or employment and includes any activity carried on by a body of persons, whether corporate or unincorporate" (L & T 1954, s. 23(2)).

3. **Exceptions from protection.** The protection of L & T 1954 does not apply:

   (*a*) where the tenant is carrying on a business in breach of a prohibition of use for business purposes generally unless the landlord or his predecessor has consented or the present landlord has acquiesced in the breach (s. 23(4));

   (*b*) in cases under the following paragraphs of s. 43(1):

      (*i*) agricultural holdings,
      (*ii*) mining leases,
      (*iii*) certain licensed premises;

   (*c*) to service tenancies as defined by s. 43(2);

(*d*) under s. 43(3) if the tenancy is for a term certain not exceeding six months unless it can be renewed or extended beyond the six months or the tenant and any predecessor in the same business have been in occupation for more than twelve months.

(*e*) the Act does not apply to persons holding under a mere licence (*see* e.g. *Addiscombe Craven Estates* v. *Crabbe* (1958)) and has been held not to apply to a tenancy at will (*Wheeler* v. *Mercer* (1957));

(*f*) the normal rules allowing termination of a lease by forfeiture or forfeiture of a superior lease or by surrender apply to business leases.

4. Contracting out of the Act. If the parties agree to exclude the tenant's right to a new tenancy by a clause in the lease or any agreement, then such a term is void (L & T 1954, s. 38). However, if such a term is approved by the court on the joint application of the persons who will be the landlord and the tenant, then it will be valid. This procedure is now quite commonly used, both parties making application to the court for approval of a draft lease containing terms excluding the provisions of the L & T Act 1954, ss. 24–28.

5. Continuation of tenancy. A tenancy under the L & T Act 1954 does not come to an end unless it is terminated in accordance with the Act (s. 24); that means it must be terminated by a tenant's notice to quit, by forfeiture or surrender or by complying with the specific provisions of the Act.

6. Termination by landlord. The landlord has to serve on the tenant a notice in the prescribed form. He must ensure also that the notice is apposite to bring to an end the contractual term. The form and content of the notice are specified under the L & T Act 1954, s. 25. The notice must give not less than six months and not more than twelve months before the specified termination date. This may be any date after the date on which the contractual tenancy may be terminated.

7. Landlord's grounds. The grounds on which a landlord may oppose a tenant's application are set out in s. 30 and are:

(a) breach of an obligation to repair or maintain such that the tenant ought not to be granted a new tenancy;

(b) persistent delay in paying rent such that the tenant ought not to be granted a new tenancy;

(c) substantial breaches of covenant or other reasons connected with the tenant's use or management such that he ought not to be offered a new tenancy;

(d) a reasonable offer by the landlord of alternative accommodation;

(e) if the tenancy is part of the property held under a superior tenancy and more rent could be had by letting as a whole rather than on separate lettings and the landlord requires possession in order to let the property as a whole;

(f) the landlord intends to demolish or reconstruct at least a substantial part of the holding or carry out substantial construction work thereon and cannot reasonably do so without obtaining possession;

(g) the landlord intends to occupy the holding at least partly for the purposes of a business carried on by him or as his residence.

(This last paragraph does not apply if the landlord's interest is one purchased or created within the last five years and since then the holding has been a business tenancy, s. 30(2).)

8. Application of ground (f). The landlord will not be able to rely on ground (f) if:

(a) the tenant will agree to the new tenancy containing a term for the landlord access to carry out his work; if the landlord could reasonably do so without obtaining possession and without substantial interference with the landlord's business tenancy; or

(b) if the tenant will accept a tenancy in an economically separable part of the building and as to that part condition (a) is satisfied or the remainder of the building is sufficient for the landlord's intended works.

9. Tenant's response. If the tenant wishes to oppose the landlord's notice to terminate, then he must take the following action:

(a) he must within two months of the giving of the landlord's notice have notified the landlord that he will not be willing to give up the tenancy (s. 23(4); s. 29(2));

(*b*) he must not less than two months and not more than four months after the landlord's notice apply to the court for the grant of a new tenancy.

10. Tenant's request for a new tenancy. The tenant can request a new tenancy himself if the grant was in the first place for a term of more than a year. The tenant can request a new tenancy by giving notice to the landlord in the form prescribed under the L & T Act 1954, s. 26. He must request a new tenancy from a specified date not earlier than the contractual tenancy could have ended or could have been ended by the tenant and not more than twelve or less than six months from the notice. If the landlord opposes this he must give notice within two months of such opposition and the tenant may then apply to the court for a new tenancy as in **9**(*b*) above.

11. Terms of new lease.

(*a*) The parties may negotiate the terms of a new lease themselves and this will be the outcome in the vast majority of cases.

(*b*) A landlord may apply to the court for an interim rent (s. 24A) while the tenancy is continued under the Act.

(*c*) The court has a wide discretion as to the terms of the new lease:

(*i*) the tenant is *entitled* only to a new lease of the part used for business but the landlord may insist that the new lease includes the whole premises (s. 32(2));

(*ii*) the maximum term is fourteen years (s. 33);

(*iii*) the rent shall be that reasonably obtainable in the open market disregarding the effect of the tenant's and his predecessor's occupation; goodwill of the tenant's business, improvements by tenant other than under an obligation to the landlord, the value of a licence of licensed premises (s. 34);

(*iv*) The new term takes effect three months after the application is finally disposed of (s. 64(1));

(*v*) within fourteen days of the court's grant of a new tenancy the tenant may apply to the court for revocation of the order and then the tenancy will continue for such time as is reasonable for the landlord to relet or dispose of the property and in taking this course the tenant will lose the protection of the Act (s. 38(2));

(*vi*) the L & T Act 1954 will apply to any new tenancy granted by the court and so the tenant can apply for a further new tenancy and so on.

12. Compensation.

(*a*) If the landlord successfully opposes in court the grant of a tenancy on grounds (*e*), (*f*) or (*g*) (*see* **7**) but on no other ground or his notice specifies no other grounds than those and the matter is not tried by the court, then the tenant is entitled to compensation. The amount is three times the rateable value of the holding unless the tenant and his predecessors in the business have occupied the premises for fourteen years in which case it is six times the rateable value (s. 37).

(*b*) Section 38(2) provides as follows. A future right to compensation cannot be excluded where the tenant and his predecessor have occupied the premises for five years. A right to compensation which has actually accrued can be modified or excluded by agreement.

13. Compensation for improvements.

(*a*) Under L & T Act 1927, s. 1 a tenant who has used premises exclusively for trade or business is entitled on quitting the holding to compensation for improvements which he has made. Compensation is available for improvements which add to the letting value of the holding. Generally compensation is not payable if the tenant was under a contractual obligation to make such improvements.

(*b*) The tenant must have given notice of his intention to effect the improvement. The landlord may object to such a notice and if agreement cannot be reached the tenant must apply to the court for a certificate that the improvement is proper.

(*c*) The parties will agree a time for completing the work or this will be fixed by the court.

(*d*) The claim for compensation must be made within three months of a notice to quit, or terminating the tenancy or of a landlord's notice opposing the tenant's request for a new tenancy (*see* **10**).

(*e*) For agreements made since 10th December 1953 it is not possible to contract out of this right to compensation.

Progress test 20

1. What is the definition of "business" under Landlord and Tenant 1954? (**2**)

2. Does the Act apply to a licence? (**3**)

3. List the landlord's grounds for opposing a new tenancy. (**7**)

4. What is the time scale for the tenant's response to a landlord's notice? (**9**)

5. How is the amount of rent fixed under a new lease? (**11**)

6. When can the tenant's right to compensation under Landlord & Tenant 1954 be excluded? (**12**)

21
Residential leases

Residential leases

1. Rent Act 1977. Residential tenancies are subject to statutory control. The 1977 Act differentiated between protected tenancies, statutory tenancies, regulated tenancies and restricted contracts. A protected tenancy must be a tenancy of a dwelling house or flat, or part of the same which is let as a separate dwelling. The essential characteristic is that the tenant has an exclusive right to the use of the essential living rooms. A kitchen but not a bathroom is a living room.

2. Rateable value limits. The rateable value must not exceed the following: generally £1,500 in Greater London, £750 outside London on the appropriate day (*see* s. 25).

3. Excluded tenancies. The following are excluded tenancies:

(*a*) Tenancies where no rent is payable or a low rent of less than two-thirds of the rateable value on the appropriate day (RA 1977, s. 5).

(*b*) Dwellings let with other land (s. 6) but note s. 26 provides that land let with a house does constitute a protected tenancy of the whole, unless the land is agricultural land exceeding two acres.

(*c*) Rent includes payment for board or attendance (s. 7). The rent must include a genuine payment for attendance, s. 7(2) provides that this will not be so unless the rent fairly attributable to attendance forms a substantial part of the rent. Attendance means a personal service to the tenant, not a service to all tenants as a group, e.g. providing central heating. Board can be partial and may even include one sandwich, but not just a morning cup of tea!

(*d*) Lettings to students by specified educational institutions, so that they can pursue courses at the Institution (s. 8).

(*e*) Holiday lettings (s. 9). The purpose here must be that tenant occupies the dwelling for a holiday and not for working purposes.

(*f*) Dwellings forming part of agricultural holdings (s. 10). Agricultural holdings are defined by the Agricultural Holdings Act 1948. It must also be occupied by a person responsible for the control of the farming. A special form of security of tenure is conferred by the 1948 Act.

(*g*) Licensed premises (s. 11). If the dwelling house is or comprises premises which are licensed for the sale of intoxicating liquor to be consumed on the premises, it is excluded.

(*h*) The immediate landlord is the Crown (unless managed by the Crown Estate Commissioner) or a government department (s. 13).

(*i*) The immediate landlord is one listed in s. 14, viz. local authorities and Commission for New Towns.

(*j*) The landlord is the Housing Corporation, a housing trust, a registered housing association (s. 15) and a housing co-operative (s. 16).

(*k*) Assured tenancies defined by Housing Act 1980, s. 56 are excluded (s. 16A). These are lettings by landlords designated as approved bodies by a statutory instrument made under this section.

(*l*) Business tenancies to which Part II of the Landlord and Tenant Act 1954 applies (s. 24(3)).

(*m*) Church of England parsonages.

(*n*) Premises let to a corporation. These are protected but as the corporation cannot reside there, there is no security of tenure once the contractual tenancy is terminated. In other ways it is protected, e.g. for registration of a fair rent (*see* 5).

(*o*) A tenancy overcrowded under the Housing Act 1957. Where the tenant is guilty of overcrowding the dwelling, re-possession restrictions are removed (s. 101(1)).

(*p*) Resident landlords (s. 12). After 14th August 1974 where the letting consists of part of a building or flat and the landlord at the date of letting (Subject Sched. 2) occupied and since then has occupied part of the same flat or building as his residence, the letting is not protected. If the building consists of purpose-built flats, even if the landlord lives in another flat in the block, s. 12 does not apply. However, if a house is later converted into flats, a resident landlord can take advantage of s. 12.

4. Duration of protected tenancies. A protected tenancy lasts only so long as the tenancy remains contractual. Once the tenancy has been determined at common law, whether by expiration of the original term, surrender, forfeiture or valid notice to quit (*see* **6**), the tenancy becomes a statutory tenancy (RA 1977, s. 2(1)(*a*)).

The statutory tenant by virtue of his previous protected tenancy has the right to remain in occupation of the dwelling so long as he pays the rent and observes the obligation of his tenancy. Even though his contractual tenancy has been terminated, he cannot be obliged to quit the premises unless the landlord obtains an order for possession under RA 1977, s. 98.

5. Determination of statutory tenancy.

(*a*) A statutory tenancy continues only so long as the tenant occupies it as his residence. It is for the landlord to prove that he has no intention to return. Once that is established, the landlord should have no difficulty in obtaining a possession order for the tenant has forfeited the protection of the Rent Acts.

(*b*) If the statutory tenant dies while occupying it as his residence, s. 2(1)(*b*) allows a surviving spouse or member of his family resident with him at his death and for the preceding six months to claim a statutory tenancy by succession (a transmission). A second transmission is also allowed.

6. Statutory tenancy on death of protected tenant. If a protected tenant dies, then s. 2(1)(*b*) also permits his spouse or member of his family (as above) to claim a statutory tenancy. A second transmission is again allowed.

All statutory tenants have the protection of RA 1977, s. 98. The protected tenant has the protection of the common law during his contractual term which must have been or have determined at common law *before* possession proceedings begin. It should be noted that if the protected tenancy was periodic, the duration of the notice to quit must be at least four weeks in length (Protection from Eviction Act 1977, s. 5) even if the common law allows a shorter period of notice, e.g. a week for a weekly tenancy. If the common law demands longer than four weeks, then the longer period must be given. The notice to quit must also contain the prescribed information (*see* Notice to Quit [Prescribed Information] Regulations 1980 S.I. 1980/1624).

7. Grounds for possession—discretionary. RA 1977, s. 98(1) provides that a court shall not make an order for possession of a dwelling house which is let on a protected *or* statutory tenancy unless the court considers it (1) reasonable to make the order and (2) *either* the court is satisfied that suitable accommodation is available for the tenant or will be available for him when the order takes effect *or* the court is satisfied that the landlord has established one of the cases for possession set out in Part I of Sched. 15.

Part I cases:

Case 1—any rent lawfully due from the tenant has not been paid or any tenancy obligation has been broken or not performed.

Case 2—the tenant or person(s) residing or lodging with him or sub-tenant has been guilty of nuisance or annoyance to adjoining occupiers or convicted of using the dwelling for immoral or illegal purposes or allowing it to be so used.

Case 3—the dwelling has deteriorated due to act or neglect of the tenant or by his sub-tenant or lodger and the court is satisfied that the tenant has not taken reasonable steps to remove that person.

Case 4—where furniture provided for use under the tenancy has deteriorated due to ill-treatment by the tenant or by someone residing or lodging with him or by his sub-tenant and the court is satisfied that he has not taken reasonable steps to remove the lodger or sub-tenant.

Case 5—the tenant has given notice to quit and in consequence the landlord has contracted to sell or let the dwelling or has taken any other steps so that he would be seriously prejudiced if he could not obtain possession.

Case 6—the tenant has assigned or sub-let the whole of the dwelling or sub-let part of the remainder being already sub-let without the landlord's consent. This applies to assignment or sub-lettings after 8th December 1965 except that for regulated furnished tenancies the date is 14th August 1974. The case applies whether or not the tenancy is protected or contractual and whether or not there is a covenant against assignment or sub-letting in the head tenancy.

Case 7—the dwelling house consists of premises licensed for the sale of intoxicating liquor and the tenant has been refused a renewal of the licence, committed an offence as licensee or has not conducted the business to the satisfaction of the licensing authorities or police or in a manner detrimental to the public interest.

Case 8—the dwelling is reasonably required for an employee or prospective employee of the landlord or of the sole tenant from him, the existing tenant being formerly a service tenant of the landlord or a previous landlord and the dwelling was let to him because of his former employment. Here it is not necessary to show that the dwelling is the only house available for the employee—it must be reasonably required.

Case 9—the dwelling is reasonably required by the landlord for occupation by:

(*a*) himself;
(*b*) his son or daughter over 18;
(*c*) his father or mother;
(*d*) his father-in-law or mother-in-law.

This case is not available if the landlord became a landlord by *purchase* after the date on which the tenancy became subject to the Rent Acts. However, the landlord's claim will fail even though it is reasonably required if tenant can show that, in all the circumstances of the case, greater hardship would be caused by granting possession than by refusing the order (Para. 1, Sched. 15, Part III).

Case 10—applies where the tenant has sub-let part of the dwelling and where the rent he is charging exceeds the maximum rent recoverable under Part III (for protected or statutory sub-tenancies) or Part IV where the sub-letting is a restricted contract.

All the above cases are discretionary for it is not enough that the landlord can bring his claim within one or more of the cases. The court must also consider whether it is reasonable to make an order.

In *Chiverton* v. *Ede* (1921) it was stated that this meant having regard "on the one hand to the general scheme and purpose of the Act, and, on one hand, to the special conditions, including to a large extent matters of a domestic and general character".

Suitable alternative accommodation

Section 98(1) provides a further discretionary ground—if the landlord can satisfy the court that suitable alternative accommodation is available. Conclusive evidence of this is a certificate to that effect from the local housing authority. If the local authority will not grant such a certificate, then he will have to show the court that accommodation is available which gives either the same security of tenure as a protected tenant or security of tenure that is broadly equivalent to that enjoyed by a protected tenant. It must also be reasonably suitable to the needs of the tenant and his family, bearing in mind the size of the family, proximity to his work and the rent and size of house a local authority would provide for a similar family. If satisfied, the court will then consider if it is reasonable to make an order.

8. Grounds for possession—mandatory. Section 98(2) states that if a landlord can bring his claim within Cases 11–20 in Part II of RA 1977, Sched. the court must make an order for possession. It has *no* power to consider if it is reasonable to make the order.

Case 11—where an owner/occupier has let the dwelling and:

(*a*) not later than the relevant date (usually the commencement of the tenancy) the landlord gave notice in writing to the tenant that possession might be recovered under Case 11; and

(*b*) the dwelling house has not, since it became a regulated tenancy, been let by the owner/occupier on a protected tenancy not subject to a Case 11 notice and the dwelling is required for one of the following:

(*i*) the owner/occupier or a member of owner/occupier's family who resided with the owner when he last occupied as his residence, or

(*ii*) owner has died and the dwelling is required as a residence by a member of his family residing with him at the date of his death, or

(*iii*) owner has died and the house is required by a successor in title (not being a successor by purchase) as his residence or for selling it with vacant possession, or

(*iv*) the dwelling is subject to a legal mortgage dated before the tenancy commenced and the mortgagee is entitled to exercise a power of sale and requires possession to dispose of the dwelling with vacant possession, or

(*v*) the dwelling house is not reasonably suitable to the needs of the owner, having regard to his place of work, and he requires it to dispose of it with vacant possession to use the proceeds of sale to buy a more suitable dwelling.

The court can dispense with the requirements of (*a*) or (*b*) or both if it thinks it just and equitable to do so subject to the caveat that it cannot dispense with (*a*) if the landlord did not originally intend to create a Case 11 tenancy.

NOTE: property may be let in successive Case 11 tenancies—Rent Act (Amendment) Act 1985.

Case 12—the landlord bought the dwelling as a retirement home and let it prior to retirement and he gave notice before the tenancy commenced that possession may be required under Case 12 *and* since August 1974 the dwelling has not been let on a tenancy not subject to a Case 12 notice *and* he has retired and requires the house as his residence or (*ii*), (*iii*) or (*iv*) above in Case 11 applies.

Case 13—the dwelling is let for a term certain not exceeding eight months and

(*a*) before the tenancy began, notice in writing was given to the tenant that possession might be required under Case 13; and

(*b*) within the twelve months preceding the commencement of the tenancy, the dwelling was occupied under a right to occupy it for a holiday.

Case 14—where the dwelling is let for a term certain not exceeding twelve months and

(*a*) before the tenancy began, the landlord gave notice in writing that possession might be required under Case 14; and

(*b*) within the twelve months preceding the commencement of the tenancy the dwelling was subject to a student letting (*see* **3** (*d*)).

Case 15—where the dwelling is to provide a residence for a minister of religion from which to perform the duties of his office and that notice has been served (as in Case 14) *and* the court is satisfied that the dwelling is required by a minister of religion as a residence from which to perform his duties.

Cases 16, 17 and 18 concern dwelling once occupied by agricultural workers where notice is served when the tenancy began that possession might be sought under the appropriate case *and* the dwelling is now required for an agricultural employee. Note that these dwellings are not "tied" cottages. Such cottages are within the ambit of the Rent (Agriculture) Act 1976. This Act gives a similar degree of security of tenure as the Rent Acts.

Case 19—shorthold tenancies (*see* **10**). The landlord must have served notice on the tenant at the beginning of the tenancy that he may take possession proceedings under Case 19. He must serve notice on the tenant not earlier than three months before the expiration of the tenancy term and expiring at least three months after the date of service that he will proceed under Case 19. He must then commence legal proceedings within three months of the expiry of the notice.

Case 20—a serving member of the armed forces who acquires a dwelling and lets it, while in the armed forces, may, if he served notice on the tenant that Case 20 may be used and if the dwelling has only been let under Case 20, recover possession if *either* he requires it for his own residence *or* (*ii*)–(*v*) in Case 11 apply.

9. Discretionary powers under RA 1977, s. 100. Where an order for possession is made under Part I cases (but not Part II cases), the court has the power to adjourn the proceedings, stay or suspend the extension of an order or postpone the day of possession, e.g. if proceedings are taken under Case 1 for non-payment of rent the court may adjourn the proceedings on condition that the tenant pays the arrears within say three months. If the tenant does so, no further action will be taken. If he does not pay the arrears, the landlord can apply for a possession order.

10. Protected shorthold tenancies. The Housing Act 1980, ss. 52–55 allowed the creation of such tenancies from 28th November 1980. This is a protected tenancy which is granted for a term certain of not less than one year and not more than five years (s. 52(1)). The term must not be capable of being brought to an end by the landlord before the expiration of the original term except by a proviso for re-entry or forfeiture for breach of covenant (s. 52(1)(*a*)). Before the grant of the tenancy the landlord must have given a notice in the prescribed form (Protected Shorthold Tenancies (Notice to Tenants) Regulations 1981).

Under s. 52(1)(*c*) if the dwelling is within Greater London either a fair rent must have been registered or a certificate must have been issued and an application made for registration before the tenancy commences.

Shorthold tenancies cannot be granted to someone who was an existing protected or statutory tenant immediately before the purported grant of a shorthold tenancy to that person (HA 1980, s. 52(2)).

11. Restricted contracts. These are defined by RA 1977, s. 19(2) as a contract whereby one person grants to another person, in consideration of a rent which includes payment for the use of furniture or for services, a right to occupy a dwelling as a residence.

The following are *not* restricted contracts:

(*a*) Regulated tenancies, i.e. protected and statutory tenancies (s. 19(5)(*a*)).

(*b*) Contracts from local authorities (s. 19(5)(*aa*)).

(*c*) Where the landlord is the Crown, government department, but a contract where the Crown Estate Commissioners manages the property can be (s. 19(5)(*b*) & (*e*)).

(*d*) Contracts where the proportions of rent payable for board is substantial (s. 19(5)(*c*)).

(*e*) Contracts where the occupier is protected under the Rent (Agriculture) Act 1976 (s. 19(5)(*d*)).

(*f*) Tenancies where the landlord is a housing association, housing trust or the Housing Association (s. 19(5)(*e*)), holiday lettings (s. 19(7)) and rent-free agreements (s. 19(2)).

No contract may be a restricted contract, if the premises fall outside the financial limits mentioned in s. 19.

The important examples of restricted contracts are:

(*a*) (*i*) where the landlord is a resident landlord within s. 12. It is the fact that the landlord is resident which is the deciding factor. It is not necessary that any part of the rent is a payment for use of furniture or services provided by the landlord (s. 20).

(*ii*) Sharing living accommodation. This can be sharing accommodation with landlord (resident or not) or with the landlord and other persons (s. 21). Living accommodation must be shared; if the tenant has his own living accommodation which he occupies exclusively but shares a kitchen with his landlord this does not bring the contract within s. 21. Sharing a bathroom does.

(*b*) A contract which is not a regulated tenancy but where a right to occupy a dwelling is given and the rent includes payment for furniture and/or services.

There is only limited security of tenure for restricted contracts. For those contracts granted before 28th November 1980 under RA 1977, s. 103(1) if a restricted contract has been referred to a Rent Tribunal (*see* **12**(*c*)), a notice to quit served before the Tribunal gives its decision or within the six months after that decision is given cannot take effect until six months have elapsed after the Tribunal decision.

Any tenant who has received a notice to quit may apply to the Rent Tribunal asking it to extend the length of the notice. Section 104 enables the Tribunal to grant an extension of up to six months, running from the day when the original notice to quit would have expired. Application must be made before the notice to quit has expired.

Restricted contracts entered into after 28th November 1980 are entitled to four weeks' (minimum) notice to quit under PEA, s. 5 (*see* **16**). Such tenants cannot ask the Rent Tribunal for an extension under either RA 1977, s. 103 or s. 104. RA 1977, s. 106A does give the County Court power to stay or suspend the execution of an order for possession for a total period of three months.

12. Rent control.

(*a*) Protected tenancies: if no rent is registered under the Rent Act, then the rent payable is that which has been agreed between the parties. If it is desired to increase the rent this can only be done by means of a rent agreement as defined by RA 1977, s. 51. If the correct procedure is not followed, then the excess over the original rent is not recoverable. Either the landlord or tenant may apply at any time for registration of a fair rent. The application is made to the rent officer who will determine what is a fair rent bearing in mind the criteria in s. 70. Once registered, the rent is the maximum that can be recovered by the landlord. If the rent being paid is less than the registered rent, the rent can only be increased to the registered rent if the terms of the tenancy allow this.

(*b*) Statutory tenancies: when no rent has been registered during the protected tenancy, then the maximum rent recoverable is that payable under the protected tenancy (s. 45(1)). If there was a fair rent registered for the protected tenancy, that applies to the statutory tenancy. Applications for registration may be made as in (*a*).

(*c*) Restricted contracts: the rent is a matter for agreement between the parties until either landlord or tenant refers the matter to the Rent Tribunal (s. 77(1)). The rent must be a reasonable rent broadly similar to the concept of a fair rent.

NOTE: registration of a fair rent means that no application can be made for an increase of rent within two years unless there is a change in the circumstances of the tenancy which means that the rent is no longer fair or it is a joint application.

(*d*) Certificates of fair rent: a landlord can apply for a certificate of fair rent when about to grant a tenancy of a house which he is building or converting to let or for which no rent has been registered within the past two years (RA 1977, s. 69). Once he is granted a certificate of fair rent, the landlord may, when the property is let, apply for registration of a fair rent. The rent officer will determine the condition of the property to ascertain if the landlord has carried out any works outstanding at the date of the certificate being granted. If he is satisfied, the rent registered will be the amount stated in the certificate.

Flats—practical points

13. Insurance. In purchasing an existing leasehold flat (or taking a new lease) it is important to note on whom the duty to issue the building rests. If the tenant covenants to insure, the covenant may require he uses a particular company or one selected by the landlord. It may also provide that the tenant is under an obligation to produce the policy and a receipt for the premiums. It may be safer and administratively simpler for the landlord to covenant to insure and to recover the premiums as service rent. In any event the lease should provide for insurance monies to be used for the re-instatement of the property.

14. Ownership and management of common parts and by other tenants. Various problems arise because of the importance to the tenant of seeking to ensure that the parts of the building not occupied by him are properly maintained and repaired:

(*a*) The lease should contain proper covenants for services in common parts and through or over other flats together with any necessary rights of access for repair.

(*b*) The tenant must ensure that there are obligations to repair and maintain the remainder of the building and that he is in a position to enforce these obligations. In particular, the tenant must have a mechanism for enforcing other tenants' obligations as well as the landlord's. This may be achieved by direct covenants between the tenants or by imposing an obligation upon the landlord to take action.

(*c*) In blocks of flats of any size it is more satisfactory to have the common parts owned by a management company controlled by the tenants.

15. Service charges. So far as service charges and other charges for repairs, maintenance or insurance are concerned, the tenant sometimes faces difficulties with possible overcharging or poor workmanship. Some protection is given by the Landlord & Tenant Act 1985, ss. 20–23 entitling the tenant to independent estimates, information as to costs and sight of accounts. Charges can be challenged on the grounds of reasonableness (L & T 1985, s. 19). Though the quite detailed provisions do provide for costs to be reasonable and "the provisions of services or the carrying out of works . . . (to be) . . . 'of a reasonable standard' " (L & T 1985, s. 19(1)(b)), the sensible tenant will ensure before entering into the lease that the mechanism for establishing and collecting the service charge and for administering the common parts is satisfactory rather than rely on this statutory protection.

Protective legislation

16. Protection from Eviction Act 1977. The following provisions assist the residential occupier in avoiding peremptory eviction:

(a) Notices to quit may have to be in a prescribed form and of a prescribed length (see 7).

(b) If premises are let as a dwelling, a right of re-entry or forfeiture cannot be enforced without court action (PEA 1977, s. 2).

(c) Unlawful eviction and harassment of a residential occupier is a criminal offence (PEA 1977, s. 1).

(d) In respect of premises formerly held under a tenancy which was not a statutorily protected tenancy or under a restricted contract created since 28th November 1980 it is not lawful to recover possession other than by court action (PEA 1977, s. 3).

(e) Premiums under RA 1977, s. 119. No person may require or receive a premium as a condition of the grant, renewal, continuance or assignment of a protected tenancy. This is a criminal offence. *Any person* is not limited simply to landlords but includes, for example, agents or collusive third parties. Premium is defined in s. 128(1) as any fine or other like sum and other pecuniary consideration. It has been described as "a cash payment made to the lessor. . . . It is in fact the purchase money which the tenant pays for the benefit which he gets under the lease" (*King* v. *Earl Cadogan* (1915)). This may include paying the landlord's legal costs. (There are somewhat similar provisions in relation to premiums and restricted contracts in s. 122.)

17. Landlord & Tenant Act 1985, ss. 11–13. This section imposes repairing covenants on the landlord where a dwelling is let for less than seven years and to a dwelling let for seven years or more which is determinable at the landlord's option within seven years. They oblige him to repair the structure and exterior and to keep in proper working order the installations for the supply of water, gas, electricity and sanitation, baths, sinks, basins, toilets and the heating apparatus for room and water.

There is no obligation on the landlord to rebuild the premises where they are damaged or destroyed by fire, tempest, flood or inevitable accident or where the necessity to repair arises from the tenant's unreasonable use of the property. Neither is there any obligation to repair the tenant's fixtures. An agreement to relieve the landlord from his statutory obligations is only valid if the leave of the court is obtained (L & T 1985, s. 12).

Note that ss. 11–13 do not apply to a lease for less than seven years where there is a right of renewal and the renewal period and the original period will exceed seven years.

Progress test 21

1. Which residential tenancies are excluded from protected tenancy status? (**3**)

2. When the court is satisfied that the landlord has established one of the cases for possession in Part I of Sched. 15, what must it then consider? (**7**)

3. What is meant by suitable alternative accommodation? (**7**)

4. What is a protected shorthold tenancy? (**10**)

5. If a restricted contract is entered into after 28th November 1980 can a Rent Tribunal grant an extension after a notice to quit has been served? (**11**)

6. Describe the repairing covenants imposed by L & T 1985, s. 11. (**13**)

7. What is a certificate of fair rent? (**12**(*d*))

8. From April to September 1985 Mary rented a cottage in Devon to various holiday makers. She intends to rent it to John who has moved to Devon looking for a job. Explain the requirements of

Case 13 and the advantages to the landlord when seeking to recover possession under a Part II case.   (7)

22
Purchase of the freehold reversion

Other than under LRefA 1967

1. Introduction. The tenant of a property may purchase the freehold reversion to his lease in one of two ways, either:

(*a*) by a bargain made between himself and the landlord; or

(*b*) by compelling the landlord to sell under LRefA 1967 (*see* **8–31**).

Where LRefA 1967 is not utilised the transaction will follow the normal stages of a freehold purchase, but the points discussed in **2–7** below should be particularly noted.

2. Preparation of draft contract and conveyance. The vendor's solicitor will prepare a draft contract in the usual way, although this is quite often dispensed with so that the parties proceed directly to the draft conveyance stage. The purchaser's solicitor would normally prepare the draft conveyance in the usual way, although frequently the vendor will insist on a form of conveyance prepared by his solicitor being accepted as a term of the contract.

3. Costs. Very commonly it will be a term of the contract that the purchaser pays the vendor's costs.

4. Covenants, grants and reservations. Where, as is the usual case, the landlord owns adjoining or neighbouring property, both parties will pay great attention to the need for relevant covenants, grants and reservations in the conveyance. Typical important points are:

 (*a*) restrictive covenants to preserve the character of the development or area;

 (*b*) particularly in terraced houses, mutual rights of access for repair and decoration of adjoining parts;

 (*c*) any necessary grants and reservations of easements for services such as drainage and sewage;

 (*d*) any required declaration as to the ownership or part ownership of boundaries and shared parts such as walls common to terraced houses, guttering and so on.

5. Declaration of merger. The purchaser's solicitor must consider whether the lease is intended to merge and be extinguished in the freehold reversion. The effect of LPA 1925, s. 185 is that whether merger takes place or not depends on the intention of the parties. If merger is intended, however, an express declaration of merger should be included in the conveyance to clarify the position.

6. Cases when merger is not possible. Merger cannot take place if there is an encumbrance on the leasehold estate. Thus, there can be no merger if the leasehold estate is subject to a mortgage. Neither evidently can there be a merger if the freehold and the leasehold estates are owned by the same person in two different capacities, e.g. the one as beneficial owner and the other as trustee.

7. Other drafting points.

 (*a*) Since the landlord will frequently own adjoining land thought must be given to the effect of LPA 1925, s. 62 in converting permissive rights into legal easements (*see Land Law*, L. B. Curzon, M & E *Handbook*, 1982).

 (*b*) Where the landlord holds other land in the same title the conveyance must include an acknowledgment for production (*see* 16:7).

 (*c*) Where the freehold reversion is subject to a mortgage then the mortgagee must join in the conveyance or otherwise release the property from the mortgage.

Under LRefA 1967

8. Terms of the Act. LRefA 1967 as slightly amended by LRefA 1979 (*see* note below) and Housing Act 1980 (Sched. 21) gives the tenant of a house in certain circumstances the right to purchase the freehold from the landlord or alternatively demand a lease for a period of fifty years from the end of the lease. The qualifying circumstances are set out in **9–11** below.

NOTE: LRefA 1979 is a short Act passed to prevent artificial inflation of the price the tenant has to pay by the landlord granting an intermediate lease of the property (*see Jones* v. *Wrotham Park Settled Estates* (1979)).

9. The property must be a house (s. 2). Thus, importantly, flats are excluded from the Act. Other points to note are as follows.

(*a*) Section 2(1) provides that "house" includes any building designed or adapted for living in and reasonably so called, notwithstanding that the building is not structurally detached.

(*b*) Section 2(2) excludes "a house which is not structurally detached and of which a material part lies above or below a part of the structure not comprised in the house". This was meant to exclude flats although the whole of a building divided into flats may still be a house (*Harris* v. *Swick Securities* (1969)). In *Gaidowski* v. *Gonville and Caius College, Cambridge* (1975) CA, the court thought that a property extended by adding one room from the ground floor of an adjoining house might be excluded from the Act by this subsection, but it was not in fact in that case because the tenant claimed enfranchisement (i.e. the purchase of the freehold reversion) only of the property without the extra room and that was a house within s. 2(1).

(*c*) In *Parsons* v. *Viscount Gage* (1974) HL, the court held that a property was excluded by s. 2(2) as "not structurally detached" where part of it was over an adjoining garage.

10. Terms of the lease.

(*a*) The tenancy must be a lease for a term of more than twenty-one years (s. 3).

(*b*) The rateable value must not exceed certain amounts, as follows.

(*i*) If the lease was created after 18th February 1966, then if it was first rated before 1st April 1973, £400 in Greater London or £200 elsewhere on 23rd March 1965 or when it was first rated; *or* if it was first rated on 1st April 1973 or later, £1,000 in Greater London or £500 elsewhere.

(*ii*) If the lease was created on or before 18th February 1966, £1,500 in Greater London or £750 elsewhere.

(*c*) The tenancy must be at a "low rent" (s. 1(1)(*a*)). This is defined in s. 4. Normally low rent means a rent of not more than two-thirds of the rateable value. In the case of a tenancy granted between the end of August 1939 and the beginning of April 1963 (other than a building lease) it is not regarded as a tenancy at a low rent if at the commencement the rent exceeded two-thirds of the letting value of the property. In *Gidlow-Jackson* v. *Middlegate Properties Ltd* (1974) it was held that the letting value meant the market value taking into account the effect of the Rent Acts.

11. Requirement of occupation. Section 1(1)(*b*) provides that the tenant must have occupied the property as his residence for the last three years or for periods amounting to three years in the last ten years. Section 7 provides that if the tenant dies while occupying the house as his residence then if a member of his family who was resident in the house becomes the tenant he may add the period of the deceased tenant's residence to his own for the purpose of calculating the period of three years' residence. For the definition of "member of his family" *see* s. 7(7). In *Duke of Westminster* v. *Oddy* (1984) a company director held a lease as bare trustee for the company. He occupied the house under a licence from the company. Held he did not occupy the lease "in right of the tenancy" and so was not entitled under the Act.

Conveyancing procedure on enfranchisement under LRefA 1967

12. Notice. The tenant must serve on the landlord written notice of his desire to purchase the freehold (s. 8(1)). The form of the notice is set out as Form 1 in LR(N)R 1967. Once the notice has been served the landlord is obliged to sell the freehold to the tenant in accordance with the other provisions of the Act. This contract is registrable as a Class C(IV) land charge.

13. Effect of tenant's notice in certain circumstances. Section 22 and Sched. 3 contain the following provisions relating to the effect of the notice.

(*a*) A tenant's notice is not effective if given after he has given notice to terminate the lease.

(*b*) A tenant's notice is not effective if given after a tenant's request for a new tenancy under the Landlord and Tenant Act 1954, s. 26, or after notice under s. 27 of that Act that he does not desire the tenancy to continue. Similarly a notice is ineffective if given after the landlord and tenant have agreed a new tenancy under s. 28 of the 1954 Act.

(*c*) If the landlord has served a notice under the Landlord and Tenant Act 1954, s. 25 (i.e. a notice to terminate the tenancy), then normally the tenant must serve a tenant's notice within two months of that if it is to be an effective notice (for details *see* Sched. 3(2)).

14. Other provisions relating to the notice.

(*a*) Section 5(7) provides that the service of a tenant's notice discharges any contract the landlord has entered into for disposal of an interest in the property.

(*b*) The tenant can serve a notice even though the landlord has commenced forfeiture proceedings and after the service of the notice the landlord cannot commence such proceedings.

(*c*) Section 5(2) provides that a tenant who sells the property after service of his notice may also assign the benefit of the notice. However, he cannot assign the benefit of the notice separately from the property.

15. Landlord's reply. The landlord must within two months of service of the tenant's notice serve a notice in reply as set out in Form 2 in LR(N)R 1967. This form acknowledges receipt of the notice and either admits the tenant's claim or refuses to admit it and states the reason for such refusal.

16. Landlord's requirements of tenant. Further procedures are laid down in LR(E&E)R 1967.

(*a*) *Deposit.* The landlord at any time after receipt of the tenant's notice may give written notice that he requires a deposit of three times the annual ground rent or £25 whichever is the greater on account of the sums which the tenant has to pay the landlord under the Act. The tenant must then pay this sum within fourteen days of the notice.

(*b*) *Proof of title and occupation.* In the same way the landlord may require the tenant to deduce his title to the lease and to supply a statutory declaration containing particulars of the occupation which the tenant relies on in giving him a right under the Act. The tenant has twenty-one days in which to comply with these requirements.

17. Proof of landlord's title.

(*a*) If the tenant has no reply to his notice within two months or after receipt of a reply he may deliver a notice to the landlord requiring him to deduce title within four weeks of receipt of the notice (LR(E&E)R 1967, Sched. 1(3)).

(*b*) After the landlord has deduced title in this way the tenant has to deliver his requisitions and objections on title within fourteen days. The landlord has to reply within fourteen days and the tenant is deemed to accept these replies if he does not object to them within seven days of their receipt (Sched. 1(4) LR (E&E)R 1967).

18. Form of conveyance and completion.

(*a*) The conveyance must be prepared in draft by the tenant and delivered to the landlord's solicitor at least fourteen days before completion is due. If the conveyance contains restrictive covenants the tenant must inform the landlord if he is granting a mortgage or other third party interest in time for the landlord to use the priority notice mechanism to protect his Class D(II) land charge (Sched. 1(9)). Schedule 1 para. 9(4) (LR(E&E)R 1967) allows the landlord to insist on duplicate conveyances if the conveyance contains covenants by the tenant or grants or reservations affecting other property of the landlord.

(*b*) One month after the price has been fixed by agreement or the court (*see* **19**) either party may give the other notice to complete the conveyance four weeks from that notice.

19. The price to be paid.

(*a*) The price is calculated according to the formula laid down in s. 9. The basic assumption is that the house is being sold on an arm's length open market sale by a willing seller on the assumption that the tenancy had been extended under the Act and the tenant and his family resident with him were not buying.

(*b*) If the parties cannot agree on the price payable it will be fixed by the Lands Tribunal in accordance with s. 21. (Legal aid is available for such proceedings—Legal Aid Act 1974.)

(*c*) Section 9(3) provides that the tenant may by written notice to the landlord withdraw from the transaction within one month of the price being ascertained in accordance with s. 9. This may have two other consequences:

(*i*) he may have to compensate the landlord in respect of the effect of his notice on the landlord's power to deal with the property;

(*ii*) the tenant can then not deliver a further valid notice for a period of three years.

20. Costs. Section 9(4) provides that in addition to the price, the tenant must pay the reasonable costs of:

(*a*) the landlord's legal costs for investigating the tenant's title and deducing title;

(*b*) the valuation of the house.

21. Release from landlord's mortgage. Section 12 provides that a conveyance under the Act discharges the property from any mortgage on the landlord's estate, and also from the operation of any court order for the enforcement of the mortgage. In order to achieve this the money due must be paid either to the mortgagee or if that

proves a difficulty then into court according to the provisions of s. 13.

22. Terms of the purchase. Section 10 deals with the rights to be conveyed to the tenant on enfranchisement, and regulates the position as to easements, reservations and restrictive covenants to be included in the conveyance to the tenant. Broadly the effect is that the tenant will hold the property with the same benefits and subject to the same incidents except those of the leasehold estate as he held it as tenant. In case of dispute as to the form of the conveyance the rather complex provisions of this section would require detailed examination. The same section gives the tenant a right to the statutory acknowledgment for production of title deeds retained by the landlord but not a right to an undertaking for their safe custody (*see also* 16:7).

23. Right to an extended lease. The procedure for obtaining an extended lease follows the same pattern as for enfranchisement. Having obtained an extended lease the tenant has a right to enfranchisement but only before the term date of the original lease and there is no right to further extension. This makes acquisition of an extended lease under the Act comparatively uncommon and therefore it is not further dealt with in this text.

Landlord's overriding rights under LRefA 1967

24. Redevelopment rights (s. 17). In certain circumstances the landlord has a right to possession where for redevelopment he wishes to demolish or reconstruct the whole or a substantial part of the property. This right is available where:

(*a*) the tenant has been granted an extended lease;

(*b*) the tenant has given notice that he wishes to have an extended lease.

The landlord can apply for possession on this ground only in the last twelve months of the unextended term (s. 17(1)).

Once the landlord has made such an application the tenant may still serve a valid tenant's notice claiming enfranchisement unless the notice is not given before the date of the court order giving possession to the landlord or unless the tenant had given notice requiring an extended lease in the twelve months before the landlord's application.

25. Residential rights (s. 18). In certain circumstances where the lease has not been extended the landlord has the right to obtain a court order granting him possession of the property as a main residence for himself or an adult member of his family.

(a) This applies only where the tenant has given notice requiring either enfranchisement or an extended lease and effect has not been given to that notice.

(b) A landlord has no rights under s. 18 if his interest in the property was purchased or created after 18th February 1966.

(c) The court may not make an order under this section if it is satisfied in the circumstances, including the availability of other accommodation for the landlord or tenant, that greater hardship would be caused by making the order than by refusing it.

26. Compensation to the tenant. Where the landlord makes a successful claim under ss. 17 or 18 (*see* **24** and **25**) the tenant is entitled to compensation. This is assessed in accordance with Sched. 2 and broadly means that the landlord will be bound to pay the tenant the market value of the site and buildings.

27. Retention of management powers. Section 19 contains lengthy provisions intended to allow the distinctive appearance, amenities or "period flavour" of a particular neighbourhood to be preserved even following enfranchisement. It applies where the property in an area is occupied under tenancies from the same landlord. In such a case the landlord could before 1st January 1970 apply to the Minister for a certificate approving a scheme for the retention of management powers by the landlord in accordance with that section.

Position of certain public bodies under LRefA 1967

28. The Crown. The Crown is not bound by the Act but will act as if it is.

29. Exceptions for development purposes. Section 28 empowers certain landlords listed in s. 28(5) (local authorities, the Commission for New Towns, development corporations and other specified public bodies) to avoid the provisions of the Act. Under this section if a Minister of the Crown certifies that the property will within ten years be required for relevant development (as defined in s. 28) then a tenant's notice will be of no effect and in certain circumstances serving the notice may give rise to the re-development rights under s. 17 taking effect (*see* **24**).

30. Restrictive covenants for future redevelopment. Section 29 allows a local authority landlord when the tenant acquires the freehold under the Act to include in the conveyance to the tenant restrictive covenants preserving the land for future redevelopment by the local authority.

31. Pre-emption. Section 30 allows a landlord who is the Commission for New Towns or a development corporation to include on enfranchisement or grant of an extended lease a right of pre-emption in its favour.

Progress test 22

1. When should a declaration of merger not be included in a purchase of the freehold reversion? (**6**)

2. What is the definition of a "house" under LRefA 1967? (**9**)

3. What is the requirement of occupation under LRefA 1967? (**11**)

4. Is a tenant's notice effective after he has given notice to terminate the lease? (**13**)

5. How should the landlord respond to the tenant's notice? (**15**)

6. How is the price to be paid on enfranchisement calculated? (**19**)

7. When is a landlord entitled to possession for redevelopment? (**24**)

8. When may a landlord of a property affected by the Act obtain possession of it as a residence for himself? (**25**)

23
Compulsory purchases

Statutory powers

1. The Local Government Acts 1933 and 1972. Sections 159 and 160 of the 1933 Act conferred a general power of compulsory purchase of land on local authorities. The procedure to be followed was set out in AL(AP)A 1946 (now the ALA 1981).

The 1972 Act (which replaced the 1933 Act) states in s. 121 that principal councils have power to purchase land compulsorily, whether it is inside or outside their area, for their functions, using the procedure specified in ALA 1981. Principal councils are county, district and London borough councils and the Greater London Council. District councils exercise the power on behalf of community councils.

2. Other legislation. Many other statutes which empower other bodies to purchase land compulsorily provide that the procedure to be followed is that laid down in ALA 1981, e.g. the Police Act 1964, s. 9(2) and the Electricity Act 1947, s. 9.

Some Acts which confer powers of compulsory purchase on organisations set out their own particular procedure, e.g. the Housing Act 1957, Part III dealing with the question of slum clearance provides in Sched. 3 details of the procedure. Other examples are to be found in the 5th Schedule to the Forestry Act 1967 and the 2nd Schedule to the Pipe-lines Act 1962. In all these cases, once the compulsory purchase order has been made, the next stages are the same as under ALA 1981.

3. **Procedures under ALA 1981.** These are examined in 4–31 below.

Draft compulsory purchase order

4. **Form of the order.** The local authority or other acquiring authority drafts a compulsory purchase order in the form prescribed by the Compulsory Purchase of Land Regulations 1982.

5. **Notification of the order.** The draft order must be publicised in the local press on two successive weeks. The form of the advertisement is specified by the Compulsory Purchase of Land Regulations 1982, and is similar to the draft order. As the advertisement does not include the map, the advertisement must state where in the locality the map can be inspected, together with the draft order. This will usually be at the offices of the local authority and, perhaps, the local library.

The period within which objection to the order must be made, i.e. twenty-one days from the date of insertion, must appear in the advertisement.

In addition, each owner, lessee and occupier (a tenant for a month or less is not an occupier (ALA 1981, s. 12)) will be sent a copy of the draft order; if after reasonable enquiries no such person can be found and there is no person on the premises to receive a notice, it may be affixed to a conspicuous part of the premises (ALA 1981, s. 6).

6. **The confirming authority.** The confirming authority is the Minister named, in the Act authorising the making of the compulsory purchase order, as the person required to confirm the order. Orders made under the Local Government Act 1972 are confirmed by the Secretary of State for the Environment.

7. **Objections to the order.** Written objections to the order, if any, are sent to the confirming authority. Unless the objections can be dealt with when compensation for the order is assessed, the Minister has to decide whether the objections will be dealt with by way of

public local inquiry (the normal method—*see* **8–12**) or a private hearing.

Public local inquiries

8. Conduct of the inquiry. If it is decided to hold an inquiry a ministry inspector is appointed to conduct it.

Where the compulsory purchase order is made under the ALA 1981 procedure and the acquiring authority is a local authority, the conduct of the inquiry must conform to the Compulsory Purchase by Public Authorities (Inquiries Procedure) Rules 1976. These Rules also apply if a private hearing is held instead of the public inquiry.

9. Notice of the inquiry. Under Rule 4(2) of the 1976 Rules, the confirming authority must give at least forty-two days' notice in writing of the date of the inquiry to the acquiring authority and the statutory objectors, i.e. any owner, lessee or occupier who has objected and has not withdrawn his objection.

Notice of the inquiry will appear in the local press and public notices of it should be posted near the affected land (Rule 4(1) and (3)).

10. Disclosure before the inquiry. Statutory objectors are obliged to notify the acquiring authority of the substance of their objections. Other objectors should do so as well if practicable.

The acquiring authority is required to go further in its disclosure. It must serve on the statutory objectors a written statement of reasons, including any statement of views by a government department on which it may be relying, at least twenty-eight days before the inquiry (Rule 4(4)). It must afford them a reasonable opportunity to inspect and copy any plans, maps or other documents which it is going to produce in evidence.

11. Procedure at the inquiry. The acquiring authority and the statutory objectors have a right to appear and be heard at the inquiry. The inspector has a discretion to allow other persons a hearing, i.e. other objectors. He is obliged to observe the rules of natural justice but is not bound by the procedural and evidential rules which apply in the courts. Expert witnesses may be called and be examined and cross-examined.

12. Inspection of the land. The inspector can, and if asked to do so by the acquiring authority or statutory objectors must, inspect the land. In either case, representatives of the acquiring authority and the statutory objectors have a right to accompany the inspector on the tour. In practice such an inspection is made almost as a matter of course.

Order comes into effect

13. The Minister's decision. The inspector makes his report to the Minister (the confirming authority). The Minister must consider the report and its recommendation, but is not obliged to follow it. The acquiring authority is notified of the Minister's decision, either that he confirms the order, with or without modification, or that he refuses to confirm it. The Tribunals and Inquiries Act 1971, s. 12 states that the Minister must give the reasons for his decision when an inquiry has been held.

14. Notification of the decision. The Minister is responsible for seeing that his decision is communicated to the parties involved.

15. Notice of confirmation. If the order is confirmed the local authority will publish a notice of this fact in the local press. In addition, notice is sent to owners, lessees and occupiers of the land affected by the order. The order comes into effect as soon as it has been notified in this way, and once confirmed it has the force of law.

Challenging the order

16. Application to High Court for review. There is no appeal from the order. However, it is possible for the order to be reviewed by the High Court. ALA 1981, s. 23 Sched. 1 provides that an aggrieved person may, within six weeks of the making of the order, apply to the High Court for an order quashing the compulsory purchase order on the grounds:

(a) that the compulsory purchase order was *ultra vires*, i.e. that there was no power to make the order, e.g. because the acquiring authority has never been given the power to acquire land in this way; or

(b) that some procedural requirement under ALA 1981 or the Tribunals and Inquiries Act 1971 has not been complied with, and that he has been substantially prejudiced thereby.

The six weeks run from the date of the publication of the compulsory purchase order in the local press.

17. Natural justice and the inquiry. Many cases concerning procedural defects have revolved around the inspector's inquiry. As already mentioned (*see* 11) this must comply with the rules of natural justice. In *Errington* v. *Minister of Health* (1935) it was said that this was so, because the inquiry had a quasi-judicial function.

The rules of natural justice require that the person holding the inquiry be impartial and unbiased. This is one reason why the inspector is a civil servant, not a local government officer.

It also means that both parties must have an adequate and reasonable opportunity to put their cases and to rebut the other side's arguments. See *Errington* v. *Minister of Health* (1935) and *Fairmount Investments Ltd* v. *Secretary of State for the Environment* (1976).

18. Application of the six weeks rule. In *Smith* v. *East Elloe Rural District Council* (1956) a compulsory purchase order was challenged on the basis of bad faith. However, this issue was not raised within six weeks of the order being made and the court held that bad faith did not mean that the court could entertain an application which was out of time. (*See also R* v. *Secretary of State for the Environment ex p. Ostler* (1977).)

Notice to treat

19. Persons on whom notice is served. Once the compulsory purchase order comes into effect (*see* 15), the acquiring authority must (unless the alternative procedure of a general vesting declaration is used, *see* 32–35) serve a notice to treat on all persons interested in, or having power to sell and convey or release, the land, so far as is known to the acquiring authority after making diligent enquiry (Compulsory Purchase Act 1965, s. 5(1)). Therefore notice is served on all persons having a legal interest in the land, other than a yearly tenant or a tenant whose tenancy has less than a year to run.

Where the property is occupied by a tenant under a yearly tenancy or one where the tenancy has less than a year to run the local authority may simply wait for the tenancy to expire. If it requires possession before this date, the local authority can serve a notice of entry on the tenant and pay him compensation for his unexpired term plus an allowance for any loss or injury sustained by him (Compulsory Purchase Act 1965, s. 20(1)).

Tenants protected by the Rent Acts may not use these Acts to resist a compulsory purchase order. However, the Land Compensation Act 1973, s. 39 imposes an obligation on the local authority to rehouse the tenant, if no other suitable accommodation is available.

20. Effect of the notice. The notice to treat is not a contract for the sale of the land but when the compensation for the sale has been agreed between the local authority and the owner or lessee, then the two together form the contract and pass the equitable title in the land to the local authority. (*See West Midland (Trust) Association (Incorporated)* v. *Birmingham Corporation* (1968).) After this stage either party can obtain specific performance of the contract.

21. The time "to treat". The recipient of the notice to treat must submit his claim for compensation to the authority within twenty-one days of service of the notice. If he does not do so the authority may submit the claim to the Lands Tribunal for assessment. If he does put in a claim but cannot reach agreement with the authority, either side may refer the matter to the Lands Tribunal (Compulsory Purchase Act 1965, s. 6). Assessment by the tribunal is final on a question of fact.

22. Serving a notice under T&C 1971, s. 180. If after the making of a compulsory purchase order it is desired by the owner to facilitate the matter, he *may* be able to take advantage of T&C 1971, s. 180. The section is really meant to deal with the situation where planning permission has been refused for the land, so that it has become incapable of reasonable beneficial use in its existing state. The owner of the land can within twelve months of the refusal serve a purchase order on the district council within which the land is situated requiring them to purchase the land. If it is accepted by the council, the body concerned is deemed to be authorised to acquire the interest of the owner compulsorily (Compulsory Purchase Act 1965, s. 181(1)).

23. Lapse of power to serve a notice to treat. The Compulsory Purchase Act 1965, s. 4 states that the powers of the acquiring authority shall not be exercised after the expiration of three years from the date on which the compulsory purchase order becomes operative. In *Marquis of Salisbury* v. *Great Northern Railway Co.* (1852) it was held that the service of a notice to treat was an exercise of those powers. Therefore the notice cannot be served outside the three-year period.

24. Ineffective notices to treat: lapse of time. As mentioned in **21**, either side may refer the question of compensation to the Lands Tribunal if agreement cannot be reached. In practice, the owner or lessee may be more concerned to prove that the notice to treat is ineffective. In the leading case of *Grice* v. *Dudley Corporation* (1958) the notice to treat was served in 1939. In 1956, no further action having being taken by the corporation, the plaintiffs sought a declaration from the High Court that the notice was invalid. It was said that the notice to treat must be enforced within a reasonable time and would only be enforceable outside that period if the delay was explained and enforcement would be equitable in all the circumstances of the case.

25. Other grounds for non-enforcement. *Grice* v. *Dudley Corporation* gave two other grounds when an order would not be enforced by the court, as follows.

(*a*) Where the acquiring body had demonstrated an intention to abandon the rights conferred by the notice to treat.

(*b*) Where the notice was *ultra vires* the local authority, e.g. because it did not have power to purchase land compulsory for the proposed purpose.

In that case Mr Justice Upjohn held there had been abandonment of the order and even if that had not been so it would have been inequitable to enforce the notice after such a delay.

26. Breach of equitable rights. The later case of *Simpsons Sales (London) Ltd* v. *Hendon Corporation* (1964) added a fourth category where enforcement would be a breach of equitable rights, i.e. bad faith, misconduct or an abuse of power. Despite the fact that the notice to treat was served in 1952 and that the plaintiffs' action began in 1959, it was held that the notice was valid because none of the four grounds was proved.

27. Action when notice invalid. Where the notice is proved invalid the acquiring authority could serve a new notice to treat, but it must bear in mind the Compulsory Purchase Act 1965, s. 4 and the three-year rule which is likely to exclude such a move. In those circumstances the only way to continue with the scheme would be to obtain a fresh compulsory purchase order.

28. Delay after the notice to treat has been served. This can be resolved, if compensation has not been fixed, by either side referring the matter to the Lands Tribunal for settlement. The owner/lessee alternatively could apply to the High Court for an order of mandamus (*see R.* v. *Hungerford Market Co Ltd ex p. Davies* (1832)). There is no advantage in using this method and it is quicker and cheaper to refer it to the Lands Tribunal.

Where the delay occurs after compensation has been settled, the aggrieved party may bring an action for specific performance (*see* **20**).

29. Withdrawal of notice to treat. The Land Compensation Act 1961, s. 31(1) allows the authority to withdraw a notice to treat within six weeks of receiving a claim for compensation from the claimant of the land or from any other claimant of the same land on whom notice has been served.

A further right of withdrawal is given to the authority by s. 31(2). The notice to treat may be withdrawn if one of the claimants has failed to submit a claim for compensation in good time. The actual withdrawal takes place at any time after the decision of the Lands Tribunal on his claim but not later than six weeks after the claim has been finally determined, unless the authority has entered into possession of the land (for entry into possession *see* **30–31**). Final determination will occur when no further proceedings in the courts are contemplated on this issue. Only after the outcome of any appeal to the Court of Appeal or House of Lords (if any) is the matter finally determined.

30. Notice of entry. At any time after serving the notice to treat, the acquiring authority may serve a fourteen-days notice of intention to enter the premises (Compulsory Purchase Act 1965, s. 11(1)). This notice entitles the authority after the expiration of the fourteen days to enter into and take possession of the premises, even though compensation has not been settled or paid. If this is done, when the compensation sum is fixed, it carries interest with it from the date of entry until the monies are paid to the relevant person.

Notice of entry is served on the owner, lessee and occupier of the land. Here "occupier" has a wider definition than that used in ALA 1981. It does include a yearly tenant and those who have periodic tenancies of less than a year, e.g. monthly or weekly.

31. Conveyance of the land. Unless a notice of entry is served, the acquiring authority will not be able to take possession of the land until the title to it has been conveyed to it by a deed of conveyance or transfer. The only difference between this compulsory conveyance and the free-market conveyance is that all costs of the conveyance, whether incurred by the local authority or the other party, are paid by the authority (Compulsory Purchase Act 1965, s. 23). The form of the conveyance may be that specified in the 5th Schedule to the Act or in any other form of deed that the acquiring authority thinks fit.

General vesting declaration

32. Introduction. CP(VD)A 1981, s. 1 states that this procedure may be used by any minister or local or public authority authorised to acquire land by means of a compulsory purchase order. The general vesting declaration is an alternative procedure to be followed after the compulsory purchase order has come into effect. Instead of serving a notice to treat and later the vendor executing a conveyance of the land, both steps are replaced by the general vesting declaration.

33. Outline of procedure. The notice of confirmation of a compulsory purchase order (*see* **15**) may also set out the procedure for the general vesting declaration. A separate notice relating to the general vesting declaration can be sent any time after the compulsory purchase order comes into effect and provided a notice to treat has not been served, for the two methods are mutually exclusive. The notice requests the recipient to give information about the land and also his name and address, and is served on all those on whom a notice to treat would otherwise be served. It will state the earliest date when the vesting declaration can be executed by the authority. This cannot be earlier than two months from the date of service of the notice. It may be that the authority will not wish to execute it until some time after that date.

34. Registration of the notice. The notice which informs the landowner of the authority's intention to execute a general vesting declaration must be registered as a local land charge (CP(VD)A 1981, s. 3(4)). The compulsory purchase order does not have to be registered. Where a joint notice has been used, the requirement of registration for the notice of intention still applies.

35. Notice of execution of the general vesting declaration. When the general vesting declaration has been executed by the authority, it is obliged to serve notice of this fact on the persons who received notice of the intention to make a general vesting declaration (*see* **33**). This notice of execution will specify when the declaration will take effect, which will be not less than twenty-eight days from the service of the notice. The effect of execution is as if the acquiring authority had conveyed the land to itself.

Although this method is quicker it does not seem to be as widely used as it could be.

Progress test 23

1. How can a community council compulsorily purchase land for its statutory functions? (**1**)

2. How long does an objector to a draft compulsory purchase order have to make known his objections? (**5**)

3. Who are the statutory objectors? (**9**)

4. What is the six weeks rule? (**16, 18**)

5. What is the effect of serving a notice to treat? (**20**)

6. When does the power to serve a notice to treat lapse? (**23**)

7. When may a notice of entry be served by the acquiring authority and on whom should it be served? (**30**)

8. On whom is a notice of an intention to make a general vesting declaration served and where must it be registered? (**33, 34**)

24

Right to buy—Housing Act 1985

Secure tenants and secure tenancy

1. Secure tenants. Under Part V of the Housing Act 1985 secure tenants have in certain circumstances the right to buy the freehold reversion or a long lease of their dwelling. The complex provisions of this right to buy are summarised here with an emphasis on the effects on conveyancing practice.

2. Definition of secure tenancy.

(*a*) *The landlord condition.* The landlord must be one of the bodies listed in s. 80 of the Housing Act 1985—a local authority; the Commission for the New Towns; a development corporation; or the Development Board for Rural Wales—or certain other landlords detailed in s. 30.

(*b*) *The tenant condition.* The tenant must be an individual or individuals occupying the dwelling house as his only or principal home.

(*c*) *Exceptions from right to buy.*

(*i*) Detailed exceptions for charitable housing trusts and certain housing associations and local authority are contained in Sched. 5.

(*ii*) Schedule 5 of the Act contains further exceptions from the right to buy of which salient examples are: housing for persons of pensionable age or disabled persons and by tenants who are bankrupt or have suffered a court order for possession of their dwelling-house.

(*d*) *Tenancies which are not secure tenancies.* It should also be noted that the lengthy list of tenancies which are said by s. 79 and Schedule 1 of the Act not to be secure tenancies are thereby excluded from the right to buy. Salient examples are: tenancies held by employees of the landlord for the better performance of their duties; long leases for terms of twenty-one years or more; tenancies held by employees of the landlord in premises that form part of a building held by the landlord for providing education or social services; student lettings provided by the landlord for students in further and higher education.

3. Qualifying conditions.

(*a*) The tenant must have been a secure tenant for periods together amounting to two years. These may include periods with different landlords or in different properties. The periods can be interrupted by periods where the tenant is not a secure tenant.

(*b*) If the property is a dwelling-house there is a right to buy the freehold; if it is a flat there is a right to a lease of a term usually of at least 125 years at a very low rent; or if the landlord is a lessee a lease with a minimum length of fifty or twenty-one years as the case may be.

(*c*) If the tenant's income is insufficient to support an outright purchase he may be entitled to a shared ownership lease. The premium payable under the lease would be 50 per cent of the freehold valuation of the property (or more if the tenant could afford it) and rent would be charged in respect of the remaining percentage interest. When the tenant can afford it he may purchase further percentage interests until he has acquired the freehold (in the case of a house) or converted to a nominal ground rent lease (in the case of a flat).

Right to buy

4. Exercise of right to buy. The tenant must serve a written notice on the landlord in a prescribed form. In this form he may claim a right to buy together with members of his family (up to three). Joint tenants all have the right to buy (s. 118(2)). A tenant has the right for his non-tenant spouse to join in a purchase; otherwise the landlord has a discretion whether to allow members of the tenant's family to join in a purchase.

5. Landlord's response. The landlord has to reply (usually within four weeks, *see* s. 124) to the tenant's claim either admitting or denying the claim. If the claim is denied the tenant may apply to the County Court to contest this refusal. If it is admitted then "as soon as possible" thereafter the landlord must serve a notice stating the price, the terms of the conveyance, the right of the tenant to appeal as to price to the district valuer, the right to a mortgage and the right of the tenant to delay completion.

6. Terms of purchase. The price on a freehold purchase is the market value discounting tenant's improvements, the fact that the tenant wishes to buy and assuming there is vacant possession. This price is then discounted by 32 per cent plus 1 per cent for each complete year in excess of three for which the tenants were secure tenants. The maximum discount is 60 per cent and other regulations provide for costs incurred on the dwelling since 31st March 1974 to be taken into account or for the Secretary of State to alter the maximum discount (*see* the Housing (Right to Buy) (Maximum Discount) Order 1980).

7. Right to a mortgage. A tenant who has the right to buy has the right to a mortgage over a twenty-five-year period. Regulations as to the income limit on such mortgages are set by the Statutory Instrument. A tenant who claims a mortgage has, if the mortgage is less than the entire purchase price and less than the permitted maximum advance, a right to defer completion by serving a notice on the authority and paying a £100 deposit. The effect of this is to peg the price for a two-year period.

The transaction

8. Completion of transaction. The terms of the conveyance or lease are specified by Sched. 6 of the Act. In respect of the conveyancing procedure it should be noted that:

(*a*) The landlord, if the land is unregistered, deduces title in accordance with s. 154 by providing a certificate that the landlord is entitled to convey the property in the manner set out in the form of conveyance or lease or in the certificate.

(*b*) On any purchase the transaction is followed by registration, whether the property is an area of compulsory first registration or not (s. 154(4)) and the Chief Land Registrar must accept as evidence of title, if appropriate, the certificate referred to in (*a*) above.

(*c*) In respect of dwelling-houses in national parks, areas of natural beauty designated under s. 87 of the National Parks and Access to the Countryside Act 1949 as areas of outstanding natural beauty, and certain other specified rural areas (*see* s. 157), the conveyance or lease may contain a term restricting the purchaser's right of disposal.

(*d*) Sections 140 and 141 provide for the timing of completion in various circumstances and will need to be studied carefully if this becomes an issue between the parties. There is a complex two-stage machinery under which the landlord can serve notices to complete on the tenant.

9. Delay by the landlord. Where tenants are having difficulty exercising their right to buy effectively and expeditiously then ss. 164–170 provide that the Secretary of State may intervene and take over the powers of that landlord. These sections were included in the Act to prevent local authorities defeating the purposes of the Act because they considered it interfered with their policies.

The case of *Norwich City Council* v. *Secretary of State for the Environment* (1982) emphasised the sweeping nature of the Secretary of State's powers of intervention.

10. Purchase of a lease. The procedure on the purchase of a lease is broadly the same as on a freehold purchase. The purchase price is on the additional assumption of a lease for 125 years with a ground rent of not more than £10 per annum. Schedule 6 deals with the detailed terms of the lease. It may be noted that the lease will contain covenants by the landlord as to exterior repair and repair of common parts, and by the tenant as to interior and decorative repair and the lease must not contain provisions prohibiting or restricting the assignment or subletting of all or part of the dwelling-house.

Progress test 24

1. What is the landlord condition for a secure tenancy? (**2**)

2. What are the qualifying occupation periods for exercise of the right to buy? (**3**)

3. How must the landlord respond to a tenant's right to buy notice? (**5**)

4. What is the rate of discount when the right to buy is exercised? (**6**)

5. If a landlord refuses to carry out the right to buy provisions what are the reserve powers under the Act? (**9**)

6. What are the terms on the purchase of a lease? (**10**)

Part four
Registered land conveyancing

25

Outline of the system of registered land

The Land Registry

1. **The Land Registry system.** Her Majesty's Land Registry was established in its present form by LRA 1925 and its more detailed rules are found in LRR 1925 as amended. The system at first developed rather slowly and then later mushroomed so that now it covers all the highly populated areas. The process of extending the system is by declaring that registration of title is compulsory following certain dealings (by and large conveyances on sale and specified leases, LRA 1925, s. 123; *see* 26:**21**) with any land within a designated part of the country. Outside those areas a voluntary registration is possible in limited classes of cases (*see* 26:**19**).

2. **The Chief Land Registrar.** The Land Registry is a department of the Civil Service. At its head is the Chief Land Registrar. Under LRA 1925 and LRR 1925 he is charged with implementing the Act and has wide discretion and powers including rule-making powers in that regard. In particular r. 298 confers on him power to hold hearings and determine disputes concerning various aspects of Land Registry practice.

3. **District Land Registries.** The Land Registry itself is situated at Lincoln's Inn Fields in London and is the administrative headquarters of the system. All applications concerning registration and registered land, however, must be made to one of the thirteen District Land Registries in the relevant part of the country. Each of

these deals with registration of title in a particular area, and is headed by a District Land Registrar who has within his area many of the powers of the Chief Land Registrar (LRR 1925, r. 133).

4. Terminology. In registered land practice the language of conveyancing is somewhat different:

(*a*) a parcel of land is referred to as a registered title;
(*b*) the owner of land is referred to as the registered proprietor;
(*c*) a conveyance of registered land is called a "transfer";
(*d*) a transaction involving registered land is known as a "dealing".

Proof of title

5. Difference between registered and unregistered conveyancing. The essential difference between registered and unregistered conveyancing concerns proof of title. In the case of unregistered land an owner shows title to a would-be purchaser by producing documentary evidence (the abstract of title and verification of the abstract) which shows historically how the title came to be and is vested in him. In the case of registered land the owner simply has to demonstrate to a purchaser that he is registered at the appropriate District Land Registry as the registered proprietor. Proof of registration is unequivocal proof of title and that title is guaranteed by the Land Registry (*see* **11, 28,** 26:**1–14** and Chap. 29 for qualifications to this) (for proof of title to registered leasehold land, *see* 26:**9–13**).

6. Identification of title. In registered land the documents of title are replaced by the fact of registration. The equivalent to a title deed are thus the various entries made on the register of title at the Land Registry. Each separate title is given a number—the title number. It is by this title number that each parcel of registered land is described and by reference to which it is referred to on the Land Registry plan.

7. Description of title. The description of each title on the register is as follows.

(*a*) It is identified by the title number.

(*b*) It is described by reference to the field plan (*see* 25).

(*c*) The various matters relevant to the title are then contained on a set of index cards for each title.

It is the Index cards, the register of title and the filed plan which are the Land Registry equivalent of title deeds.

8. Land Certificate. In unregistered conveyancing the owner has possession of his title deeds. However the register of title and the filed plan are retained by the Land Registry. The registered proprietor is instead issued with a Land Certificate (*see* 15–16) containing a facsimile copy of his registered title. If the land within a particular title number is subject to a registered mortgage (*see* 28:21–31) the Land Certificate is kept at the Land Registry and the mortgagee is issued instead with a Charge Certificate (*see* 17).

The register of title

9. The three registers. Each title consists of entries on a series of index cards at the appropriate District Land Registry. For each title there are three registers: the Property Register (*see* 11–12), the Proprietorship Register (*see* 13) and the Charges Register (*see* 14). The three registers of a specimen title are illustrated in Fig. 2.

10. Meaning of "register". To avoid confusion the reader must note that in all accounts of the Land Registry the word "register" has three different meanings. Depending on the context it may mean:

(*a*) the entire collection of Land Registry titles;

(*b*) the entire register of a particular title;

(*c*) as in this chapter, the three "registers" of which each title is made up.

11. The Property Register. (LRR 1925, r. 2.) This is the first register and is roughly the equivalent of the "parcels clause" in unregistered conveyancing (*see* 13:13).

(*a*) *Description of land.* The register consists of a verbal descrip-

H.M. LAND REGISTRY

Edition 1	TITLE NUMBER SO19834	SPECIMEN
opened 14.8.1965	*This register consists of* 2 *pages*	

A. PROPERTY REGISTER

containing the description of the registered land and the estate comprised in the Title

ADMINISTRATIVE AREA   PARISH OR PLACE
(County, County Borough, etc)

SOUTHUMBERLAND   OLDCASTLE

The Freehold land shown and edged with red on the filed plan of the above
title registered on 14 August 1965 known as 97 Acacia Gardens, together with a
right of way over the part of the driveway at the side not included in the
title.

NOTE 1:-The land edged and numbered in green on the filed plan has been
removed from this title and registered under the title number or numbers
shown in green on the said plan.

NOTE 2:-There is appurtenant to the land in this title the following right
reserved by the Transfer dated 12 March 1971 referred to in Entry No.4
of the Charges Register:-

"EXCEPT AND RESERVING to the Transferor for the benefit of the Transferors'
retained land the full and free right to the uninterrupted passage and
running of water and soil through the drains and sewers now existing or
within 21 years hereafter to be constructed in or under the land hereby
transferred."   (15.4.1971)

The land is now in the County of Southumbria, Oldcastle District.   (15.1.1976)

B. PROPRIETORSHIP REGISTER

stating nature of the Title, name, address and description of the proprietor of the land and any entries affecting the right of disposing thereof

TITLE ABSOLUTE

Entry number	Proprietor, etc.	Remarks
1.	~~PERCY BYSSHE SHELLEY of 97 Acacia Gardens, Oldcastle, Southumberland, Steel Erector, registered on 14 August 1965.~~	~~Price paid~~ £4250
2.	ROBERT BROWNING, Sales Representative, and ELIZABETH BARRETT BROWNING, his wife, both of 97 Acacia Gardens, Oldcastle, Southumbria, OL3 5PJ., registered on 15 January 1979.	
3.	RESTRICTION registered on 15 January 1979:-No disposition by one proprietor of the land (being the survivor of joint proprietors and not being a trust corporation) under which capital money arises is to be registered except under an Order of the registrar or of the Court.	

Any entries struck through are no longer subsisting

Figure 2 *Property Register, Proprietorship Register and Charges Register of a
specimen title.*

TITLE NUMBER SO19834 *(H.M. LAND REGISTRY)* SPECIMEN

C. CHARGES REGISTER

Page 2   *containing charges, incumbrances, etc., adversely affecting the land and registered dealings therewith*

Entry number	The date at the beginning of each entry is the date on which the entry was made on this edition of the register.	Remarks
1.	14 August 1965–The part of the driveway at the side included in the title is subject to rights of way.	
~~2.~~	~~14 August 1965–CHARGE dated 12 July 1965 registered on~~ 14 August 1965 to secure the moneys including the further advances therein mentioned. 15·1·1979	
3.	~~PROPRIETOR–HIGH STREET BANK LIMITED~~ of 44 High Street, Oldcastle, Southumberland, registered on 14 August 1965.	*WD1*
4.	15 April 1971–A Transfer of the land edged and numbered SO22463 in green on the filed plan dated 12 March 1971 by Percy Bysshe Shelley to John Keats contains the following covenant by the transferor:– "The Transferor hereby covenants with the Transferee and his successors and assigns as owners for the time being of the land hereby transferred that he the Transferor will not at any time use the land remaining in title number SO19834 or permit the same to be used for any purpose other than as the site for a single private dwellinghouse with the usual garages outbuildings and appurtenances."	*WD7*
5.	15 January 1979–CHARGE dated 18 December 1978 registered on 15 January 1979 to secure the moneys including the further advances therein mentioned.	
6.	PROPRIETOR–WEYFORD BUILDING SOCIETY of Society House, The Avenue, Weyford, Blankshire, registered on 15 January 1979.	*WD8*

Figure 2   *(contd.)*

tion of the land in the title and a reference to the plan (*see* **25**) which is an integral part of the description. Because of the importance in registered titles of the filed plan the verbal description is usually rather brief. In the example in Fig. 2 it simply refers to the "land ... edged with red on the filed plan" and the address of the property: "97 Acacia Gardens".

   (*b*) *Interests and benefits.* The register also contains notes as to:

      (*i*) any exemptions from overriding interests (*see* **27**:5–9);

(*ii*) any easements, rights and privileges of which the land has the benefit or to which it is subject.

Thus, in the example in Fig. 2 the description states that the registered land has the benefit of the specified right of way. If the Registrar is not satisfied that such a right is demonstrated sufficiently clearly to be guaranteed by the Land Registry then it will be referred to in a qualified way, e.g. "the conveyance to AB of 6th July 1979 states that the land has the benefit of a right of way therein mentioned".

(*c*) *Mines and mineral rights.* The registry will also contain a note of who owns mines and minerals under the land. If no mention is made of mineral or mining rights in the Property Register then the ownership of these by the registered proprietor is not guaranteed (LRA 1925, s. 83(5)(b)).

(*d*) *Restrictive covenants.* The registered proprietor may have the benefit of restrictive covenants taken on a previous transfer. It is not customary for the Registrar to include a mention of this in the register. He may do so if requested by an applicant for registration. If the benefit of such a covenant is mentioned the Land Registry does not guarantee that the covenant has the effect claimed.

12. Property Register in leasehold title. LRR 1925, r. 5 provides that in the case of leasehold title the Property Register must also contain:

(*a*) a reference to the registered lease (this will be the parties thereto, the term, and the rent);

(*b*) exceptions or reservations from the lease;

(*c*) if the lessor's title is registered, that title number.

13. The Proprietorship Register. (LRR 1925, r. 6.) The second register is analogous to the "habendum" in unregistered conveyancing (*see* 13:**19**).

(*a*) *Type of title.* It first states the type of registered title owned by the registered proprietor. There are seven classes of title (*see* 26:**1**–**13**). The example in Fig. 2 states that the land is registered with "Title Absolute". Since it is not stated to be leasehold it is freehold.

(*b*) *Name and address.* Next the register states the full name and address of the registered proprietor or proprietors. A description, e.g. occupation (as in the example), title or honorary designation (e.g. gentleman) may be given although this is unnecessary and is usually omitted from applications for registration. The address is important as it is to the address given that the Registrar will send any notice affecting the land. A proprietor may have up to three addresses including that of his solicitor entered (LRR 1925, r. 315). The address may be updated free of charge by producing the Land Certificate to the Land Registry and this should not be omitted.

(*c*) *Date.* Following the address the date of registration of the proprietor as proprietor is shown.

(*d*) *Price paid.* In the remarks column it was the practice to record the price paid by the new proprietor (*see* entry 1 in the example in Fig. 2). In order to cut down the administrative burden the Land Registry has dispensed with this practice unless requested by the proprietor to make such an entry.

(*e*) *Other entries.* The register may also contain various entries intended to protect third party interests or restrict dealings with the registered land. These are:

(*i*) cautions (*see* 27:**14–18**) giving the cautioner a right to notice before any dealing is entered;

(*ii*) restrictions (*see* Fig. 2 and 27:**19–20**) preventing any dealing with the land from being registered unless specified formalities are complied with;

(*iii*) inhibitions (*see* 27:**22–23**): whilst still in force these prevent the registration of any dealing with the land they affect.

14. The Charges Register. (LRR 1925, r. 7.) This contains the encumbrances affecting the registered property as follows.

(*a*) All encumbrances subsisting at the date of first registration. Where these are lengthy they are referred to briefly in the register and then set out at length in a schedule or by referring to an annexed copy of the relevant document.

(*b*) All subsequent charges or encumbrances. A typical example of this would be a registered mortgage made by the proprietors (*see* 28:**21–31**).

(*c*) Notes of any adverse interests; notes relating to conditions and covenants and of dealings with registered charges and encumbrances. An example of the first of these would be "a conveyance of 26th November 1896 between AB and CD contained restrictive covenants, but an abstract of these was not produced on the application for First Registration".

The Land or Charge Certificate

15. Issue of the Land Certificate. When a new title is registered or there is a change of registered proprietors then the new proprietor is issued by the Land Registry with a Land Certificate. This is in a prescribed form (LRR 1925, r. 261, Form 78). The Land Certificate is popularly regarded as the registered-land equivalent of title deeds. To some extent this is misleading because the Land Certificate is only a facsimile of the official register and may not be up to date. In addition, there may be matters of title not contained wholly on the register (*see* leasehold title, 26:**9**; possessory title, 26:**4**).

16. Form of the Land Certificate. The front cover is a certificate that the land described within is registered under the given title number. It also contains a warning against any person altering or adding to the certificate. Any such unofficial alteration or addition is of no effect. The certificate is impressed with the official seal of the appropriate District Land Registry (LRA 1925, s. 126(7); s. 132(4)).

On the inside cover there is a date stamp showing the date when the certificate was last compared with the register at the Land Registry. The certificate then contains various notes intended to explain to the layman the effect of and the exceptions from the effect of registration.

Inside the cover there is sewn up a facsimile copy of the entries on the registers of the relevant property current at the date the certificate was last compared with the registers in the Land Registry. In respect of the period up until this date no verification of the certificate with the register is necessary.

17. Charge Certificate. If the property within a particular title is subject to a registered charge (mortgage) then the Land Certificate for that title is held by the Land Registry. The proprietor of the registered charge (the lender) is issued instead with a Charge Certificate. This is the same in form as the Land Certificate except that it also has sewn within it a copy of the relevant charge.

18. Need to produce the Land Certificate.

(*a*) The Land Certificate must be produced to the correct District Land Registry whenever there is a disposition of the land (LRA 1925, s. 64(1)(a)). This means a disposition affecting the registered title, not, for example, a disposition with a registered proprietor's equitable interest (*see* 27:**1–4**). The relevant powers of disposition are contained in LRA 1925, s. 18 and include sales or gifts of the legal estate, and the grant of legal easements or restrictive covenants.

(*b*) LRA 1925, s. 64(1)(b) provides that the Land Certificate must be produced at the time of any registered transmission of the land. Transmission occurs on death or bankruptcy (LRA 1925, ss. 41–47) (*see* 28:**17, 18**).

(*c*) LRA 1925, s. 64(1)(c) provides that the Land Certificate must be produced before a notice is entered on a title (*see* 27:**11**) but not on the entering of a caution (*see* 27:**14**), inhibition (*see* 27:**22**) or creditor's notice (*see* 28:**18**), or the entry of notice of a lease at a rent without taking a fine.

19. Need to produce the Charge Certificate. A Charge Certificate must be produced in the same way in the same circumstances as described in **18**(*a*), (*b*) and (*c*) where these affect the registered interest belonging to the proprietor of the registered charge. It should be noted that if the dealing is with the interest of the registered freehold proprietor and does not affect the charge, e.g. a dealing with the equity of redemption only, then the Charge Certificate does not have to be produced and the Land Certificate is of course already held by the Land Registry.

20. Registrar's discretion to order production. The Registrar has discretion to order production of the Land or Charge Certificate (LRR 1925, r. 266) on any application for registration made by or with the consent of the proprietor and to refuse to proceed until it is produced.

21. Lost certificates. If it is proved that a certificate is lost or destroyed or cannot be produced then a new certificate may be issued (LRR 1925, r. 270). Notice must be given in the London Gazette and the Registrar may take such indemnities and order such further advertisements (which will be at the expense of the applicant) as he sees fit. An application for a new certificate in such circumstances may be made by letter and should be supported by the statutory declaration of somebody (e.g. a solicitor) with knowledge of the relevant history.

22. Deposit of Land or Charge Certificate (LRR 1925, r. 269). When a proprietor effects a disposition he may not always hand over the Land Certificate to the other party. This will be the case if he sells part only of his registered land in that title or grants a right of way or a restrictive covenant in favour of some adjoining owner. That purchaser or covenantee will seek to have his purchase or interest registered but will not have the relevant certificate of title. Thus, r. 269 provides that a proprietor may deposit his certificate and give the Land Registry written directions of the purpose for which it is deposited so that it will not be deemed to be deposited in the Land Registry for any other purpose.

Maps and verbal descriptions of registered land

23. The index map and parcels index. LRR 1925, r. 8 provides that a map should be kept showing the position and extent of all registered titles. Rule 8(2) provides for the keeping of an index of the separate parcels of registered land—the parcels index. The map kept under this rule is called the Public Index Map and is open to inspection by any person. It may be inspected personally or by an official search (r. 12; r. 286—the procedure and purpose of this search called a "Form 96 search" is discussed further in 1:**14**).

24. Descriptions of registered land. All registered land must be described by the applicant in such a way as "by plan or otherwise, to enable the land to be fully identified on the Ordnance Map or the General Map". LRA 1925, s. 76 provides for a variety of methods of describing registered land. The description may be:

(*a*) a verbal description plus a plan based on the ordnance survey map;

(*b*) by reference to a document filed at the Land Registry which contains a sufficient description and a plan;

(*c*) in any other way an applicant for registration desires which the Registrar or the court may approve.

However, the key to the system of plans and descriptions which provides the uniformity and clarity which is a great strength of the system is found in LRR 1925, r. 272 which states simply that "The Ordnance Map shall be the basis of all registered descriptions of land." This system, which means that all land is referred to by reference to a plan which, so far as it goes (*see* 27) is of renowned accuracy, has a great effect on registered land conveyancing. It means that once land is registered it can usually be described by reference to the title number and a very brief verbal description—usually the address is sufficient in a contract or transfer. On an application for first registration the transfer is almost invariably by reference to a plan. It may be noted that where there is a transfer of part of the land in a registered title by reference to a plan (r. 98, Form 20) then the "plan must be signed by the transferor and by or on behalf of the transferee".

25. The General Map or the filed plan. Each parcel of land is described by reference to one of these two types of plan. The General Map is one plan referring to and used in the Land Certificates of a large number of properties. The disadvantage of this is that each time the map changes each title on that map has to have its Land Certificate updated and the system is thus a cumbersome one. For this reason the use of the General Map has been superseded by use of filed plans. A filed plan means a plan prepared for use on a particular title and on which the land in that title is edged red (*see* Fig. 3). A copy of the filed plan is bound up in the Land or Charge Certificate and this gives us the common description of registered land: "The Freehold land shown and edged with red on the filed plan of the above Title" shown in the specimen Property Register reproduced in Fig. 2.

26. Colouring on the filed plan. The Land Registry uses a consistent code of colour references on the filed plan and it is obviously sensible (as Ruoff and Roper, *Registered Conveyancing*, strongly urge) for solicitors to use the same system. (It would be sensible also for the same references to be used uniformly in unregistered transactions particularly as that land too will one day be registered.)

The colouring scheme is as follows.

(*a*) Red edging marks the extent of land within a particular title.

(*b*) Green edging marks land removed from a title.

(*c*) Green tinting shows excluded islands of land within the area of the title.

(*d*) Brown tinting shows land over which the registered land has a right of way.

(*e*) Blue tinting shows land within the title subject to a right of way.

(*f*) For further references colours are utilised in the following order:

(*i*) tinting in pink, blue, yellow and mauve;

(*ii*) edging with a blue, yellow or mauve band;

(*iii*) hatching with a colour other than black or green;

(*iv*) numbering or lettering of small self-contained areas.

In addition when reading a filed plan it may be noted that a boundary represented by a feature shown on the ground or on the existing ordnance survey is represented by a continuous dark line. A boundary not representing such a feature is shown by a broken dark line.

27. Scale of the filed plan. The scale of the filed plan is usually 1/1,250 enlarged from the survey 1/2,500. In the case of detailed divisions of property, e.g. flying freeholds and terraced houses with small adjoining lanes, dustbin areas, garage spaces, drying areas and the like, this scale does not show detail clearly enough. In such a case the plans provided, e.g. on a lease, may be used as the description or an enlargement of the filed plan or of part may be issued with the Land Certificate.

28. The "general boundaries rule". (LRR 1925, r. 278.)

(*a*) At the request of the proprietor the exact boundary of land

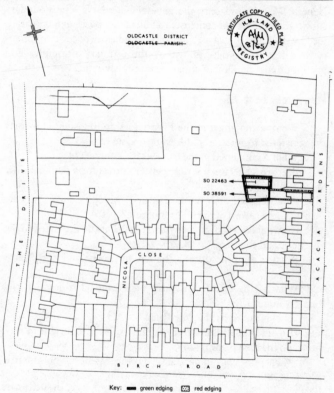

Figure 3 *Filed plan of a specimen title.*

within a title may be fixed (r. 276 and r. 277). This is a time-consuming and expensive business for which the applicant must pay. It is in fact extremely uncommon and such a request would be discouraged by the Land Registry.

(b) In every other case the boundary shown on the filed plan or General Map shows only the general boundary. The boundary shown is therefore not conclusive and its exact position not guaranteed by the Land Registry. The exact boundary between two parcels is thus left to be determined by the ordinary principles and presumptions common to unregistered conveyancing (*see* 13:**16**).

Progress test 25

1. What is contained in the Proprietorship Register? How may the registered proprietor's address be updated?   (**13**)

2. What is contained in the Charges Register?   (**14**)

3. Prepare a specimen set of register entries for a fictional title. (**11–14**, Figs. 2, 3)

4. How does one discover the date up to which a Land Certificate is an accurate record of the register of title?   (**16**)

5. On what occasions must a Land Certificate be produced to the District Land Registry?   (**18, 20**)

6. What is the procedure in the case of a lost Land Certificate? (**21**)

7. What is the effect of deposit of a Land Certificate in the Registry under LRR 1925, r. 269?   (**22**)

8. What is meant by the "filed plan"?   (**25**)

9. How is land within a title which is subject to a right of way shown on the filed plan?   (**26**)

10. What do you understand by the "general boundaries rule"?   (**28**)

26
Types of registered title and registration procedures

Introduction

1. Types of registered title. As has been seen (25:6) each separate registered title has a separate title number. A separate registered title may exist in respect of the following interests: freehold, leasehold and rentcharge. Rentcharges are not dealt with in this part because they are rarely if ever covered in examinations, and are of practical importance in only two localities and are being phased out by the Rentcharges Act 1977. The various kinds of freehold and leasehold title and the way in which they are guaranteed by the Land Registry are discussed below.

Registered freehold title

2. Types of registered title. There are three types of registered freehold title:

(a) freehold absolute (*see* **3–4**);
(b) possessory freehold (*see* **5**);
(c) qualified freehold (*see* **6**).

3. Freehold absolute. This is the title equivalent to the fee simple absolute of unregistered conveyancing. Absolute title is "without question, the most reliable and marketable title that exists, because it is virtually indefeasible and cannot be bettered" (Ruoff and Roper, *Registered Conveyancing*). In this claim lies the whole strength of the registered land system. The titles once registered are guaranteed according to their tenor. It may be noted, too, that all forms of registered title are subject to the possibility of rectification and indemnity in certain circumstances (*see* Chap. 29).

4. Effect of registration. The effect of registration with an absolute freehold title varies slightly depending on whether the proprietor is a first proprietor or the purchaser of land already registered.

(*a*) *Effect of registration as first proprietor.* Registration at the Land Registry confers on the proprietor a legal estate in fee simple in possession in the land together with all rights, privileges and appurtenances belonging to that land (LRA 1925, s. 5). The registered title is subject to the following (s. 5):

(*i*) registered encumbrances (*see* 25:**14**);

(*ii*) overriding interests affecting the land (*see* 27:**5–9**);

(*iii*) if the registered proprietor is not beneficially entitled to the land, then any minor interests of which he has notice.

For example, if A purchases from B a house with unregistered title in an area of compulsory registration (*see* **20**) with notice that C, B's mother-in-law, contributed to the price when B bought the house, then when A is registered as proprietor he takes subject to C's equitable interest if any (for further discussion and examples, *see* 27:**2–3**).

(*b*) *Effect of registration as the transferee of an absolute freehold title.* The effect of registration is to vest in the new proprietor a legal fee simple absolute in possession. This is also subject to registered encumbrances and overriding interests affecting the land. LRA 1925, s. 20(4) provides that a purchaser who does not purchase for value takes subject to minor interests subject to which the transferor held the title. A purchaser for value takes free of such interests irrespective of notice (*see* 27:**3**). Of course, the transferee will be subject to any equities to which he was himself already liable.

For example, F is trustee of the Aber Taff Estate. He purchases Taff Hall from Lord T, the tenant for life and registered proprietor. When he is registered the apparent effect of registration is to free him from minor interests. Nevertheless F holds the land subject to the right of the beneficiaries to have a purchase by a trustee set aside. Since F is now registered as proprietor the beneficiaries' claim

umbrances and interests. The proprietor of an absolute
title holds the land subject to:

egistered encumbrances (*see* 25:**14**);
overriding interests affecting the land in title (*see* 27:**5–9**);
perhaps minor interests of which he has notice (*see* 27:**1–4**);
all the incidents of his leasehold interest.

Procedures. In all classes of leasehold title short particulars of
ease are contained in the Property Register. If the lessor's title is
stered then the title number is also stated. Otherwise the Land
tificate is issued to the registered proprietor in the same way as
freehold titles except that the original lease stamped as being
istered at the Land Registry is also issued to the proprietor and
kept in the Land Registry.

2. Good leasehold. (LRA 1925, ss. 8 and 10.) This type of title is
granted when the title of the freeholder or an intermediate estate has
not been approved by the Registrar. The effect of registration with
good leasehold title is the same as registration with absolute
leasehold title except that the right of the lessor to grant the lease is
not guaranteed. The registered proprietor thus takes subject to any
right in derogation of the landlord's title to grant the estate.

For example, S dies leaving land settled on his wife with
remainders over. The land is unregistered and is properly vested in
the wife as tenant for life under the settlement. When the land is in
an area of compulsory registration the wife grants T a lease which is
not within the powers of a tenant for life under SLA 1925 (e.g. a
lease exceeding fifty years which is not a building, mining or forestry
lease—SLA 1925, s. 41(iv)). When T obtains registration of his lease
with good leasehold title (assuming the freehold title was not
deduced at the time of the lease to him) then his title is subject to the
right (if any) of the trustees or beneficiaries of the settlement to have
the lease set aside.

13. Possessory leasehold. (LRA 1925, ss. 8 and 11.) Like possessory freehold title this has the same effect as registration with title
absolute except that registration does not prejudice the enforcement

would be to have the register rectified (*see* Chap. 29; and Ruoff and
Roper, *Registered Conveyancing*).

5. Possessory freehold. (LRA 1925, s. 6.) The effect of registration
with possessory title is the same as that of registration with an
absolute title except as follows.

(*a*) The first proprietor with possessory title takes subject to any
interest adverse to or in derogation of his title which exists or is
capable of arising at the time of his registration.

(*b*) A transferee of a possessory title is in a similar position to the
transferee of an absolute title but is also subject to any interest
adverse to or in derogation of the title of the first registered
proprietor subsisting or capable of arising at the time of registration
of *the first registered proprietor* (LRA 1925, s. 20(3)).

On an application for first registration (which will invariably be
for registration with an absolute title) the Registrar may refuse an
absolute title but register a possessory title. In support of the
possessory title the Registrar may require a statutory declaration as
to the applicant's possession (LRR 1925, r. 37) and similarly he may
require a statutory declaration concerning the deeds or the lack of
deeds produced in support of the application (r. 38).

6. Qualified freehold. (LRA 1925, s. 7.) This type of title is
uncommon. If a would-be proprietor applies for an absolute title,
the Registrar may enter on the register a qualification of his interest.
Such a qualification excludes from the effect of registration (so that
the proprietor when registered is bound thereby) any estate, right or
interest:

(*a*) arising before a specified date; *or*

(*b*) arising under a specified instrument or otherwise particularly
described in the register.

For example, V purchases a parcel of unregistered land in a
non-compulsory area from trustees who had themselves purchased
the trust estate. Shortly afterwards P purchases the land, now in an
area of compulsory registration, from V. The Registrar may, on P's
application for registration, qualify his title so as to exclude from the

effect of registration the right, if any, of the beneficiaries under the trust to have the conveyance to the trustees set aside.

Registered leasehold title

(*See also* Preface)

7. Classification of leaseholds. Before setting out the types of registered leasehold title it may be helpful to give a synopsis of the classification of leaseholds in Land Registry practice and refer to the sections where the problems raised thereby are discussed further. The treatment of leaseholds in registered land can be a source of considerable confusion. Leasehold interests can be divided into the following seven categories depending on their status under LRA 1925.

(*a*) *Leases not exceeding twenty-one years either subject to no rent or granted in consideration of a premium.* Such a lease cannot be registered under a separate title number. A grant of such a lease out of a registered title takes effect as a minor interest under LRA 1925, s. 101. This means that the lease binds a purchaser of the registered title only if it is protected by entry of a notice or caution (*see* 27:**11, 14**) on the registered title. If the tenant is in actual possession of the land the lease may be an overriding interest within LRA 1925, s. 70(1)(g) (*see* 27:**6, 9**). If that is so then the lease cannot also be a minor interest. The effect of s. 3(xv) is that the two categories are mutually exclusive.

(*b*) *Leases not exceeding twenty-one years granted at a rent without taking a fine.* These cannot be registered under a separate title number of their own. They are, however, protected as overriding interests within LRA 1925, s. 70(1)(k) (*see* 27:**6**).

(*c*) *A new lease (other than a lease falling within paragraphs (e) or (f) below) for a term of more than twenty-one years granted out of land which is already registered.* Such leases must be registered under a separate title number with the appropriate type of leasehold title ("substantive registration"). This is so whether the freehold property is situate in a compulsory or a non-compulsory area (*see* 25:**16, 17**).

(*d*) *A grant of a lease of not less than forty years or the assignment of a lease with at least forty years to run* (unless the lease is one within

paragraph (*e*) or (*f*) below). In either of th[...] registered as a separate title if the land is in [...] (LRA 1925, s. 123).

(*e*) *Leases containing an absolute prohibition* [...] *vivos* (*LRA 1925, s. 8(2))* *and equitable leases* [...] Neither of these types of lease is capable of bei[...] separate title number. They may be protected [...] interests within s. 70(1)(k) or s. 70(1)(g) (*see* 2[...] they may be protected by registration of a notice o[...]

(*f*) *A mortgage of registered land by demise or su[...]* take effect as a charge by way of legal mortgage (LRA[...] As in unregistered land the mortgagee does not take [...] in the land.

(*g*) *If a lease which does not at the time require substantiv[...] is granted out of unregistered land and the reversion to [...] subsequently registered,* the lease is protected as an overridi[...] or otherwise by entry of notice of the lease on the registere[...] 27:**5–9, 11**).

8. Types of leasehold title. There are three types of leasehold

(*a*) absolute leasehold (*see* **9–11**);
(*b*) good leasehold (*see* **12**);
(*c*) possessory leasehold (*see* **13**).

9. Absolute leasehold. (LRA 1925, ss. 8 and 9.) Where a lease requires registration it is registration which makes the lease a legal leasehold interest just as is the case with registration of freehold land. Absolute leasehold is the securest form of leasehold title. It is available only if the titles to the freehold and to any intermediate leasehold are already registered or are deduced to the satisfaction of the Land Registry.

Since the reversionary title will have been accepted by the Land Registry, registration with absolute leasehold can guarantee both the lease and the title to the reversion. Thus the effect of such registration is to guarantee that the proprietor is the owner of the lease and that the lease was validly granted.

10. Enc
leasehol[...]
(*a*) [...]
(*b*) [...]
(*c*) [...]
(*d*) [...]

11. [...]
the l[...]
regi[...]
Cer[...]
for[...]
re[...]
n[...]

of any rights in derogation of or adverse to that of the registered proprietor which exist at the time of registration.

14. Covenants and easements. In all types of leasehold title the title may be subject to covenants and easements and other rights affecting the freehold or other reversionary title. In the case of absolute leasehold title those subsisting at the date of first registration will be noted on the leasehold title.

Conversion of title
(*See also* Preface)

15. Introduction. In certain circumstances land which is registered with a possessory or qualified title may be converted to a superior type of title. The circumstances are specified in **16–17**.

16. On a transfer for valuable consideration. LRA 1925, s. 77(2) provides that on a transfer for valuable consideration the Registrar may upgrade a qualified, possessory or good leasehold title to an absolute title or good leasehold title as appropriate providing he is satisfied as to the title shown.

17. After the passage of time.

(*a*) *Possessory freehold to absolute freehold.* In the case of freehold land registered with possessory title the Registrar has power to register the proprietor on his own application and on the giving of satisfactory evidence of possession as the holder of an absolute title once fifteen years have elapsed since registration with a possessory title.

(*b*) *Possessory leasehold to good leasehold.* In the same way the title to leasehold land may be upgraded from possessory to good leasehold title ten years after registration.

(*c*) *Good leasehold to absolute leasehold.* The Registrar may convert good leasehold to absolute leasehold title once it has been registered for ten years providing the proprietor or his predecessors have been in possession during that period.

An application for conversion of good leasehold to absolute leasehold may be made before ten years have elapsed if either the freehold title becomes registered or the freehold title can be deduced to the Registrar.

First registration

18. Introduction. First registration of title to a piece of land may take place either compulsorily following a transaction with the land (*see* **20–21**) or voluntarily (*see* **19**).

19. Voluntary first registration. The registered land system originally allowed generally for first registration on a voluntary basis. LRA 1966, s. 1 provided that from 13th January 1967 voluntary registrations need be accepted by the Land Registry only in such cases as the Registrar should from time to time specify.

The present list of cases where a voluntary first registration may be made came into effect on 4th May 1983. The cases are as follows.

(*a*) *Lost or destroyed deeds* where either:

(*i*) the deeds have been lost or destroyed by enemy action in the Second World War or in some other national disaster or by fire, theft or criminal act; *or*

(*ii*) title deeds are lost or destroyed wholly or partially while in the custody of a solicitor, building society or clearing bank.

(*b*) *Building estates.* The estate must comprise at least twenty units, and a certificate in a specified form must be given to the Land Registry.

(*c*) *Applications by local authorities and development corporations.* These relate to developments by such bodies of freehold or long leasehold housing estates.

(*d*) *Registered leaseholds.* The proprietor may apply for registration of the immediate reversion where merger is to take place.

20. Compulsory first registration. Compulsory first registration is required following specified transactions with unregistered land in those areas which are specified as areas of compulsory registration by Order in Council (LRA 1925, s. 120). Compulsory first registration now extends to the bulk of urban areas in England and Wales. It should be carefully noted that when the right to buy under the

Housing Act 1985 is exercised the title must be registered even if the land is in a non-compulsory area.

21. Specified transactions. LRA 1925, s. 123 provides that in an area of compulsory registration the following transactions must *within two months of completion* be followed by an application for compulsory registration:

(*a*) a freehold sale;

(*b*) the grant of a registrable lease (for non-registrable leases *see* **7**) for a term of years absolute for a term of at least forty years from the grant;

(*c*) the assignment on sale of a term of years absolute having not less than forty years to run from the date of the assignment.

The expression "sale" is defined by LRA 1925, s. 123(3) as including an exchange where there is equality money. Also included are compulsory acquisitions by deed poll and conveyances in consideration of shares or in consideration of securities, an annuity or a rentcharge. Not included are gifts, mortgages, partitions and exchanges without equality money, and assents. No definitive list is published by the Land Registry. (A useful more detailed list is found in Wontner and Quickfall, *Land Registry Practice*.)

22. Effect of non-registration. LRA 1925, s. 123 provides that the relevant deed giving rise to a requirement of compulsory registration shall "become void so far as regards the grant or conveyance of the legal estate" if registration does not take place within the statutory period of two months. Thus, the deed dealing as it does with unregistered land does pass the legal estate at the time of the grant in the ordinary way. If registration then does not take place within the two months the deed becomes ineffective for that purpose.

For example, in a compulsory area A sells Whiteacre to B. B's solicitor by an oversight does not notice that the land is now in a compulsory area. The transaction is completed in the ordinary way and a legal fee simply passes to B. Two months after completion when B's solicitor still has not registered his title, s. 123 operates to annul the passing to B of the legal estate. Since the legal estate cannot disappear it presumably reverts to A who holds it on trust for B pending eventual registration of B's title.

23. The danger of non-registration. The penalty stated in s. 123 (i.e. the annulment of passing of the legal estate) is the only penalty for failure to effect compulsory registration. The main danger is that some other person may be registered as proprietor of the particular parcel of land whether under a title wrongfully made by the vendor (who still holds the legal estate) or gained by possession. In addition, since the purchaser now has only an equitable title he may be bound by equities prior in time which bind the vendor but from which a purchaser for value of a legal estate would take free.

24. Curing non-registration. Under s. 123 the Chief Land Registrar or the court on appeal from the Registrar may accept a late application. An explanation must be given when submitting a late application, but a simple one will be accepted, e.g. oversight by the purchaser's solicitor. There is a small late fee to pay (at present £1). Applications to the Registrar are invariably accepted and although appeal from a refusal by the Registrar is possible "no such application has ever been rendered necessary and it is unlikely that one ever will" (Ruoff and Roper, *Registered Conveyancing*). The late registration is effective to vest the legal estate in the new proprietor at the actual date that it is effected in the same way as any other registration (*see* **4**).

The mechanics of first registration

25. Conveyancing procedures up to completion. When land is purchased in a compulsory area but the title is not yet registered, even where the transaction must be followed by a first registration the procedure until completion is identical with the procedure in unregistered conveyancing.

26. Establishing that registration is required. The purchaser will know that he must effect a first registration from his Form 96 search of the index map (*see* **1:14**). In addition the reply to one of the standard enquiries of the district council in which the land is situate will reveal whether or not the area is one of compulsory registration (*see* 2:**12**). Where the transaction is a protracted one so that there is some lapse of time after these searches are made the purchaser's solicitor may find that the land in question falls within a compulsory area by the time of completion. The Land Registry publishes a practice leaflet showing which areas are from time to time subject to compulsory registration and the solicitor must make a careful scrutiny of any published amendments to this.

27. Form of transfer. In a purchase where first registration is required the purchaser's solicitor may, instead of preparing a draft conveyance in the traditional form, utilise the much simpler form of a registered land transfer (LRR 1925, r. 72). The form of transfer will be a suitably amended Form 19 (*see* Chap. 28, Fig. 5).

28. Application for registration. Following completion and the usual stamping of the transfer document (*see* 28:**2**) the first registration is effected by forwarding the deeds to the appropriate District Land Registry. The application must include the following.

(*a*) The correct Land Registry cover. For each type of application for first registration (freehold, leasehold, good leasehold and so on) the correct printed form of application must be used. This form is called a "cover" since it is a double-sided, folding, two-page form inside which the documents sent for registration are placed. For a first registration of freehold land Form 1B is used (reproduced in Fig. 4). The similar form for first registration of freehold land by a company is Form 1E. The Land Registry cover contains a certificate by the solicitor signing the certificate that he has properly investigated the title for the statutory period; a statement that any land charges entries revealed by the official search either do or do not affect the land concerned and if they do a note of the document by which they were created; and a schedule of encumbrances (e.g. charges, leases, etc.) which affect the property.

(*b*) The transfer or conveyance together with a certified copy thereof.

(*c*) All searches (including the local search), title deeds, epitomes and abstracts, requisitions on title, counsel's opinion and other documents relating to the title in the applicant's possession.

Form 1B
HM Land Registry

Land Registration Acts, 1925 to 1971

APPLICATION BY SOLICITORS FOR FIRST REGISTRATION OF FREEHOLD LAND ON BEHALF OF
*RECENT PURCHASER(S) OTHER THAN A COMPANY OR CORPORATION

*Where the applicant(s) is/are not (a) purchaser(s) under a conveyance/transfer dated within one year of the application, form 1C should be used.

FOR OFFICIAL USE ONLY		
Date stamp	Title number	Record of fee paid

Details in the panels below to be supplied by solicitors	Acknowledged by

PROPERTY

County_____ District or Borough_____
(insert local authority name)

Short Description_____
(include parish or place)

☐ A13 list

☐ Postcard

Initials _____

Date _____

LAND REGISTRY FEES

Notes:
1. Fees are assessed under the current Land Registration Fee Order and are payable on the delivery of applications.
2. Cheques should be made payable to "HM Land Registry".
3. No fee is payable for the registration of any mortgage on the land that accompanies this application.

Particulars of
underpayments or
overpayments of fees

	Value £	Fee scale	£	p
Land and buildings _____		1		
Other fees _____				
(As to mortgages, see note 3 above.)		Total fees paid		

A. We, _____

of _____

solicitors, hereby apply for the registration of _____
(In BLOCK LETTERS, enter full name(s), postal address(es) and occupation(s) of applicant(s) for entry on the register)

_____

_____

_____

_____

(1) *Strike out word(s) not applicable.*

(hereinafter called the applicant(s)) as proprietor(s), with **Absolute** title, of the freehold land described

above assured by the accompanying *conveyance/transfer* dated_____

_____19_____ made between:

(1) _____

( ) _____

( ) _____

( ) the applicant(s)

B. We certify as follows:

   a. We acted for the applicant(s) on the purchase inducing this registration.

   b. We investigated, or caused to be investigated, the title in the usual way on behalf of the applicant(s) for a period of not less than 15 years commencing with a good root of title, and made or caused to be made, all such searches or official searches as were proper.

(OVER)

Figure 4   *Form 1B: application for first registration of freehold land.*

c. [2] *The applicant (being a sole owner) is entitled to the land for his own benefit.*

OR

c. [2] *The applicants (being joint owners) are entitled to the land holding for themselves as:*

(3) Insert "X" in the appropriate box.

[3] ☐ *beneficial joint tenants*   [2] ☐ *tenants in common*

OR

c. [2] *The applicant(s) is/are entitled to the land as estate owner(s) within the meaning of section 4*

(4) Insert, e.g., "personal representative(s)", "trustees on behalf of charity", "trustees for sale upon the trusts of ", "tenant for life" or "statutory owners".

of the Land Registration Act 1925, as [4] _____

_____

d. We are not aware of any question or doubt affecting the title to the land or any part thereof, or of any matter or thing whereby the title is or may be impeached, affected or called in question in any manner whatsoever.

e. The deeds and documents accompanying this application and mentioned in the accompanying list in triplicate signed by us and dated the _____ day of _____ 19___ are all the deeds and documents relating to the title which the applicant(s) has/have in his/their possession or under his/their control, including opinions of counsel, abstracts, contracts for sale, requisitions, replies, official certificates of the result of search in the Land Charges Department and other like documents in regard to the title.

f. Any abstracts of title are marked by solicitors to show that they have been examined with the original deeds and all particulars of wills, grants of probate or letters of administration, marriages and deaths set out therein as separate items have been verified and are so marked. Such abstracts contain a copy or full extract of all restrictive covenants, stipulations, easements, rentcharges and other incumbrances to which the land is subject, similarly marked as examined.

g. Any copy deeds have been verified with the originals and are so marked.

(5) Strike out or amend word(s) as requisite.

h. [5] *None of the/Only the following* entries which are either disclosed in the official certificates of the result of search in the Land Charges Department or referred to in an abstract of title affect the land:

_____

_____

[5] *The instruments creating the entries are those dated* _____

_____

_____

which, or abstracts of which, accompany this application.

C. As a result of our investigation, we believe that:

a. The conveyance/transfer validly conveyed/transferred to the applicant(s) the estate and interest thereby purported to be conveyed/transferred, free from any adverse rights or incumbrances (including restrictive covenants) which were not shown by the conveyance/transfer.

b. The applicant(s) has/have not been entered into or created any contract for sale, lease or agreement for lease, easement, mortgage, charge, lien, rentcharge, restrictive covenant or other right or incumbrance, except as stated in the said conveyance/transfer or in the schedule below, affecting the land or any part thereof.

c. There is no person in possession or occupation of the land or any part thereof adversely to the estate or interest of the applicant(s) therein and the land is not subject to any matters not disclosed by this application.

(6) Only required if merger of a lease is applied for. If such lease is registered, the land certificate thereof must be produced.

(*) *We hereby apply that no note be made on the register of the lease dated* _____ _____ *which has been determined by merger. We are not aware of any* [7] *sub-lease or other incumbrance affecting the said lease.*

(7) If there is a sub-lease the application should be amended accordingly and the counterpart produced.

Signature of solicitor(s)
to the applicant(s) _____

Date _____ 19___

Figure 4 *(contd.)*

THE SCHEDULE OF INCUMBRANCES

(This schedule should include any incumbrances of the kinds mentioned in paragraph b of Part C
above which affect the land including any charges created by the applicant(s). If there are no such
incumbrances, enter the word " NONE " below.)

_____

_____

_____

_____

_____

_____

_____

_____

_____

_____

_____

_____

_____

INSTRUCTIONS REGARDING DOCUMENTS

Note: A certified true copy of **a.** the conveyance/transfer to the applicant and **b.** any subsisting mortgage that is to be entered
on the register must be supplied for filing: the originals will be returned on completion of the registration in accordance with
the directions given in Panels 1 and 2 below. It is essential that these panels be completed correctly so that the acknowledgment
of receipt of this application is sent to the right solicitor(s) and the documents to be issued on completion of the registration
are sent to the person(s) entitled to have them.

1. **Name and address of solicitor(s) to whom the acknowledgement of the application and all requisitions made by the Land
    Registry, including requests for unpaid fees, are to be sent:**

**BLOCK
LETTERS**
Name _____

Address _____

_____

Solicitor's reference_____ Telephone number_____

IMPORTANT

The documents not retained in the Land Registry, together with the land certificate (or charge certificate(s) as the case may be)
will, on the completion of the registration, be returned to the above address. If a particular document is required to be issued
to some other person or firm upon completion of the registration or in connection with any requisition which may arise, please
complete panel 2 below.

2. Additional instructions (if any) for the issue of any document to some person or firm other than as mentioned in panel 1
    above:

**BLOCK
LETTERS**
Description of document_____

Name _____

Address _____

_____

Reference_____

Figure 4 *(contd.)*

THIS PAGE IS FOR OFFICIAL USE ONLY

MAPPING PARTICULARS

Index Map or Map Section reference	Provisionally indexed and G93 sent to Pending List	SC	R28	FE
_____ sheet ____ section ____ card	_____ _____ *Plans drafter* *Date*	☐	☐	☐ *Tick appropriate box*

	Sent		Returned		Adjoining registrations:
Referred for:	Date	Initials	Date	Initials	_____
Survey ... ... (and C.46 sent) Map revision ...					Indexed on Map Section and Parcel Index entries brought up to date, or Indexed on Public Index Map and entered on G64.
Tracing					Mapped by_____ Date _____ *Plans drafter*
Prints					Indexing
O.S. sheets					checked by _____ Date _____ *Plans drafter*
,, ,, ...					

Special instructions _____

_____

_____

_____

_____

To Legal Staff

The following information relates to the grant of rights of way and other easements

Reference on deed	Deed dated	Title No. or 'not registered'	Existing Reference on F.P. of that title or 'not referenced'	Previous freehold registrations
				Previous leasehold registrations
				Title shown Index number

(The above information checked by_____*Plans drafter*)

The land coloured_____on the plan on the *conveyance/transfer* dated_____

is_____included in the undermentioned deeds_____

The land edged red on the filed plan is within that shown on a plan or described in the parcels of the undermentioned deeds.

Conveyance/Transfer to applicant(s) dated_____*Counterpart lease dated*_____

1. Deed dated_____   Abstract page_____

2. ,, ,, _____   ,, ,, _____

3. ,, ,, _____   ,, ,, _____

4. ,, ,, _____   ,, ,, _____

5. ,, ,, _____   ,, ,, _____

_____

_____

_____

_____

_____

Checked and passed by Plans settler_____Date_____
(*Name in full*)

Oyez Publishing Limited, Norwich House, 11/13 Norwich Street, London EC4A 1AB, a subsidiary of The Solicitors' Law Stationery Society, Limited.   F24782 2/79 ★ ★ ★ ★

Figure 4   (*contd.*)

(*d*) A schedule in triplicate of all the documents enclosed.

(*e*) If the purchaser has entered into a charge, the charge deed and a certified copy thereof.

(*f*) The correct fee for the transaction.

If the purchaser is a company the certificate given in the application form also states that the company has power to enter into the transaction in question and that the company has not created any debentures or debenture stock. If this certificate cannot be given then a certified copy of the company's memorandum of association and articles must be supplied. A copy of any debentures and any trust deed securing them must be forwarded with the application together with the certificate of registration under s. 95 of the Companies Act 1948.

The application must be delivered to the correct District Land Registry.

Progress test 26

1. What is the effect of first registration with an absolute freehold title? (**3**)

2. What is meant by qualified freehold title? (**6**)

3. Which leases are capable of substantive registration? (**7** (*c*), (*d*))

4. What is meant by good leasehold title? (**12**)

5. When is voluntary registration of title now possible? (**19**)

6. When must compulsory first registration take place? (**20–21**)

7. What is the effect of failure to effect a compulsory first registration and how may this be cured? (**22, 24**)

8. How will a purchaser know that first registration must take place? (**26**)

9. What documents must be forwarded with an application for first registration and what additional information must be provided on behalf of a company applying for first registration? (**28**)

Third party rights in registered land

Introduction

1. Classification of interests. "Minor interests" are defined by LRA 1925, s. 3(xv) as "interests not capable of being disposed of or created by registered dispositions and capable of being overriden (whether or not a purchaser has notice thereof) by the proprietors unless protected as provided by this Act, and all rights and interests which are not registered or protected on the register and are not overriding interests". The definition goes on expressly to include interests behind a trust for sale or a strict settlement.

Thus, the scheme of things in registered land is to provide for:

(*a*) interests registrable with a title number of their own (24:**7**);

(*b*) overriding interests which are not registrable or in need of protection by any entry on the register (*see* **5–9**);

(*c*) other interests which require protection by entry of some indication thereof on the registered title claimed to be affected (*see* **11–23**).

2. What third party rights affect a proprietor?

(*a*) A first registered proprietor is subject only to entries on the register and overriding interests unless he is not entitled to the land for his own benefit in which case he takes subject to all minor interests of which he has notice (LRA 1925, s. 5(d)).

(*b*) A person dealing with registered land is not affected by notice of any trust (LRA 1925, s. 74). In addition, LRA 1925, s. 20

provides that the effect of registration of a disposition of a freehold (s. 23 deals with leasehold) is to give a title free from all interests except overriding interests and those protected by an entry on the register.

(*c*) However, s. 20(4) (for freeholds) and s. 23(5) (for leaseholds) provide that if the disposition is not for valuable consideration then the new proprietor holds subject to the same minor interests as the transferor.

3. The possibility of a constructive trust. Even if a new registered proprietor purchased the land for valuable consideration he may be subject to an equitable interest not amounting to an overriding interest or protected on the register but imposed on him by a constructive trust: thus, in *Peffer* v. *Rigg* (1977) it was suggested that a registered proprietor could be subject to an equitable interest subject to which the vendor to him had held the land where it would be unconscionable for him to take free from that interest; and in *Lyus* v. *Prowsa Ltd* (1982) it was similarly suggested that a registered proprietor could take subject to an unregistered estate contract entered into by a previous proprietor if it was unconscionable for him to take free therefrom.

4. The minor interests index. The Land Registry is obliged to maintain a separate index of dealings with minor interests. It contains entries relating to dealings with equitable interests such as life interests, reversions and interests existing behind a trust for sale in registered land. The index is concerned only with these equitable interests and has no relevance to or effect on dealings with registered titles. Thus, LRR 1925, r. 11 provides for the maintenance of the index and r. 11(2) provides that "the entries therein shall not form part of the register, nor shall any purchaser be concerned with that index". The index may be searched by letter by anyone interested in an equitable interest in a registered title. In practice the index is very little utilised and the number of entries and searches a year is very small. (*See also* Preface.)

Overriding interests

5. Definition. These are defined by LRA 1925, s. 3(xvi) as "all the incumbrances, interests, rights and powers not entered on the register but subject to which registered dispositions are by this Act to take effect". This is therefore a category of interests which automatically affect a registered title and hence require no protection by an entry on the register. If a matter which would otherwise be an overriding interest is entered on the register of a title (e.g. an easement protected by notice on the register) then it is no longer an overriding interest, but is instead protected by that entry on the register.

6. List of overriding interests. LRA 1925 contained a complete list of overriding interests but subsequent legislation has added a little to this. The bulk are still found in LRA 1925, s. 70 and are as follows.

(*a*) Section 70(1)(a) contains a "jumble of rights" (Ruoff and Roper, *Registered Conveyancing*). These are easements and profits, public rights, rights of sheepwalk, rights of way, water and other easements not being equitable easements requiring to be protected by notice.

(*b*) Section 70(1)(b): mostly obsolete liabilies arising from tenure.

(*c*) Section 70(1)(c): liability to repair the chancel of any church.

(*d*) Section 70(1)(d): liability in respect of embankments and sea and river walls.

(*e*) Section 70(1)(e): payments in lieu of tithe and tithe redemption annuities.

(*f*) Section 70(1)(f): subject to other provisions of the Act, rights acquired or in the course of being acquired under the Limitation Acts.

(*g*) Section 70(1)(g): the rights of every person in actual occupation of the land or in receipt of the rents and profits thereof, save where enquiry is made of such person and the rights are not disclosed.

(*h*) Section 70(1)(h): the various matters excepted from the effect of registration in the case of possessory, qualified or good leasehold title.

(*i*) Section 70(1)(i): rights under local land charges unless and until registered or protected on the register in the appropriate manner.

(*j*) Section 70(1)(j): rights of fishing and sporting and various manorial rights.

(*k*) Section 70(1)(k): leases for any term or interest not exceeding twenty-one years granted at a rent without taking a fine (*see* Preface).

(*l*) Section 70(1)(l): various mineral and mining rights. It may be noted that the rights of the National Coal Board and mines and coal are overriding interests (*see* Coal Industry Nationalisation Act 1946, ss. 5 and 8).

Some detailed points on certain of these overriding interests are discussed in **7–9** below.

7. Section 70(1)(a). It will be seen that this category consists largely of legal easements and profits. These interests will very frequently be protected by being noted on the Property Register (*see* 25:**11–12**). In that case they are not overriding interests.

8. Section 70(1)(f). The following two cases illustrate this type of overriding interest.

(*a*) *Chowood Ltd* v. *Lyall* (1930). A company was registered as first proprietor but the title was rectified to remove part of the land from the title because before the company's purchase Mrs Lyall had acquired a title to that land by adverse possession.

(*b*) *Bridges* v. *Mees* (1957). P in 1936 had contracted to purchase a plot of land. He paid the purchase money and went into occupation but never took a conveyance of the land. In 1955 the company vendor was in liquidation and the liquidator sold the land to D who was registered with title absolute. The court held that D's title was subject to P's rights as occupier for twenty years.

9. Section 70(1)(g). This has proved the most controversial type of overriding interest and the following cases must be carefully examined.

(*a*) *London & Cheshire Insurance Co. Ltd* v. *Laplagrene Co. Ltd and Another* (1971). In this case a vendor had remained in occupation after the sale as lessee under a leaseback arrangement. The purchaser mortgaged the land, but the vendor remained unpaid. It was held that the vendor could enforce the unpaid vendor's lien against the purchaser's mortgagee. The vendor was still in actual occupation and it did not matter that this occupation was by virtue of the lease and not by virtue of the lien which it was sought to enforce. Neither was the vendor's claim defeated by the fact that this occupation had ceased by the time of the court action.

(b) *Hodgson* v. *Marks* (1971). A had a lodger, B, in whom she had (misplaced) confidence. She transferred her house to him and he was registered as the proprietor. The transfer was for no consideration; B was simply supposed to look after the house for A and was thus a bare trustee. He mortgaged the property. It was held that the mortgagee took subject to A's interest. She was in occupation of the property, even though B appeared also to be in occupation and her occupation may only have been of part of the property. (*See also* 8:**16**.)

(c) *Williams & Glyn's Bank* v. *Brown; Williams & Glyn's Bank* v. *Boland* (1980). These two important cases were dealt with together by the House of Lords. In each the matrimonial home was registered in the name of the husband although the wife had made contributions to the purchase price. In each case it was held that the wife was in equity entitled to a one-half share in the property. Each house had been mortgaged to the bank who had made no enquiries of the husband or the wife as to whether the wife had any interest in the house and if so what that interest was. The court held that the wife's equitable interest was an interest capable of falling within LRA 1925, s. 70(1)(g). The court held that whether a wife in these circumstances was in actual occupation was a question of fact, and if she was physically living in the matrimonial home then she was in actual occupation (judicial opinion to the contrary on this point in *Caunce* v. *Caunce* (1969) and *Bird* v. *Syme Thomson* (1978) was expressly disapproved). The bank as mortgagee was thus subject to the wife's equitable interest and could not as against her obtain possession of the property. (*See also* 8:**16**.)

(d) *Blacklocks* v. *J. B. Developments (Godalming) Ltd* (1981). It was held that where a person had a right of rectification this was capable of being an overriding interest under s. 70(1)(g). Thus, where P had a claim for rectification against X and X sold his land to D then P's claim was capable of being an overriding interest which bound D when he became registered as proprietor.

(*e*) In *City of London Building Society* v. *Flegg* (1985) the Court of Appeal held that beneficial co-owners in actual occupation could have an overriding interest which was not overreached by a sale by two trustees. Previously it was thought a sale by two trustees would be overreaching under s. 2 and s. 27 LPA 1925. The Court held this was subject to the interests of persons in occupation under s. 14 LPA 1925.

(*f*) In *Winkworth* v. *Edward Bevan Ltd* (1985) a wife was held to acquire an equitable interest in property purchased by her husband's company where she paid a substantial sum into the company's bank to reduce its borrowing. Her interest bound a subsequent mortgage as an overriding interest since she was in actual occupation.

The system of notices, cautions, restrictions and inhibitions

10. Introduction. Notices, cautions, restrictions and inhibitions are the names of various entries made on the register of title to protect the interests of third parties in the land.

11. Notices. (LRA 1925, ss. 48–52.) A notice is a specific entry on the Charges Register (*see* 25:**14**) of a title. It gives notice of some estate, right or claim and any person taking an interest in the land takes subject thereto.

Notices can be used to protect any interest which would be registrable under LCA 1972 (though their use is not restricted to these) if the land were unregistered, e.g. restrictive covenants, estate contracts or an unpaid vendor's lien.

12. Need for Land or Charge Certificate. LRA 1925, s. 64(1)(c) provides that if the Land or Charge Certificate is outstanding (i.e. not presently in the Land Registry), it must be produced in the appropriate District Land Registry at the time of the application to register the notice. This means that unless the certificate is in the Land Registry the proprietor's co-operation is needed to obtain the registration of a notice (*see also* **14**).

13. Effect of registration. LRA 1925, s. 52(2) states the effect of registration of a notice. Registration operates *by way of notice only*.

Thus, as in the land charges system, dispositions of the land concerned take effect subject to the notice and are thus bound by the estate, interest or claim *to the extent that it is valid*. Registration does not have any constitutive effect; it does not validate an otherwise invalid claim against the land.

For example, suppose A as the registered proprietor of land agrees to sell it to B. B (since the Land Certificate is in the Land Registry) obtains registration of notice of this contract. A further purchaser from A is affected by this notice, but if, for example, the contract is unenforceable because of non-compliance with LPA 1925, s. 40 (*see* 5:2) registration does not alter this unenforceability.

14. Cautions. (LRA 1925, ss. 53–57.) A caution is used to protect the same type of interest as a notice. An application to register a caution need not be accompanied by the Land or Charge Certificate and is thus used when the proprietor's co-operation in producing this is not forthcoming. Registering a caution is therefore commonly described as a hostile step compared to registering a notice.

15. Application. An application for a caution to be registered must be accompanied by a statutory declaration setting out briefly the basis of the claim, e.g. referring to an estate contract for which protection is sought (LRR 1925, r. 215).

16. Effects. The effect of a caution is that when any application is made to register a dealing with land in the title, the Registrar is obliged to serve notice on the cautioner. The notice gives the cautioner a specified period (usually fourteen days; in any event not less than seven days—LRR 1925, r. 218) to show cause why the caution should continue to be effective or the dealing not be registered. Unless the cautioner does so the caution will cease to be effective at the end of the specified period. The cautioner may show cause either in writing to the Registrar or at an oral hearing and the Registrar may cancel the caution and allow the pending application to proceed or protect the cautioner's interest by the appropriate entry on the register.

17. Liability for loss. LRA 1925, s. 56(3) provides that if a person lodges a caution without reasonable cause he may be liable in damages to anyone thereby suffering loss.

18. Caution against first registration. LRA 1925, s. 53(1) allows anyone claiming an interest in land which would allow him to object to a disposition of it to register a caution against registration. This ensures that the Registrar will notify the cautioner of any application for registration of the land and the cautioner will have an opportunity to show cause why the registration should not proceed by making an objection thereto within a specified period.

19. Restrictions. (LRA 1925, s. 58.) A restriction is an entry on the Proprietorship Register and operates to prevent a disposition which does not conform to the terms of the restriction. The entry of a restriction is most commonly found to protect a minor interest in land and the following three examples will illustrate its use.

(*a*) In the case of settled land the beneficiaries will be protected by an entry to the following effect:

"*Restriction:* No disposition under which capital money arises is to be registered unless the money is paid to AB and CD (the trustees of the settlement . . . .) or into court.

Except under an order of the Registrar, no disposition is to be registered unless authorised by the Settled Land Act 1925."

(*b*) Where land is transferred to two or more persons and it appears from the transfer document or the application for registration that the survivor of them cannot give a valid receipt for capital money, the Registrar is obliged to enter a restriction as follows:

"*Restriction:* No disposition by one proprietor of the land (being the survivor of joint proprietors and not being a trust corporation) under which capital money arises is to be registered except under an order of the Registrar or of the court."

(*c*) Where a charity is registered as proprietor of land a restriction is entered as follows:

"*Restriction:* No disposition or other dealing is to be registered without the consent of the Charity Commissioners . . . or an order of the Registrar."

20. Voluntary restrictions. Voluntary restrictions may be entered by the proprietor or otherwise on production of the Land or Charge Certificate. They may be used:

   (*a*) to ensure a named person's consent is obtained to a dealing;

   (*b*) to prevent the land being sold without the consent of a registered chargee;

   (*c*) to protect any other kind of interest in the land.

Voluntary restrictions may be removed on application in the appropriate form by the persons appearing to be interested in the restriction (LRR 1925, r. 235).

21. Compulsory restrictions. In various circumstances the entry of a restriction by the Registrar is compulsory. This applies to the three examples in **19**. Such restrictions are not removable voluntarily but generally only on the registration of a transfer made in accordance with the terms of the restriction.

22. Inhibitions. (LRA 1925, s. 57.) Any interested person may apply to the Chancery Division of the High Court by originating summons or to the Registrar for an inhibition to be registered on the register of a title. The effect of entry of an inhibition is to prevent any further dealing with the land being registered until the inhibition is removed. Where the inhibition is entered by the Registrar application may be made at any time to the Registrar for its cancellation or discharge (LRR 1925, r. 231). If the inhibition was entered pursuant to a court order an application for its discharge must be made to the court.

23. Bankruptcy inhibitions. Inhibitions other than bankruptcy inhibitions are rare. When a receiving order is made the Official Receiver will apply for an inhibition to be entered against any land appearing to be affected. The entry is made on the Proprietorship Register and is as follows:

"*Bankruptcy inhibition (date):* No disposition or transmission is to be registered until a trustee in bankruptcy is registered."

Progress test 27

1. What is meant by the expression "minor interest"? (**1**)
2. What is the minor interests index? (**4**)
3. What is an "overriding interest"? (**5**)
4. Give four examples of overriding interests. (**6**)
5. Explain the decision in *Williams & Glyn's Bank* v. *Brown* (1980). (**9**(*c*))
6. What is the effect of registration of a notice? (**13**)
7. Explain how registration of a caution operates to protect the interest of a cautioner. (**16**)
8. Give two examples of restrictions that may be entered on the register. (**19**)
9. What is the effect of registration of an inhibition? (**22**)

28
Dealings with and transmissions of registered land

Introduction

1. The registered proprietor's powers. The registered title is a creature of statute and the proprietor's powers of dealings with this title are contained in LRA 1925. Section 18 confers, in respect of registered freeholds, the power to transfer the legal estate "in the prescribed manner" and to create legal estates out of the registered land and legal encumbrances over the land. Section 21 contains provisions for disposition of leasehold titles analogous to those in s. 18. Section 25 confers a power to create charges of registered land.

Section 101 confers on the registered proprietor or other person "having sufficient interest or power in or over registered land" the power to create overreachable "minor interests" affecting the registered land. These interests do not appear on the register of title, take effect in equity and are protected by appropriate notices, cautions, inhibitions and restrictions (*see* 27:**11–23**).

2. General procedure with dealings. A transaction with registered land which requires registration at the Land Registry is called a "dealing". In respect of any dealing with registered land which should be entered on the register, e.g. a sale, mortgage or grant of a legal right of way, the procedure is as follows.

(*a*) Following completion of the transaction similar requirements as to stamping and production of deeds to the Inland Revenue apply as in unregistered conveyancing.

(*b*) The transaction is registered at the appropriate District

Registry (*see* **32**).

(*c*) The application for registration must be delivered to the correct District Land Registry within the priority period of the official search (*see* **13**) if priority is to be obtained.

Sales and purchases of registered land

3. The vendor's role.

(*a*) *Draft contract.* The vendor's solicitor will prepare a draft contract in the same way as for unregistered land. The parcels clause will be much simpler in that the property will generally be described by reference to the title number together with a brief description. In the case of a private house the address is usually quite sufficient providing the boundaries have not changed since registration occurred. If the sale is of part of the land within a title the description will be by reference to a plan (*see* **25:24**).

(*b*) *Deducing title.* This is provided for by LRA 1925, s. 110. The vendor must provide the following.

(*i*) An authority to inspect the register. This is the registered proprietor's written authorisation for the purchaser to examine the state of the register of title, bespeak copy documents and make official searches.

(*ii*) copies of the subsisting entries on the register. This is usually done by providing the purchaser with a set of official office copies of the register of title although a photocopy of the Land or Charge Certificate may be, and is occasionally, provided instead.

If part of the property sold is unregistered or there are rights, e.g. unregistered leases (*see* **26:7**), as to which the register is not conclusive then title to that extent is deduced in the traditional way.

Section 110(1)(a) provides that if the purchase money does not exceed £1,000 the purchaser must carry the cost of providing the copy entries.

(*c*) *Registration of vendor.* LRA 1925, s. 110(5) provides that if the vendor is not registered as the proprietor of the registered land being sold he must, notwithstanding any stipulation to the contrary, at his own expense procure his registration or the purchaser's consent to his not so doing.

4. The purchaser's role. The purchaser has a considerably simpler task in the case of registered land than unregistered. The procedure is the same as in the case of unregistered land save largely as follows.

(*a*) Examination of title is unnecessary to the extent that title is registered. It must simply be seen that the vendor is the registered proprietor of the title contracted to be sold. The official office copy entries provided by the vendor are guaranteed to be accurate and conclusive as to the facts stated therein (**LRA 1925, s. 113**) (but *see* Chap. 29).

(*b*) For the same reason requisitions on title are generally unnecessary although they may arise from matters appearing on the Land Registry search or from matters excluded from registration (*see* **11**; **26:7**).

(*c*) On completion again there is no time spent in examining deeds or marking abstracts. The purchaser simply has to ensure that he receives the Land or Charge Certificate relating to the title contracted to be sold, i.e. that the title number on the certificate handed over is the same as that in the office copy entries.

(For the procedure for redeeming a registered mortgage on or following completion, *see* **26**.)

5. Forms of transfer. A "transfer" is the registered land equivalent of a conveyance. LRR 1925 lay down different forms for different transactions. Form 19 is the commonest form and is used for the transfer of the whole of the land (whether freehold or leasehold) within a title (*see* Fig. 5). This form shows the considerable simplicity of registered land transfers compared to their counterparts in unregistered conveyancing. In practice printed forms are generally used and the details merely filled in.

Where there is no suitable prescribed form, one of the prescribed forms may be adapted or the equivalent unregistered form suitably altered. A typical, and well drafted, transfer of a single plot on a large estate is reproduced in Fig. 6. This form shows how covenants, grants and exceptions are included in a transfer.

6. Procedure. The transfer is prepared by the purchaser's solicitor in the same way as in unregistered conveyancing and submitted as a draft to the vendor's solicitor. However, in simple cases where a printed form is used it is quite often agreed that an engrossment be prepared without the prior submission of a draft to the vendor's solicitor.

7. Execution and parties. A transfer is executed in the same way as any other conveyancing deed. It appears, though, from the forms printed as part of LRR 1925 that, in contrast to the position with unregistered land (*see* 13:**33**), a witness to execution is obligatory.

Where a transfer (or other document, e.g. the grant of an easement) deals with only part of the land in a title, then the plan must be signed by the transferor and by the transferee or his solicitor on his behalf.

Where two or more persons are the transferee the restriction set out in 27:**19**(*b*) will be entered on the register unless the transfer or the application for registration provides that the surviving co-owner is able to give a valid receipt for capital money arising on a disposition of the property.

Searches in respect of registered land

8. Local land charges searches. A local search will be made in the same way, at the same time and to the same effect as in unregistered conveyancing (*see* 2:**5–8**).

9. Searches of the Land Charges Department of the Land Registry. These are not relevant in the case of registered land and will be made only in the following circumstances.

(*a*) In dealing with unregistered land even in an area of compulsory registration a land charges search will be effected before completion in the usual way (*see* 12:**1–12**).

(*b*) A land charges search may be required even for land which is already registered in respect of title which has to be deduced in the ordinary unregistered way. For example:

(*i*) if V contracts to sell to P a possessory title then P should if possible search against the previous estate owner;

Form 19

H.M. Land Registry

Land Registration Acts, 1925 to 1971

Stamp pursuant to section 28 of the Finance Act, 1931, to be impressed here	When the transfer attracts Inland Revenue duty, the stamps should be impressed here before lodging the transfer for registration

(1) For a transfer by a company or corporation form 19(Co) is printed and for a transfer to joint proprietors form 19(JP) is printed.

(¹) TRANSFER OF WHOLE
(Rule 98 or 115, Land Registration Rules 1925)

County and district (or London borough) }

Title number(s)

Property

Date_____19___ In consideration of_____

(2) Strike out if not required.

pounds (£_____) (²) *the receipt whereof is hereby acknowledged*

(3) In BLOCK LETTERS, enter full name(s), postal address(es) and occupation(s) of the proprietor(s) of the land.

I/We(³)

(4) If desired or otherwise as the case may be (see rules 76 and 77).

_____(⁴) *as beneficial owner(s)* hereby transfer to:

(5) In BLOCK LETTERS, enter full name(s), postal address(es) and occupation(s) of the transferee(s) for entry on the register.

(⁵)

(6) Any special clause should be entered here.

the land comprised in the title(s) above mentioned (⁶) (⁷)

(7) A transfer for charitable uses should follow form 36 in the schedule to the Land Registration Rules, 1925 (see rules 121 and 122).

(continued overleaf)

Figure 5 *Form 19: form used for the transfer of the whole of the land within a title.*

(8) If a certificate of value for the purposes of the Stamp Act, 1891, and amending Acts is not required, this paragraph should be deleted.

(8) It is hereby certified that the transaction hereby effected does not form part of a larger transaction or series of transactions in respect of which the amount or value or aggregate amount or value of the consideration exceeds £_____

Signed, sealed and delivered by the said   **Seal**

_____

_____

in the presence of

Name _____

Address _____

Occupation _____

Signed, sealed and delivered by the said   **Seal**

_____

_____

in the presence of

Name _____

Address _____

Occupation _____

Oyez Publishing Limited, Norwich House, 11/13 Norwich Street, London EC4A 1AB, a subsidiary of The Solicitors' Law Stationery Society, Limited   ★★★★ F24543 10 '79

Figure 5 (contd.)

　(ii) if V contracts to sell a good leasehold title P may search against the unregistered freehold title.

10. Official search of the index map. The purpose of this search is discussed in 1:**14**. The index map is discussed in 25:**23**. Cautions against first registrations are discussed in 27:**18** and compulsory first registration in 26:**20**.

11. Official searches of the register. It is the official search of the register which in registered land replaces the land charges search. The search is made on a specified printed form: Form 94A (see Fig. 8) for a search of the whole of the land in a title; Form 94B (see Fig. 7) for a search of part of the land of a title; Form 94C for a search

H.M. LAND REGISTRY

LAND REGISTRATION ACTS, 1925 TO 1971

Stamp pursuant to Section 28 of the Finance Act, 1931 to be impressed here	When the Transfer attracts Inland Revenue duty, the stamps should be impressed here before lodging the Transfer for registration

TRANSFER OF FREEHOLD LAND
(PART)

County and District
(or London Borough) :

Title Number :

Property
(short description) :

Dated the   day of   19

   1. In consideration of
pounds (£   ) the receipt whereof is hereby acknowledged GEORGE WIMPEY & CO., LIMITED whose registered office is at 27 Hammersmith Grove London W6 7EN (hereinafter called "the Company") as Beneficial Owner hereby transfers to

(hereinafter called "the Transferee") the land (hereinafter called "the Property") shown coloured red and blue and numbered   on the accompanying plan being part of the land comprised in the Title above referred to Together with the dwelling-house (and garage if any) thereon known as

TOGETHER with full right and liberty for the Transferee his tenants servants and licensees (in common with all other persons having the like right) at all times hereafter :—

  (a)   for the purpose of access to or egress from the Property to pass and repass with or without vehicles along the roads and on foot only along the footpaths which are now or may within twenty one years from the date hereof be constructed on the Company's Estate (hereinafter called "the Estate" which expression shall in this Transfer mean all the land in respect of which the Company is or was the registered proprietor under the Title Number above referred to) PROVIDED ALWAYS that this sub-clause shall not apply to the land shown coloured brown on the said plan (hereinafter called "the Brown Land");

  (b)   for the purpose of access to or egress from the Property to pass and repass with or without vehicles over any part of the Brown Land which forms part of a forecourt and on foot only over any other parts of the Brown Land subject to the payment of a fair and proper proportion of the expense from time to time of maintaining repairing and renewing the surface of the Brown Land;

Approved by H.M. Land Registry for the purpose of Form C.168
TR/FH shared access – 7/74
Legal 41

Figure 6   *Typical form for transfer of a single plot on a large estate.*
This form is copyright and is reproduced by permission of Wimpey Group Services Limited.

(c)   to the free passage and running of water soil gas electricity and other services through all drains channels sewers pipes wires cables watercourses gutters and other conducting media (hereinafter called "the Service Installations") in on or under or belonging to any land comprised in the Estate and now used by the Property subject to the payment of a fair and proper proportion of the expense from time to time of cleaning maintaining repairing and renewing the same;

(d)   to keep the eaves gutters spouts downpipes chimney cappings foundations and any similar structures (hereinafter together referred to as "the Projections") incidental to the user of the buildings on the Property which overhang or protrude beneath the adjoining land comprised in the Estate;

(e)   to enter after the giving of reasonable notice at all reasonable times (except in the case of emergency) upon the adjoining land comprised in the Estate so far as may be necessary for the purposes of inspecting cleaning maintaining repairing and renewing the buildings walls fences and other boundary structures on the Property the Service Installations and the Projections causing as little damage as possible and making good to the reasonable satisfaction of the registered proprietors from time to time of the said adjoining land any damage caused.

TOGETHER ALSO with the benefit of all covenants made with the Company by any other person who is the registered proprietor of any land comprised in the Estate.

2.   The Property is transferred subject to the rights (which so far as not already created are hereby reserved) of the registered proprietors from time to time of:—

(a)   any land comprised in the Estate to the free passage and running of water soil gas electricity and other services from and to such land through all of the Service Installations in on under or belonging to the Property subject to the payment of a fair and proper proportion of the expense from time to time of cleaning maintaining repairing and renewing the same;

(b)   the adjoining land comprised in the Estate to keep the Projections incidental to the user of the buildings on the said adjoining land which overhang or protrude beneath the Property;

(c)   the adjoining land comprised in the Estate to enter after the giving of reasonable notice and at all reasonable times (except in the case of emergency) upon the Property so far as may be necessary for the purposes of inspecting cleaning maintaining repairing and renewing the buildings walls fences and other boundary structures on the said adjoining land and the Service Installations and the Projections referred to in this Clause causing as little damage as possible and making good to the reasonable satisfaction of the Transferee any damage caused.

3.   The part of the Property shown coloured blue on the said plan (hereinafter called "the Blue Land") is also transferred subject to the rights (which so far as not already created are hereby reserved) of the registered proprietors from time to time of any land comprised in the Estate to which access is to be gained over the Blue Land to pass and repass with or without vehicles over any part of the Blue Land which forms part of a forecourt and on foot only over any other parts of the Blue Land subject to the payment of a fair and proper proportion of the expense from time to time of maintaining repairing and renewing the surface of the Blue Land.

4.   There is hereby also reserved to the registered proprietors from time to time of any land comprised in the Estate the right to grant for the benefit of the Estate all easements wayleaves licences rights and privileges needed by County and District Councils Electricity Boards other Statutory Authorities Oil Supply Companies and Television and Radio Service Companies in connection with the services usually provided or maintained by them.

5.   The Transferee to the intent and so as to bind the Property into whosesoever hands the same may come hereby covenants with the Company and also (subject to the right of waiver and modification hereinafter reserved to the Company) as a separate covenant with every other person who is now the registered proprietor of any land comprised in the Estate for the benefit of the Estate and each and every part thereof that:

(a)   no building on the Property shall be used for any purpose other than as or incidental to a private dwellinghouse;

(b)   nothing shall be done which may lessen the support or protection given by any party walls referred to in Clause 6 hereof;

(c)   if any garage on the Property is joined to the dwellinghouse thereon and also to any building on the adjoining land comprised in the Estate then no building or other structure shall be erected over or upon such garage.

Figure 6   *(contd.)*

6. The Transferee hereby further covenants with the Company at all times hereafter to maintain repair and renew the fence or other boundary structure on the side or sides of the Property marked "T" within the boundary on the said plan provided that any retaining wall erected along a boundary of the Property with the adjoining land comprised in the Estate and that part of any wall of the buildings on the Property supporting any building on adjoining land comprised in the Estate are deemed party walls and shall be maintained jointly by the Transferee and the registered proprietor for the time being of such adjoining land.

7. The Transferee for the purpose of affording to the Company a full and sufficient indemnity hereby further covenants with the Company to observe the covenants contained or referred to in the Register of the Title above referred to so far as the same relate to the Property and are still subsisting and capable of being enforced and to indemnify and keep indemnified the Company against all actions claims and demands whatsoever in respect of the non-observance of the said covenants.

8. IT IS HEREBY AGREED AND DECLARED as follows:—

(a) The Transferee shall not by implication prescription or otherwise become entitled to any right of light or air which would restrict or interfere with the free use of the land comprised in the Estate or adjoining or neighbouring land of the Company for building or other purposes and the Company may at any time hereafter release waive or modify any of the covenants imposed by it upon any such land or any part thereof.

(b) Where the context so admits the expressions "the Company" and "the Transferee" shall be deemed to include the successors in title of the Company and the Transferee respectively.

(c) Where there are two or more persons included in the expression "the Transferee" the covenants expressed to be made by the Transferee shall be deemed to be made by such persons jointly and severally and as between such persons they shall hold the Property upon trust for themselves as joint tenants
so that the survivor of them is   entitled to give a valid receipt for capital monies arising on a disposition of the Property.

9. It is hereby certified that the transaction hereby effected does not form part of a larger transaction or of a series of transactions in respect of which the amount or value or the aggregate amount or value of the consideration exceeds £

The COMMON SEAL of GEORGE WIMPEY)
& CO., LIMITED was hereunto)
affixed in the presence of:—)

Authorised Signatory

SIGNED SEALED and DELIVERED)
by the Transferee in the)
presence of:—)

Signature _____

Address _____

_____

Occupation _____

Figure 6 *(contd.)*

in respect of which no priority is conferred, i.e. a search on behalf of a person who is not a purchaser, a lessee or a chargee in good faith for valuable consideration. Unless the application is made by the registered proprietor or his solicitor the applicant must hold a written authority to inspect the register signed by the proprietor or his solicitor.

12. Period to be covered by a search. The purchaser who has been provided with office copies of the register (*see* **3**(*b*)) knows the exact state of the register at the date of those office copies. Accordingly the purpose of a search is to inform him if there have been any entries made from the date of those office copies to the time of the search. If the purchaser has not been supplied with official office copies then he should either have obtained them himself and search for the same period as before or attend at the vendor's office to inspect the Land Certificate and search in respect of the period from the time when the certificate was last compared with the register (*see* 25:**16**) to the time of the search.

13. Priority conferred by a search. The search discloses to the searcher any entry made in the period covered by the search. A search on behalf of a purchaser, lessee or chargee in good faith for valuable consideration confers upon the searcher priority over any application made during the priority period of his search. Priority is conferred provided that the application pursuant to the search affecting the same property is made within the priority period and *completed in due course by registration* (Land Registration (Official Searches) Rules 1981, r. 5). The priority period is now thirty working days.

14. Extension of the priority period. A fresh search may be made using the same authority to inspect as many times as wished before completion. A further priority period is obtained each time a search is made.

After completion has taken place it is not possible to extend the priority period by making a further search.

Form 94B   H.M. Land Registry
Duplicate

Land Registration (Official Searches) Rules 1981

Application by Purchaser for Official Search with priority in respect of PART of the land in a title

(Numbers in brackets relate to notes overleaf.)

....District Land Registry

(For an official search of whole of the land in a title, use form 94A.)

County and district (or London borough)	
Title number	
Enter full name(s) of the registered proprietor(s)	
Application is made to ascertain whether any adverse entry has been made in the register affecting the undermentioned property since the date shown opposite being EITHER the date on which an office copy of the subsisting entries in the register was issued OR the last date on which the land or charge certificate was officially examined with the register.	
Enter full name(s) of the applicant(s) *(i.e. purchaser(s) lessee(s) or chargee(s))*	

I/We *as solicitors acting* for the above mentioned applicant(s) certify that the applicant(s) intend(s) to:-

(Enter X in the appropriate box opposite)

- [P] purchase
- [L] take a lease of
- [C] lend money on the security of a registered charge on

the undermentioned PART OF the land in the above title

Property to be purchased, leased or charged.
State either

(a) where an estate layout plan has been approved in the Land Registry
  (i) the plot number(s) and
  (ii) the date of approval of the estate plan

or (b) IN ALL OTHER CASES
the short description of the property referring to a plan . *Please attach a copy of the plan to the duplicate search.*

(a) .... Plot number(s)

.... Date of approval

(b) ....
....
shown ....on the attached plan

A   WHERE A SOLICITOR IS ACTING FOR THE APPLICANT(S)

I/We certify that I/We hold the duly signed written authority of (or of the solicitor(s) for) the above mentioned registered proprietor(s) to inspect the register of the above title OR that I/We also act as solicitor(s) for the registered proprietor(s).

Indicate this by entering X in this box

[A]

B   WHERE A SOLICITOR IS NOT ACTING FOR THE APPLICANT(S)

The duly signed written authority of (or of the solicitor(s) for) the registered proprietor(s) to inspect the register of the above title accompanies this application.

Indicate this by entering X in this box

[B]

Key number	

Signed: ....

Date ....

Telephone number

Reference

This panel must be completed using BLOCK LETTERS and inserting the name and address to which the official certificate of result of search is to be sent.

Figure 7   *Form 94B: application by purchaser for official search with priority in respect of **part** of the land in a title.*

Form 94D   H.M. Land Registry   Land Registration (Official Searches) Rules 1981

This page is to be completed only by H.M. Land Registry

| Official search no. to be |
| impressed here. |

Official Certificate of the Result of Search

It is hereby certified that the official search applied for has been made with the following result:

Since...19.................

1. Is the land searched included in this title?		2. What plan references affect it?	
Date stamp	Pending official searches	Pending dealings	Remarks

Search drafted ....   Search checked ....

ADDRESSES OF DISTRICT LAND REGISTRIES

District Land Registry	Address	Telephone No.	Telex Call No.
Birkenhead	76 Hamilton Street, Birkenhead, Merseyside L41 5JW	051-647 5661	628475
Croydon	Sunley House, Bedford Park, Croydon CR9 3LE	01-686 8833	917288
Durham	Aykley Heads, Durham DH1 5TR	0385 61361	53684
Gloucester	Bruton Way, Gloucester GL1 1DQ	0452 28666	43119
Harrow	Lyon House, Lyon Road, Harrow, Middx. HA1 2EU	01-427 8811	262476
Lytham	Lytham St Annes, Lancs FY8 5AB	0253 736999	67649
Nottingham	Chalfont Drive, Nottingham NG8 3RN	0602 291111	37167
Peterborough	Aragon Court, Northminster Road, Peterborough PE1 1XN	0733 46048	32786
Plymouth	Plumer House, Tailyour Road, Crownhill, Plymouth PL6 5HY	0753 701234	45265
Stevenage	Brickdale House, Danestrete, Stevenage, Herts. SG1 1XG	0438 4488	82377
Swansea	37 The Kingsway, Swansea SA1 5LF	0792 50971	48220
Tunbridge Wells	Tunbridge Wells, Kent TN2 5AQ	0892 26141	95286
Weymouth	1 Cumberland Drive, Weymouth, Dorset DT4 9TT	03057 76161	418231

Services To Lawyers Limited   828

Figure 7 *(contd.)*

Form 94A HM Land Registry
(Duplicate)
Land Registration (Official Searches) Rules 1981

Application by Purchaser for Official Search with priority in respect of the WHOLE of the land in a title

......................................District Land Registry

(For an official search of part of the land in a title, use form 94B).

County and district (or London borough)	
Title number	
Enter full name(s) of the registered proprietor(s)	
Application is made to ascertain whether any adverse entry has been made in the register since the date shown opposite being EITHER the date on which an office copy of the subsisting entries in the register was issued OR the last date on which the land or charge certificate was officially examined with the register.	
Enter full name(s) of the applicant(s) *(i.e. purchaser(s) lessee(s) or chargee(s))*	
I/We *as solicitors acting for* the above mentioned applicant(s) certify that the applicant(s) intend(s) to:- *(Enter X in the appropriate box opposite)*	P purchase · L take a lease of · C lend money on the security of a registered charge on · the WHOLE of the land in the above title

A WHERE A SOLICITOR IS ACTING FOR THE APPLICANT(S)

I/We certify that I/We hold the duly signed written authority of (or of the solicitor(s) for) the above mentioned registered proprietor(s) to inspect the register of the above title OR that I/We also act as solicitor(s) for the registered proprietor(s).

Indicate this by entering X in this box

A

B WHERE A SOLICITOR IS NOT ACTING FOR THE APPLICANT(S)

The duly signed written authority of (or of the solicitor(s) for) the registered proprietor(s) to inspect the register of the above title accompanies this application.

Indicate this by entering X in this box

B

Key number	
	Signed: ....
	Date: ....
	Telephone number
	Reference
	This panel must be completed using BLOCK LETTERS and inserting the name and address to which the official certificate of result of search is to be sent.

Figure 8 *Form 94A: application by purchaser for official search with priority in respect of the **whole** of the land in a title.*

Form 94D HM Land Registry

Land Registration (Official Searches) Rules 1981

This page is to be completed only by HM Land Registry	*Official search no. to be impressed here:*

Official Certificate of the Result of Search

It is hereby certified that the official search applied for has been made with the following result:

Since .... 19 ....

Date stamp	Pending official searches	Pending dealings	Remarks

Search drafted ....

Search checked ....

ADDRESSES OF DISTRICT LAND REGISTRIES

District Land Registry	Address	Telephone No.	Telex Call No.
Birkenhead	76 Hamilton Street, Birkenhead, Merseyside L41 5JW	051-647 5661	628475
Croydon	Sunley House, Bedford Park, Croydon CR9 3LE	01-686 8833	917288
Durham	Aykley Heads, Durham DH1 5TR	0385 61361	53684
Gloucester	Bruton Way, Gloucester GL1 1DQ	0452 28666	43119
Harrow	Lyon House, Lyon Road, Harrow, Middx. HA1 2EU	01-427 8811	262476
Lytham	Lytham St Annes, Lancs. FY8 5AB	0253 736999	67649
Nottingham	Chalfont Drive, Nottingham NG8 3RN	0602 291111	37167
Peterborough	Aragon Court, Northminster Road, Peterborough PE1 1XN	0733 46048	32786
Plymouth	Plumer House, Tailyour Road, Crownhill, Plymouth PL6 5HY	0752 701234	45265
Stevenage	Brickdale House, Danestrete, Stevenage, Herts. SG1 1XG	0438 4488	82377
Swansea	37 The Kingsway, Swansea SA1 5LF	0792 50971	48220
Tunbridge Wells	Tunbridge Wells, Kent TN2 5AQ	0892 26141	95286
Weymouth	1 Cumberland Drive, Weymouth, Dorset DT4 9TT	03057 76161	418231

oyez The Solicitors' Law Stationery Society, plc, Oyez House, 237 Long Lane, London SE1 4PU

F1670 9-81
★ ★ ★ ★ ★

Figure 8 *(contd.)*

Settled land and trusts for sale

15. Settled land. Settled land is registered in the name of the tenant for life or if none the statutory owner or SLA personal representative as the case may be. The rights of those interested in the settlement are minor interests (*see* 27:**1**). Dealings with these minor interests may be the subject of entries in the minor interests index (*see* 27:**4**) although in fact this index has fallen almost into disuse. As in the case of unregistered land the beneficiaries are protected by the rules in SLA 1925 regulating the machinery of dealings with settled land (*see* 10:**4** and 27:**19**). Compliance with these rules is ensured by the entry of an appropriate restriction on the register of title.

16. Trusts for sale. The position of the beneficiaries behind a trust for sale has been discussed in 27:**3**. An example of a restriction used to protect the beneficiaries in one case of co-ownership is given in 27:**19**. Other restrictions (e.g. requiring a named person's consent to a sale) may be employed in appropriate cases.

Transmissions of registered land

17. Transmission on death. Where a registered proprietor dies his personal representatives may obtain registration in their names. This is done by forwarding the appropriate application form (Form 82) together with a certified copy of the probate or letters of administration, the Land or Charge Certificate and where appropriate the Inland Revenue certificate of non-liability to capital transfer tax. Once registered as proprietors the personal representatives may deal with the land in the same way as any other registered proprietor.

Alternatively personal representatives may deal with the land without themselves being registered as proprietors. The transfer by them will be in the standard form and the transferee may obtain registration in the usual way (*see* **32**) including with his application for registration a certified copy of the probate or grant of administration.

18. Transmission on bankruptcy. LCA 1972 does not apply to registered land. Registered land is affected by bankruptcy proceedings only if an appropriate entry is made on the register of title. A bankruptcy petition is protected by a creditor's notice registered by the Chief Land Registrar (LRA 1925, s. 61(1)). Thereafter any dealing with the land takes effect subject to the rights and claims of the proprietor's creditors as the entry takes effect by way of notice (*see* 27:**13**).

19. Bankruptcy inhibition. Once a receiving order is made the Registrar must enter a bankruptcy inhibition which prevents any dealing with the land until the inhibition is vacated (LRA 1925, s. 61(3) and *see* 27:**23**).

20. Registration of Official Receiver or trustee. When a proprietor of registered land is adjudicated bankrupt his registered property vests automatically in the trustee-in bankruptcy in the same way as his other property (LRA 1925, s. 61(5)). The Official Receiver or the trustee appointed to administer the estate may be registered in place of the bankrupt on production of the order of adjudication or certificate of appointment as trustee respectively (LRR 1925, r. 174 and r. 175). LRA 1925, s. 43 provides that the Official Receiver or trustee will then hold the land to be dealt with in accordance with ordinary bankruptcy law and subject to the same minor interests as the bankrupt held the land.

Mortgages of registered land

21. Introduction. There are several methods of mortgaging registered land reflecting more or less the range of mortgages available in the case of unregistered land (*see* Curzon, *Land Law*).

22. The registered charge. The most important kind of mortgage of registered land is the registered charge. LRA 1925, s. 25 confers on the registered proprietor a power to charge the land in his title by deed. The instrument may be in any form but is commonly in the same form as a mortgage by deed of unregistered land.

23. Procedure. A registered charge when it is registered takes effect as a charge by way of legal mortgage (LRA 1925, s. 27(1)). The registered charge takes effect as such when the charge is entered in the Charges Register of the relevant title. Thus, the same points arise as to applying within the priority period of the Land Registry search and with the papers in order to the correct District Land Registry as in the case of other dealings (*see* **13**, **32**). The application for registration is made on Form A4 (or Form A5 if it is a charge of part of the land in a title), *see* Fig. 9.

24. Charge Certificate. After registration the chargee is issued with a Charge Certificate which is a facsimile of the entries on the register of that title bound together with the original charge (LRR 1925, r. 262; the form of Charge Certificate is discussed in 25:**17**). The Land Certificate is retained in the Land Registry until the charge is discharged.

25. Companies. When a charge is created by a company the charge must also be registered at the Companies Registry (*see Company Law*, M. C. Oliver, Macdonald & Evans, 1982) and then at the Land Registry. The application to the Land Registry must be accompanied by the certificate of registration under s. 95 of the Companies Act 1948 (LRR 1925, r. 145), and should also contain a certificate from the company secretary, solicitor or director that the charge does not contravene any provision of the company's memorandum and articles of association.

A floating charge by a company cannot be a registered charge. A registered charge must be a charge of specified registered land. The proper way to protect a floating charge is by notice (*see* 27:**11**) if the Land or Charge Certificate can be produced or otherwise by caution (*see* 27:**14**).

26. Discharge of a registered charge. This is effected by sending the Land Registry form of discharge (Form 53, or Form 53Co. in the case of a corporate mortgagee—in both cases a simple form acknowledging that the mortgage debt has been discharged) to the Land Registry. This is sent under cover of Form A4 (*see* Fig. 9) or A5 and must be accompanied by the Charge Certificate.

27. Equitable mortgages of registered land. This is one of the areas of Land Registry law and practice where least clarity has been achieved. The overriding principle to bear in mind is that the registered proprietor may, as well as having the power to create a registered charge under LRA 1925, s. 25, charge the land in the same variety of ways as in the case of unregistered land (*see* Curzon, *Land Law*) by virtue of the power of disposition vested in him by LRA 1925, s. 101.

The possible methods of protecting equitable mortgages are discussed in **28–31** below.

28. Notice of deposit of Land or Charge Certificate. LRA 1925, s. 66 gives the registered proprietor power to create a lien on the registered land by deposit of a Land Certificate. This is equivalent to the mortgage by deposit of the title deeds in the case of unregistered land. The lien takes effect, subject to any overriding interests and any interests on the register to the contrary, in the same way as an unregistered owner's deposit of his title deeds.

The proprietor of a registered charge can in the same way and to the same effect create a lien on his charge by deposit of the Charge Certificate (LRA 1925, s. 66).

Such a lien by deposit is protected by notice of deposit or of intended deposit entered on the Charges Register of the relevant title. Notice of the deposit (or an intended deposit by a prospective proprietor) is given to the Land Registry (the Land or Charge Certificate need not be sent with the application) and the Registry makes the necessary entry on the Charges Register. Once entered on the register the notice takes effect as a caution and gives the depositee the opportunity to object to any application for a dealing with the land (*see* 27:**14**).

The depositee in any event has possession of the Land or Charge Certificate. This gives him the additional protection that no dealing requiring production of the certificate can be registered without his consent (*see* 25:**18, 19**).

29. *Re White Rose Cottage* (1965). In this case it was held in the Court of Appeal that notice of deposit could be registered even though the registered proprietor signed a memorandum of deposit as well as handing over the Land Certificate. Where a mortgage is

A4   H.M. LAND REGISTRY

APPLICATION TO REGISTER DEALINGS WITH THE <u>WHOLE</u> OF THE LAND COMPRISED
IN REGISTERED TITLE(S)

FOR OFFICIAL USE ONLY		
Date stamp	Application number	Record of fee paid

THE PANELS BELOW SHOULD BE COMPLETED BY THE
APPLICANT OR HIS SOLICITOR.

By post or under hand
Received Stamp
Ackd. by _____
Date _____

County and District
(or London borough)

Title number(s)(¹)

Pending application numbers

(1) *If this application affects more than eight title numbers,*
attach a separate list of them (in triplicate) to this page
and write "see list" in the space opposite.

Nature and priority of applications	Value	Fee scale para. or abatement	£	p	Particulars of underpayments or overpayments
		Total fees paid			

Fees are assessed under the current Land Registration Fee Order, and are payable on delivery of applications. They may be paid by cheque or postal order, drawn in favour of "H.M. Land Registry".

Panel 1

DOCUMENTS LODGED HEREWITH
Please list all documents and treat each original and copy as a separate item

(i)	(iv)	(vii)
(ii)	(v)	(viii)
(iii)	(vi)	(ix)

Name and address of solicitor or applicant to whom the acknowledgement of the application and all
requisitions made by the Land Registry including requests for unpaid fees are to be sent:

BLOCK
LETTERS

Name _____
Address_____

Solicitor's reference_____   Telephone number_____

IMPORTANT

The documents not retained in the Land Registry, together with the land certificate (or charge certificate(s) as the case may be), will, on the completion of the registration, be returned to the above address. If a particular document is required to be issued to some other person or firm upon completion of the registration or in connection with any requisition which may arise, please complete panel 2 below.

Panel 2 Additional instructions (if any) for the issue of any document to some person or firm other than that mentioned in panel 1 above:

BLOCK
LETTERS

Description of document_____
Name _____
Address_____
Reference_____

THE PARTICULARS REQUESTED ON PAGE 4 MUST ALSO BE SUPPLIED

Figure 9 *Form A4: application to register a dealing with the whole of the land*
in a title.

THESE PAGES ARE FOR

Edition _____
Opened _____

(Write all names and addresses in BLOCK CAPITALS)

	A. PROPERTY REGISTER

Entry
no.

B. PROPRIETORSHIP REGISTER

TITLE

(CANCEL_____)

Entry
no.

C. CHARGES REGISTER   Remarks

(Date)   Charge dated_____
registered on_____

to secure $\left\{ \begin{array}{l} \textit{the moneys} \\ \textit{the moneys including the further advances} \end{array} \right\}$ therein mentioned

PROPRIETOR—_____

registered on_____

(CANCEL_____and insert date)

Figure 9   *(contd.)*

OFFICIAL USE ONLY

DRAFT ENTRIES FOR $\{$ NEW EDITION OF REGISTER MODEL.............................. / ADDITIONS TO EXISTING REGISTER.

	Name	Stn.	Date
Drafted			
Checked			

Title No._____

(lowest, if several affected)

Type after _____

Send out after _____

Special Instructions

C_____ sent on_____

*enclosing (for return)*_____

Make repro. copy of $\{$ (a)_____ / (b)_____ *and plan (tinted/untinted)*
(Strike out instructions not applicable)

SETTLED BY_____ Date_____

Subject to:

REVIEWED BY_____ Date_____

NOTE
The typist will require the following documents for copying purposes:

1_____

2_____

TO SETTLER:
1 Points arising:_____

Points to be attended to on reply to requisitions

1_____

2_____

3_____

INSTRUCTIONS TO TYPIST (Strike out instructions not applicable)

Enter Make up/Prepare L.C., C.C. No._____ Prepare C.C. No._____(Xerox form)
Prepare Comb/Comp. C.C. No._____for this and titles_____
Make up/Prepare A.54 and duplicate.
Sew up outside/inside_____C.C. No._____original charge dated_____

(Re)-sew up in L.C./C.C. No. _____ $\{$ Copy of new edition with old/new plan. / office copy transfer(s)/conveyance(s)/abstract(s) of_____(and plan(s)) / dated / original A.54/(existing) schedule or copy of restrictive covenants.

Prepare envelope label and copy for address in panel 1/panel 2/Deposit No._____(see A.15)
Typed by_____Stn._____Date_____

INSTRUCTIONS TO COMPARER (Strike out instructions not applicable)

Make copy $^{transfer}_{charge}$ an office copy. Mark copy transfer with office copy stamp.
Sew up in C.C. No._____Xerox sheets and original charged dated_____
Mark lease dated_____"Lease determined, register closed."
Mark_____dated_____"Notice registered."
See that office copy transfer dated_____has not been (re)sewn up in L.C., C.C. No._____
and cancel the office copy transfer.
N.B.—See that any cancellations appear on both thin sheet and register.
Compared by_____Stn._____Date_____

Stamp old register
"Closed see new edition"
Cancel $\{$ L.C. (cover) / C.C. No._____

INSTRUCTIONS TO DESPATCHER (Strike out instructions not applicable)

(a) **MISCELLANEOUS INSTRUCTIONS**
(i) See that $\{$ instructions (if any) as to marking of deeds have been carried out. / instructions (if any) to typist as to sewing up of documents have been carried out.
(ii) Instruct Day List to mark off this application and official search_____and_____D.
(b) **DOCUMENTS TO BE RETAINED**
(i) Cancelled L.C. (cover).
(ii) Cancelled C.C. No._____and charge (mortgage) dated_____
(iii) All documents in panel 1, page 1, marked with *.
(iv) L.C. or C.C. No._____on deposit *vide*_____
(c) **DOCUMENTS TO BE ISSUED**
(i) Issue to name and address in panel 1, page 1:
L.C._____C.C. No._____
Documents (if any) mentioned in panel 1 not marked *
(ii) Issue document(s) as directed in panel 2, page 1.
(iii) Issue document(s) as directed in Deposit No._____
(iv) Issue C43, to_____
CERTIFICATE COMPARED WITH REGISTER
AND DESPATCHED BY_____Stn._____Date_____

TO FILING BRANCH: Add to R.R. file the following:_____	Notices		
	To	Form No.	RD No.
form 63/duplicate A.54/original transfer dated_____			
Remove from C file/R.R. file the following:_____			
copy charged dated_____			

Figure 9 *(contd.)*

FURTHER PARTICULARS TO BE SUPPLIED WHERE APPROPRIATE

3. Full Postal **address** including any postal code for entry on the register is:

As to new proprietor(s) of the land (if any)	*As to new proprietor(s) of a charge (if any)*

4. IF THE TRANSFER OR ASSENT IS TO JOINT TENANTS can the survivor of them give a valid receipt for capital money arising on a disposition of the land ? _____ (State YES or NO)

5. ON APPLYING TO REGISTER A COMPANY(1) AS PROPRIETOR OF LAND OR OF A CHARGE, a copy of the memorandum and articles of association, certified as a true copy by the secretary or solicitor of the company, should be produced (rule 259). However, production can usually be dispensed with if the company's solicitor supplies the following confirmation.

(A) (ON APPLYING TO REGISTER A COMPANY AS PROPRIETOR OF LAND)

We, solicitors to _____ Limited, hereby confirm that:
(insert name of company)

(a) the company is a company trading for profit and has been incorporated in England or Scotland under the Companies Acts;

(b) the memorandum and articles of association contains provisions entitling the company to hold and sell, mortgage, lease and otherwise deal with land and to borrow, lend and invest money;

(c) the company is (not)(2) an insurance company authorised to carry on long term business.

(2)(d) the charge(s) by the company lodged herewith do(es) not contravene any of the provisions of the memorandum and articles of association of the company.

(2)(e) the Company's registered number is _____ and we hereby apply for the entry thereof on the register.

Signature of **company's** *solicitors* _____

(B) (ON APPLYING TO REGISTER A COMPANY AS PROPRIETOR OF A CHARGE

We, solicitors to _____ Limited, hereby confirm that:
(insert name of company)

(a) the company is a company trading for profit and has been incorporated in England or Scotland under the Companies Acts;

(b) the memorandum and articles of association contains provisions entitling the company to hold and sell, mortgage, lease and otherwise deal with land and to borrow, lend and invest money;

(c) the lending of money:
(2) is not the primary object of the company and the company is not a moneylender as defined in the Moneylenders Act, 1900, s. 6.

or

(2) is the primary object of the company and
(i) a note or memorandum in writing of the contract was signed by the borrower and a copy of it was delivered to him pursuant to section 6 of the Moneylenders Act, 1927;
(ii) there has been no contravention of any of the other provisions of the said Act, in connection with the transaction to which the charge relates.

or

(2) is the primary object of the company but the company is exempt from the provisions of the Moneylenders Acts because _____

(Here give the grounds of the exemption, e.g., that the company carries on the business of banking, or has an exemption order of the Department of Trade and Industry.)

(2)(d) the Company's registered number is _____ and we hereby apply for the entry thereof on the register.

Signature of **company's** *solicitors* _____

(1) The term "company" is here used to refer to companies registered under the Companies Acts.
(2) Strike out if inapplicable.

6. IF A DISCHARGE OF THE ONLY REMAINING CHARGE. As solicitors for the registered proprietor of the land, we hereby apply for the issue of the land certificate to us.

Signature _____

REMINDERS

Please see that:
1. Charges are accompanied by copies certified by a solicitor (or in the name of the firm) as true copies. **Certification by clerks is not sufficient.**
2. **All material dates and particulars have been inserted in charges especially in the printed forms of building society and insurance company mortgages.**
3. Evidence of death or change of name is lodged where required.
4. The lease is lodged in support of an application for merger.

I/We have supplied the information required and hereby apply for the registration of the dealings in the order of priority shown on page 1 and request that, if practicable, the register be cleared so as to show only subsisting entries. *A cheque or postal order value* _____ *accompanies this application.*

Signature of applicant or his solicitors _____ Date _____

Oyez Publishing Limited, Norwich House, 11/13 Norwich Street, London EC4A 1AB, a subsidiary of The Solicitors' Law Stationery Society, Limited

★ ★ ★ ★ F26801 1/70

Figure 9 *(contd.)*

made by deed it cannot be protected by notice of deposit but only by registration as a registered charge, LRA 1925, s. 106 and *Barclays Bank Ltd* v. *Taylor* (1973).

30. Notices, cautions and restrictions. A mortgage of registered land which is not protected by registration as a registered charge may be protected by a notice (27:**11**), a caution (27:**14**) or a restriction (27:**19**) in an appropriate form, e.g. providing that the property cannot be dealt with without the consent of the mortgagee, if such is indeed a term of the mortgage agreement (LRA 1925, s. 106).

Registration of a dealing

31. Documents. The following documents must be sent to the relevant District Land Registry to register a dealing.

(*a*) The correct application form, i.e. Form A4 for a dealing with the whole of the land in a title (*see* Fig. 9); Form A5 for a dealing with part of the land in a title.

(*b*) The relevant Land or Charge Certificate unless this is on deposit in the Registry.

(*c*) The transfer or other document, e.g. mortgage, grant of right of way, etc., and a certified copy of this if it imposes restrictive covenants or where it is a legal charge.

(*d*) The correct fee.

Progress test 28

1. How may personal representatives of a deceased proprietor obtain registration as proprietors? (**3**)

2. What extra formalities are necessary when a company creates a registered charge? (**9**)

3. How is discharge of a registered charge effected? (**11**)

4. What is the effect of registration of a notice of deposit? (**15**)

5. How may a mortgage of registered land not protected by registration as a registered charge be protected? (**18**)

29

Rectification and indemnity

Introduction

The system of land registration provides a guarantee that once a proprietor is registered the legal estate is vested in him (by virtue of LRA 1925, s. 69(1)). The strength of the system is in the reliance that can be placed in the indefeasibility of this title once registration is obtained. Nevertheless there must be jurisdiction to correct the register in the case of mistakes or fraud. Where the register is so corrected, in specified cases compensation ("indemnity") may be payable.

Minor errors and omissions and alterations

1. Formal alterations. LRR 1925, r. 249 gives the Registrar power to make formal alterations of the register "as to any change in the name, address, or description of any proprietor or otherwise as he may deem proper".

2. The "slip rule". LRR 1925, r. 13 (known as the "slip rule") allows the Registrar to correct "any clerical error or error of a like nature . . . in the register, or any plan or document referred to therein". The correction must be one that can take effect without any detriment to any registered interest. The Registrar may give notices, call for evidence or seek any assent to the correction as he deems proper.

3. Registration in error. LRR 1925, r. 14 deals with the case where the whole or part of the land has been registered in error. The Registrar may enter notice of this on the register and cancel the registration, either wholly or to the extent required, either:

(*a*) with the consent of the proprietor and all persons appearing to be interested in the land; or

(*b*) after giving notice to such persons and holding such enquiry as he considers proper.

4. No indemnity. In the three cases of minor errors and omissions discussed in **1**, **2** and **3**, no question of indemnity will ordinarily arise.

Rectification

5. Powers. The power of rectifying serious errors or omissions or to give effect to proper legal claims is contained in LRA 1925, s. 82. It may be exercised by either the Registrar or the High Court. Appeal is possible from the Registrar to the High Court.

6. Circumstances when rectification may be ordered. The circumstances when rectification may be ordered are as follows (subject as below, *see* **7**).

(*a*) Where a court so orders to give effect to some person's proven estate, right or interest in the land.

(*b*) Where a court so orders to give effect to the grievance of any person in respect of some entry, omission, default or unnecessary delay in an entry.

(*c*) Where all interested parties consent.

(*d*) Where an entry has been obtained by fraud.

(*e*) Where two or more persons are mistakenly registered as proprietor of the same land.

(*f*) Where a mortgagee has been registered as proprietor of the land, instead of the charge, and there is a subsisting right of redemption.

(*g*) Where the wrong person has been registered as estate owner.

(*h*) In any other case where it may be deemed just to rectify the register.

7. Rectification against proprietor in possession. LRA 1925, s. 82(3) provides that the register will not be rectified against a proprietor in possession except in the following three cases.

(a) If the proprietor is a party to or has substantially contributed to the error or omission *by fraud or lack of proper care*.

(b) If for any reason it is considered it would be unjust not to order the rectification (s. 82(3) as amended by the Administration of Justice Act 1977, s. 24).

(c) To give effect to an overriding interest or an order of the court.

Indemnity

8. Availability. The right to indemnity is contained in LRA 1925, s. 83. Indemnity is available to one who suffers loss:

(a) through rectification (s. 83(1));

(b) by an error or omission where there is no rectification (s. 83(2));

(c) by the loss or destruction of a document lodged at the Land Registry (s. 83(3));

(d) by an error in an official search (s. 83(3)).

9. Indemnity excluded. LRA 1925, s. 83(5) (as amended by the Land Registration and Land Charges Act 1971) excludes the right to an indemnity in the following cases.

(a) Where the applicant substantially contributed to the mistake by fraud or lack of proper care; or where his predecessor has done so unless the applicant claims through a disposition for valuable consideration which is protected on the register.

(b) In respect of any mineral rights unless such are specifically included in the register of title.

(c) In respect of costs incurred in taking or defending proceedings without the consent of the Registrar.

10. Amount of indemnity. LRA 1925, s. 83(6) provides that the amount of indemnity may not exceed:

(a) the value of the relevant interest at the time of the mistake *in any case where rectification is not ordered*;

(*b*) the value of the relevant interest immediately before rectification *in any case where rectification is ordered*.

Decisions on rectification and indemnity

11. *Re Chowood's Registered Land* (1933). Mrs Lyall acquired a title to the disputed land ("the land") by adverse possession. C Co. Ltd purchased land including "the land" and was registered as proprietor. Mrs Lyall's claim for rectification succeeded (of course she was in possession). C Co. Ltd's claim for indemnity failed. It had lost nothing—its registration had in any event been subject to subsisting overriding interests (LRA 1925, s. 70(1)) of which Mrs Lyall's adverse possession was one (*see also* 27:**8**).

12. *Re 139 High St, Deptford* (1951). A sold to B a shop plus an annexe. B was registered as proprietor thereof. In fact the annexe belonged not to A but to BTC and BTC's claim for rectification was successful. (Today the claim for rectification would not be successful unless B had contributed to the mistake by fraud or lack of proper care or it was otherwise just, Administration of Justice Act 1977, s. 24). B was awarded an indemnity as he would be today, if rectification was awarded; he loses his claim to indemnity only if he has "caused or substantially contributed to the mistake through *fraud or lack of proper care*" (LRA 1925, s. 83(5)).

In *Argyle BS* v. *Hammond* (1984) it was held (CA) that the charges register could be rectified against a mortgagee where the transfer to the mortgagors had been forged. This was so even though the mortgagee had acted in good faith.

Progress test 29

1. Explain what is meant by "the slip rule". (**2**)

2. What are the circumstances when rectification of a serious error may be ordered? (**6**)

3. When can rectification be ordered against a proprietor in possession? (**7**)

4. In what four circumstances is an indemnity available? (**8**)

5. In what circumstances is the right to indemnity excluded? (**9**)

6. How is the amount of indemnity calculated? (**10**)

Appendix 1
Glossary of terms

Students of conveyancing often find the jargon of conveyancers mysterious. This appendix therefore explains some of the terms which appear in the text and which will be encountered in other textbooks.

Abstract. The abstract of title is the evidence the vendor produces of his title (in unregistered conveyancing). Traditionally this took the form of abbreviated transcriptions of the chain of documents tracing his title from the root of title (*q.v.*). Nowadays photocopies of these documents are used instead.

Assent. A document (either a deed or under hand) by which personal representatives convey property to the person entitled to the property which is part of a deceased estate they are administering.

Assurance. An old-fashioned word still sometimes used instead of "conveyance".

Caution. An entry on the title of registered land notifying that someone claiming an interest or encumbrance therein is entitled to notice of any dealing therewith before it can be registered.

Charge. In registered conveyancing a registered charge is a mortgage protected by entry on the register of the mortgaged property.

Conveyance. A deed transferring the legal estate in land. Expression usually reserved for sales of land, the deed for a voluntary transaction being called a "deed of gift" or a "settlement".

Counterpart. An exact copy of the deed used when a deed is to be executed in duplicate so that each party will have an original to keep (e.g. a lease kept by the tenant and the counterpart lease kept by the landlord).

Dealing. A transaction with registered title.

Deed poll. A deed made by one party alone (an expression no longer generally current). Contrast with "indenture" which means a deed made by more than one party (*inter partes*) and was formerly written out in duplicate and the two halves separated by cutting a jagged edge or indenture which could thereafter be fitted together as proof of identity.

Encumbrance. An interest adverse to a particular legal or equitable estate, e.g. a mortgage.

Engrossment. The fair copy which is to be used as the actual deed.

Epitome. List of documents of title in chronological order stating the date, type of document and parties and whether or not the original will be retained by the vendor on completion or not.

Escrow. A deed delivered conditionally, i.e. which does not become an effective deed ("delivered absolutely") until the condition is satisfied.

Fittings and fixtures. Fittings are the chattels in property which do not form part of the realty; fixtures are things which are or have become part of the realty. Thus, in the absence of a contrary stipulation the former are not included in the contract for the sale of land and buildings and the latter are. To become a fixture a chattel must be affixed substantially to the land for the purpose of improving the land as land.

Habendum. The part of the deed which shows how the purchaser is to hold the land, e.g. TO HOLD the same unto the purchaser in fee simple.

Indenture. *See* Deed poll.

Inhibition. An entry on the title of registered land preventing any dealing with the land being registered.

Memorandum.

(*a*) A note on a deed or other instrument recording some dealing with the land or estate to which that instrument is pertinent, e.g. a memorandum on a grant of probate of a sale of some land which is part of the deceased estate.

(*b*) Some written evidence, e.g. of a contract for the sale of land.

Recital. A non-operative introductory part of a deed telling the story of the transaction or the title concerned.

Restriction. An entry on the title of registered land preventing any dealing with the land unless the conditions of the restriction (e.g. requiring the consent of a mortgagee) are complied with.

Root of title. The deed or event from which in unregistered conveyancing the vendor undertakes (or, in the absence of an express stipulation, is bound) to trace his title.

Stakeholder. A person who holds money (usually a deposit) pending the outcome of an event and not as agent for one of the parties involved.

Statutory declaration. A declaration under oath in accordance with the Statutory Declarations Act 1835. A false declaration is punishable as perjury under the Perjury Act 1911, s. 5. Used in conveyancing to explain, for example, lost or missing title deeds or other defects in title or ambiguities in deeds such as the extent of land thereby formerly conveyed.

Tacking. This refers to the doctrine which may allow a first mortgagee who makes a further advance to have priority over an intervening second or subsequent mortgage. The further advance is thus "tacked" to the first mortgage.

Testimonium. A formal introduction to the attestation clause in a deed.

Transfer. A conveyance of registered land.

Transmission. The passing of registered title on the death or bankruptcy of the registered proprietor.

Undertaking. A promise to do or not to do something, e.g. pay money or produce a document. An undertaking by a solicitor is enforceable even though not a contractual promise (*see* 18:5). An undertaking by some other person is not enforceable in the same way and should not be relied upon.

Appendix 2
Conditions of sale

THE LAW SOCIETY'S GENERAL CONDITIONS OF SALE (1984 REVISION)

1 DEFINITIONS
In these conditions—
(a) "completion notice" means a notice served under condition 23(2)
(b) "the contract rate" means the rate specified in a special condition or, if none is so specified, the rate prescribed from time to time under section 32 of the Land Compensation Act 1961 for interest payable thereunder
(c) "contractual completion date" has the meaning given in condition 21
(d) "conveyance" includes an assignment and a transfer under the Land Registration Acts
(e) "lease" includes underlease
(f) "normal deposit" means the sum which, together with any preliminary deposit paid by the purchaser, amounts to ten per centum of the purchase money (excluding any separate price to be paid for any chattels, fixtures or fittings)
(g) "working day" means any day from Monday to Friday (inclusive) other than—
(i) Christmas Day, Good Friday and any statutory bank holiday, and
(ii) any other day specified in a special condition as not a working day
(h) a reference to a statute includes any amendment or re-enactment thereof.

2 SERVICE AND DELIVERY
(1) Section 196 of the Law of Property Act 1925 applies to any notice served under the contract, save that—
(a) a notice shall also be sufficiently served on a party if served on that party's solicitors
(b) any reference to a registered letter shall include a prepaid first class ordinary letter
(c) if the time at which a letter containing a notice would in the ordinary course be delivered is not on a working day, the notice shall be deemed to be served on the next following working day
(d) any notice shall also be sufficiently served if (i) sent by telex or by telegraphic facsimile transmission to the party to be served, and that service shall be deemed to be made on the day of transmission if transmitted before 4 p.m. on a working day, but otherwise on the next following working day (ii) when the addressee is a member of a document exchange (as to which the inclusion of a reference thereto in the solicitors' letterhead shall be conclusive evidence) delivered to that or any other affiliated exchange, and that service shall be deemed to have been made on the first working day after that on which the document would, in the ordinary course, be available for collection by the addressee.
(2) Sub-condition (1) applies to the delivery of documents as it applies to the service of notices.

3 MATTERS AFFECTING THE PROPERTY
(1) In this condition—
(a) "competent authority" means a local authority or other body exercising powers under statute or Royal Charter
(b) "requirement" includes (whether or not subject to confirmation) any notice, order or proposal
(c) "relevant matter" means any matter specified in sub-condition (2) whenever arising.

(2) The property is sold subject to—
(a) all matters registrable by any competent authority pursuant to statute
(b) all requirements of any competent authority
(c) all matters disclosed or reasonably to be expected to be disclosed by searches and as a result of enquiries formal or informal, and whether made in person, by writing or orally by or for the purchaser or which a prudent purchaser ought to make
(d) all notices served by or on behalf of a reversioner, a tenant or sub-tenant, or the owner or occupier of any adjoining or neighbouring property.
(3) (a) Notwithstanding sub-condition (2), the vendor warrants that he has informed the purchaser of the contents of any written communication received by, or known to, the vendor on or before the working day preceding the date of the contract relating to any relevant matter. Failure to give such information before the contract is made shall be deemed to be an omission in a statement in the course of the negotiations leading to the contract, but shall give rise to no right to compensation to the extent that the purchaser has a claim for damages against a competent authority
(b) In the event of any conflict or variation between information in fact received from any competent authority relating to any relevant matter and any statement made by the vendor in respect of the same matter, the purchaser shall rely on the information received from the competent authority to the exclusion of that given by the vendor
(c) The vendor shall forthwith inform the purchaser of the contents of any written communication received by him after the working day preceding the date of the contract and before the day of actual completion which if received on or before the former day would have fallen within paragraph (a).
(4) The purchaser (subject to any right or remedy arising from sub-condition (3)) will indemnify the vendor in respect of any liability under any requirement of a competent authority (whether made before or after the date of the contract), including the reasonable cost to the vendor of compliance after reasonable notice to the purchaser of the vendor's intention to comply, such sum to be payable on demand. The provision of this sub-condition shall prevail in the event of conflict with any other condition.

4 OPPORTUNITY TO RESCIND
(1) This condition only applies if a special condition so provides.
(2) Within such period as is specified in a special condition or, if none is so specified, within twenty working days from the date of the contract (as to which, in either case, time shall be of the essence), the purchaser shall be entitled notwithstanding condition 3(2), to rescind this contract by service of notice on the vendor specifying a matter to which this condition applies affecting the property.
(3) This condition applies to any of the following matters of which the purchaser had no knowledge on or before the working day preceding the date of the contract—
(a) a financial charge which the vendor cannot, or has not at the purchaser's written request agreed to discharge on or before actual completion
(b) a statutory provision prohibiting, restricting or imposing adverse conditions upon the use or the continued use of the property for such purpose as is specified in a special condition, or, if none is so specified, the purpose for which the vendor used it immediately before the date of the contract
(c) a matter which is likely materially to reduce the price which a willing purchaser could otherwise reasonably be expected to pay for the vendor's interest in the property in the open market at the date of the contract.
(4) For the purposes of this condition, the purchaser's knowledge—
(a) includes everything in writing received in the course of the transaction leading to the contract by a person acting on his behalf from the vendor, a person acting on the vendor's behalf, or a competent authority (as defined in condition 3(1)(a))
(b) does not include anything solely because a statute deems that registration of a matter constitutes actual notice of it.

5 EASEMENTS, RESERVATIONS, RIGHTS AND LIABILITIES
(1) The vendor warrants that he has disclosed to the purchaser the existence of all easements, rights, privileges and liabilities affecting the property, of which the vendor knows or ought to know, other than the existence of those known to the purchaser at the date of the contract or which a prudent purchaser would have discovered by that date.
(2) Without prejudice to the generality of sub-condition (1)—
(a) the purchaser shall purchase with full notice of the actual state and condition of the property and shall take it as it stands, save where it is to be constructed or converted by the vendor
(b) the property is sold, and will if the vendor so requires be conveyed, subject to all rights of way, water, light, drainage and other easements, rights, privileges and liabilities affecting the same
(3) (a) In this sub-condition "the retained land" means land retained by the vendor—
(i) adjoining the property, or
(ii) near to the property and designated as retained land in a special condition.

(b) The conveyance of the property shall contain such reservations in favour of the retained land and the grant of such rights over the retained land as would have been implied had the vendor conveyed both the property and the retained land by simultaneous conveyances to different purchasers.

6 TENANCIES

(1) This condition applies if the property is sold subject to any lease or tenancy and shall have effect notwithstanding any partial, incomplete or inaccurate reference to any lease or tenancy in the special conditions or the particulars of the property.

(2) Copies or full particulars of all leases or tenancies not vested in the purchaser having been furnished to him, he shall be deemed to purchase with full knowledge thereof and shall take the property subject to the rights of the tenants thereunder or by reason thereof. The purchaser shall indemnify the vendor against all claims, demands and liability in respect of such rights, notwithstanding that they may be void against a purchaser for want of registration.

(3) The vendor gives no warranty as to the amount of rent lawfully recoverable from any tenant, as to the effect of any legislation in relation to any lease or tenancy or as to the compliance with any legislation affecting the same.

(4) The vendor shall inform the purchaser of any change in the disclosed terms and conditions of any lease or tenancy.

(5) If a lease or tenancy subject to which the property is sold terminates for any reason, the vendor shall inform the purchaser and, on being indemnified by the purchaser against all consequential loss, expenditure or liability, shall act as the purchaser directs.

7 ERRORS, OMISSIONS AND MISSTATEMENTS

(1) No error, omission or misstatement herein or in any plan furnished or any statement made in the course of the negotiations leading to the contract shall annul the sale or entitle the purchaser to be discharged from the purchase.

(2) Any such error, omission or misstatement shown to be material shall entitle the purchaser or the vendor, as the case may be, to proper compensation, provided that the purchaser shall not in any event be entitled to compensation for matters falling within conditions 5 (2) or 6 (3).

(3) No immaterial error, omission or misstatement (including a mistake in any plan furnished for identification only) shall entitle either party to compensation.

(4) Sub-condition (1) shall not apply where compensation for any error, omission or misstatement shown to be material cannot be assessed nor enable either party to compel the other to accept or convey property differing substantially (in quantity, quality tenure or otherwise) from the property agreed to be sold if the other party would be prejudiced by the difference.

(5) The purchaser acknowledges that in making the contract he has not relied on any statement made to him save one made or confirmed in writing.

8 LEASEHOLDS

(1) This condition applies if the property is leasehold.

(2) In all cases the immediate title to the property shall begin with the lease. Where the lease, unless registered with absolute title, is dated not more than fifteen years before the date of the contract and was granted for a term exceeding twenty-one years, the freehold title and all other titles superior to the lease shall be deduced for a period beginning not less than fifteen years prior to the date of the contract and ending on the date of the lease.

(3) A copy of the lease and a copy of, sufficient extract from, or abstract of, all superior leases the contents of which are known to the vendor having been supplied or made available to the purchaser, he shall be deemed to purchase with full notice of the contents thereof, whether or not he has inspected the same.

(4) Where any consent to assign is necessary—

(a) the vendor shall forthwith at his own cost apply for and use his best endeavours to obtain such consent

(b) the purchaser shall forthwith supply such information and references as may reasonably be required by the reversioner before granting such consent

(c) if any such consent is not granted at least five working days before contractual completion date, or is subject to any condition to which the purchaser reasonably objects, either party may rescind the contract by notice to the other.

(5) Any statutory implied covenant on the part of the vendor shall not extend to any breach of the terms of the lease as to the state and condition of the property and the assignment shall so provide. This sub-condition applies notwithstanding that a special condition provides for the vendor to convey as beneficial owner.

(6) Where the property is sold subject to an apportioned rent specified as such in a special condition, the purchaser shall not require the consent of the reversioner to be obtained, or the rent to be otherwise legally apportioned.

(7) The purchaser shall assume that any receipt for the last payment due for rent under the lease before actual completion was given by the person then entitled to such rent or his duly authorised agent.

9 DEPOSIT

(1) The purchaser shall on or before the date of the contract pay by way of deposit to the vendor's solicitors as stakeholders the normal deposit, or such lesser sum as the vendor shall have agreed in writing. On a sale by private treaty, payment shall be made by banker's draft or by cheque drawn on a solicitors' bank account.

(2) Upon service by the vendor of a completion notice, the purchaser shall pay to the vendor any difference between the normal deposit and any amount actually paid (if less).

(3) If any draft, cheque or other instrument tendered in or towards payment of any sum payable under this condition is dishonoured when first presented the vendor shall have the right by notice to the purchaser within seven working days thereafter to treat the contract as repudiated.

10 OPTIONAL METHODS OF EXCHANGE

(1) Exchange of contracts may be effected by a method authorised by condition 2 for the service of notices. If so effected, the contract shall be made when the last part is, as the case may be, posted or delivered to a document exchange.

(2) Where contracts have not been exchanged, the parties' solicitors may agree by telephone or telex that the contract be immediately effective and thereupon the solicitors holding a part of the contract signed by their client shall hold it irrevocably to the order of the other party.

11 INSURANCE

(1) If the property is destroyed or damaged prior to actual completion and the proceeds of any insurance policy effected by or for the purchaser are reduced by reason of the existence of any policy effected by or for the vendor, the purchase price shall be abated by the amount of such reduction.

(2) Sub-condition (1) shall not apply where the proceeds of the vendor's policy are applied towards the reinstatement of the property pursuant to any statutory or contractual obligation.

(3) This condition takes effect in substitution for section 47 of the Law of Property Act 1925.

(4) The vendor shall be under no duty to the purchaser to maintain any insurance on the property, save where the property is leasehold and the vendor has an obligation to insure.

12 ABSTRACT OF TITLE

(1) Forthwith upon exchange of contracts the vendor shall deliver to the purchaser—

(a) where the title is not registered, an abstract of the title to the property or an epitome of the title together with photocopies of the relevant documents;

(b) where the title is registered—

(i) the documents, particulars and information specified in sub-sections (1) and (2) of section 110 of the Land Registration Act 1925, save that copies of the entries on the register, the filed plan and any documents noted on the register and filed in the registry shall be office copies, and

(ii) such additional authorities to inspect the register as the purchaser shall reasonably require for any sub-purchaser or prospective mortgagee or lessee.

(2) Where the title is not registered, the vendor shall at his own expense produce the relevant documents of title or an abstract, epitome of title or copy thereof (bearing in each case original markings of examination of all relevant documents of title or of examined abstracts thereof).

(3) Where before the date of the contract any abstract, epitome or document has been delivered to the purchaser, he shall not, save as provided by conditions 6 (2) or 8 (3) be deemed to have had notice before the date of the contract of any matter of title thereby disclosed.

13 IDENTITY AND BOUNDARIES

(1) The vendor shall produce such evidence as may be reasonably necessary to establish the identity and extent of the property, but shall not be required to define exact boundaries, or the ownership of fences, ditches, hedges or walls, nor, beyond the evidence afforded by the information in his possession, separately to identify parts of the property held under different titles.

(2) If reasonably required by the purchaser because of the insufficiency of the evidence produced under sub-condition (1), the vendor shall at his own expense provide and hand over on completion a statutory declaration as to the relevant facts, in a form agreed by the purchaser, such agreement not to be unreasonably withheld.

14 MORTGAGES IN FAVOUR OF FRIENDLY AND OTHER SOCIETIES

Where the title includes a mortgage or legal charge in favour of trustees on behalf of a friendly society, a building society or a society registered under the Industrial and Provident Societies Acts, the purchaser shall assume that any receipt given on the discharge of any such mortgage or legal charge and apparently duly executed was in fact duly executed by all proper persons and is valid.

15 REQUISITIONS
(1) In this condition "abstract" means all of the documents particulars and information required to be delivered by the vendor under condition 12.
(2) Subject to sub-condition (4), the purchaser shall deliver any requisitions or objections relating to the title, evidence of title or the abstract, in writing within six working days of receipt of the abstract (or, in the case of an abstract delivered before the date of the contract, within six working days of the date of contract). Within four working days of such delivery the vendor shall deliver his replies in writing.
(3) The purchaser shall deliver any observations on any of the vendor's replies in writing within four working days of their receipt.
(4) Where some but not all parts of the abstract have been delivered, and defects in title are not disclosed by such parts of the abstract as have been delivered, then in respect only of the undelivered parts or undisclosed defects (as the case may be) the abstract shall be deemed to be received for the purpose of sub-condition (2) at the time or respective times when any previously undelivered part is delivered.
(5) Time shall be of the essence of the contract for the purposes of this condition.

16 RESCISSION
(1) If the vendor is unable, or on some reasonable ground unwilling, to satisfy any requisition or objection made by the purchaser, the vendor may give the purchaser notice (specifying the reason for his inability or the ground of his unwillingness) to withdraw the same. If the purchaser does not withdraw the same within seven working days of service, either party may thereafter, notwithstanding any intermediate negotiation or litigation, rescind the contract by notice to the other.
(2) Upon rescission under any power given by these conditions or any special condition—
(a) the vendor shall repay to the purchaser any sums paid by way of deposit or otherwise under the contract with interest on such sums at the contract rate from four working days after rescission until payment.
(b) the purchaser shall forthwith return all documents delivered to him by the vendor and at his own expense procure the cancellation of any entry relating to the contract in any register.

17 PREPARATION OF CONVEYANCE
(1) The purchaser shall deliver the draft conveyance at least twelve working days before contractual completion date, and within four working days of such delivery the vendor shall deliver it back approved or revised.
(2) The purchaser shall deliver the engrossment of the conveyance (first executed by him, where requisite) at least five working days before contractual completion date.
(3) The purchaser shall not, by delivering the draft conveyance or the engrossment, be deemed to accept the vendor's title or to waive any right to raise or maintain requisitions.
(4) Save to the extent that a covenant for indemnity will be implied by statute, the purchaser shall in the conveyance covenant to indemnify the vendor and his estate (and any estate of which the vendor is personal representative or trustee) against all actions, claims and liability for any breach of any covenant, stipulation, provision or other matter subject to which the property is sold and in respect of which the vendor or any such estate will remain liable after completion.
(5) The vendor shall give an acknowledgment for production and, unless in a fiduciary capacity, an undertaking for safe custody of documents of title retained by him. Where any such document is retained by a mortgagee, trustee or personal representative, the vendor shall procure that such person shall give an acknowledgment for production, and the vendor, unless in a fiduciary capacity, shall covenant that if and when he receives any such document he will, at the cost of the person requiring it, give an undertaking for safe custody.
(6) The vendor shall be entitled on reasonable grounds to decline to convey the property to any person other than the purchaser, by more than one conveyance, at more than the contract price or at a price divided between different parts of the property.

18 OCCUPATION BEFORE COMPLETION
(1) This condition applies if the vendor authorises the purchaser to occupy the property before actual completion, except—
(a) where the purchaser already lawfully occupies any part of the property, or
(b) where the property is a dwellinghouse and the authority for the occupation is only for the purpose of effecting works of decoration, repair or improvement agreed by the vendor,
(2) The purchaser occupies the property as licensee and not as tenant. The purchaser may not transfer his licence or authorise any other person save members of his immediate family to occupy any part of the property.
(3) The purchaser shall not, by taking such occupation, be deemed to accept the vendor's title or to waive any right to raise or maintain requisitions.
(4) While the purchaser is in occupation of the whole or any part of the property under this condition, he shall—
(a) pay and indemnify the vendor against all outgoings and any other expenses in respect

of the property and pay to the vendor in respect of such occupation a sum calculated at the contract rate on the amount of the purchase money (less any deposit paid)
(b) be entitled to receive any rents and profits from any part of the property not occupied by him
(c) insure the property in a sum not less than the purchase price against all risks in respect of which premises of the like nature are normally insured.
(5) The purchaser's licence to occupy the property shall end—
(a) on contractual completion date, or
(b) upon termination of the contract, or
(c) upon the expiry of five working days' notice given by either party to the other, and thereupon the purchaser shall give up occupation of the property and leave the same in as good repair as it was in when he went into occupation.
(6) If the purchaser, after his licence has ended under sub-condition 5(a), remains in occupation with the express or implied consent of the vendor, he shall thereafter occupy on the other terms of this condition and on the further term that the vendor's rights under condition 22 shall not thereby be affected.

19 APPORTIONMENTS

(1) In this condition—
(a) "the apportionment day" means—
(i) if the property is sold with vacant possession of the whole, the date of actual completion
(ii) in any other case, contractual completion date
(b) "payment period" means one of the periods for which a sum payable periodically is payable, whether or not such periods are of equal length.
(2) This condition shall not apply to any sum if—
(a) the purchaser cannot, by virtue only of becoming the owner of the property, either enforce payment of it or be obliged to pay it, or
(b) it is an outgoing paid in advance, unless the vendor cannot obtain repayment and the purchaser benefits therefrom or is given credit therefor against a sum that would otherwise be his liability.
(3) On completion the income and outgoings of the property shall, subject to sub-condition (2) and conditions 3 and 22(4) and to any adjustment required by condition 18(4), be apportioned as at the apportionment day.
(4) For the purposes of apportionment only, it shall be assumed—
(a) that the vendor remains owner of the property until the end of the apportionment day, and
(b) that the sum to be apportioned—
(i) accrues from day to day
(ii) is payable throughout the relevant period at the same rate as on the apportionment day.
(5) Sums payable periodically shall be apportioned by charging or allowing—
(a) for any payment period entirely attributable to one party, the whole of the instalment payable therefor
(b) for any part of a payment period, a proportion on an annual basis.
(6) (a) This sub-condition applies to any sum payable in respect of any period falling wholly or partly prior to the apportionment day, the amount of which is not notified to either party before actual completion
(b) A provisional apportionment shall be made on the best estimate available. Upon the amount being notified, a final apportionment shall be made and one party shall thereupon make to the other the appropriate balancing payment.

20 ENDORSEMENT OF MEMORANDUM

Where the vendor does not hand over all the documents of his title, he shall at completion endorse a memorandum of the sale to the purchaser on the last such document in each relevant title and thereupon produce the endorsed documents for inspection.

21 COMPLETION

(1) Contractual completion date shall be as stated in the special conditions but if not so stated shall be the twenty-fifth working day after the date of the contract. Completion shall take place in England or Wales either at the office of the vendor's solicitors or, if required by the vendor at least five working days prior to actual completion, at the office of the vendor's mortgagee or his solicitors.
(2) The vendor shall not be obliged to accept payment of the money due on completion other than by one or more of the following methods—
(a) legal tender
(b) a banker's draft drawn by and upon a settlement bank for the purposes of the Clearing House Automated Payments System or any other bank specified in a general condition
(c) an unconditional authority to release any deposit held by a stakeholder
(d) otherwise as the vendor shall have agreed before actual completion.
(3) If completion is effected otherwise than by personal attendance the time for completion is when on a working day

(a) the money due on completion is paid to the vendor or his solicitors, and
(b) the vendor's solicitors hold to the order of the purchaser all the documents to which he is entitled on completion.
(4) For the purposes of this condition money is paid when the vendor receives payment by a method specified in sub-condition (2). Where the parties have agreed upon a direct credit to a bank account at a named branch, payment is made when that branch receives the credit.
(5) (a) This sub-condition applies if the money due on completion is not paid by 2.30 p.m. on the day of actual completion or by such other time on that day as is specified in a special condition
(b) For the purposes of condition 22 only, completion shall be deemed to be postponed by reason of the purchaser's delay from the day of actual completion until the next working day
(c) The purchaser shall not as a result of the deemed postponement of completion be liable to make any payment to the vendor unless the vendor claims such payment by giving notice at completion or within five working days thereafter (as to which period time shall be of the essence). Payment shall be due five working days after receipt of such notice.

22 COMPENSATION FOR LATE COMPLETION
(1) For the purposes of this condition—
(a) "delay" means failure to perform or lateness in performing any obligation of the contract which causes or contributes to lateness in completion
(b) a party is "in default" if and to the extent that the period, or the aggregate of the periods, of his delay exceeds the period, or the aggregate of the periods, of delay of the other party
(c) "the period of default" means the length of the excess defined in paragraph (b) or, if shorter, the period from contractual completion date to the date of actual completion.
(2) If the sale shall be completed after contractual completion date, the party in default (if any) shall be liable to compensate the other for loss occasioned to him by reason of that default.
(3) Before actual completion, or within five working days thereafter (as to which period time shall be of the essence), the party entitled to compensation may, by notice to the other party, opt to be paid or allowed a sum calculated at the contract rate on the amount of the purchase money (less any deposit paid) for the period of default as liquidated damages in settlement of his claim for compensation.
(4) If the vendor is entitled to compensation, he may, before actual completion, by notice to the purchaser, opt to take the net income of the property for the period of default in lieu of such compensation.
(5) The right to recover any compensation under this condition shall not be prejudiced by completion of the sale, whether before or after the commencement of proceedings.

23 COMPLETION NOTICE
(1) This condition applies unless a special condition provides that time is of the essence in respect of contractual completion date.
(2) If the sale shall not be completed on contractual completion date, either party, being then himself ready able and willing to complete, may after that date serve on the other party notice to complete the transaction in accordance with this condition. A party shall be deemed to be ready, able and willing to complete—
(a) if he could be so but for some default or omission of the other party
(b) notwithstanding that any mortgage on the property is unredeemed when the completion notice is served if the aggregate of all sums necessary to redeem all such mortgages (to the extent that they relate to the property) does not exceed the sum payable on completion.
(3) Upon service of a completion notice it shall become a term of the contract that the transaction shall be completed within fifteen working days of service and in respect of such period time shall be of the essence.
(4) If the purchaser does not comply with a completion notice—
(a) the purchaser shall forthwith return all documents delivered to him by the vendor and at his own expense procure the cancellation of any entry relating to the contract in any register
(b) without prejudice to any other rights or remedies available to him, the vendor may—
  (i) forfeit and retain any deposit paid and/or
  (ii) re-sell the property by auction, tender or private treaty.
(5) If on any such re-sale contracted within one year after contractual completion date the vendor incurs a loss and so elects by notice to the purchaser within one month after the contract for such re-sale, the purchaser shall pay to the vendor liquidated damages. The amount payable shall be the aggregate of such loss, all costs and expenses reasonably incurred in any such re-sale and any attempted re-sale and interest at the contract rate on such part of the purchase money as is from time to time outstanding (giving credit for all sums received under any re-sale contract on account of the re-sale price) after contractual completion date.
(6) If the vendor does not comply with a completion notice, the purchaser, without prejudice to any other rights or remedies available to him, may give notice to the vendor forthwith to pay to the purchaser any sums paid by way of deposit or otherwise under the contract and

interest on such sums at the contract rate from four working days after service of the notice until payment. On compliance with such notice the purchaser shall not be entitled to specific performance of the contract, but shall forthwith return all documents delivered to him by the vendor and at the expense of the vendor produre the cancellation of any entry relating to the contract in any register.

(7) Where after service of a completion notice the time for completion shall have been extended by agreement or implication, either party may again invoke the provisions of this condition which shall then take effect with the substitution of "seven working days" for "fifteen working days" in sub-condition (3).

24 CHATTELS

The property in any chattels agreed to be sold shall pass to the purchaser on actual completion.

25 AUCTIONS

(1) This condition applies if the property is sold by auction.

(2) The sale is subject to a reserve price for the property and, when the property is sold in lots, for each lot.

(3) The vendor reserves the right—

(a) to divide the property into lots and to sub-divide, re-arrange or consolidate any lots

(b) to bid personally or by his agent up to any reserve price

(c) without disclosing any reserve price, to withdraw from the sale any property or lot at any time before it has been sold, whether or not the sale has begun.

(4) The auctioneer may—

(a) refuse to accept a bid

(b) in the case of a dispute as to any bid, forthwith determine the dispute or again put up the property or lot at the last undisputed bid.

(5) The purchaser shall forthwith complete and sign the contract and pay, but not necessarily by the means specified in condition 9(1), the normal deposit.

The National Conditions of Sale

THESE CONDITIONS ARE COPYRIGHT AND MAY NOT BE REPRODUCED

20th Edition
first published
December 1981

Construction of the conditions

In these conditions, where the context admits—

(1) The "vendor" and the "purchaser" include the persons deriving title under them respectively.

(2) "Purchase money" includes any sum to be paid for chattels, fittings or other separate items.

(3) References to the "Special Conditions" include references to the particulars of sale and to the provisions of the contract which is made by reference to the conditions.

(4) The "prescribed rate" means the agreed rate of interest or, if none, then the rate of interest prescribed from time to time under Land Compensation Act 1961, s. 32.

(5) "Solicitor" includes a barrister who is employed by a corporate body to carry out conveyancing on its behalf and is acting in the course of his employment.

(6) "Working day" means a day on which clearing banks in the City of London are (or would be but for a strike, lock-out, or other stoppage, affecting particular banks or banks generally) open during banking hours Except in condition 19(4), in which "working day" means a day when the Land Registry is open to the public.

(7) "Designated bank" means a bank designated by the Chief Registrar under Building Societies Act 1962, s. 59.

(8) The "Planning Acts" means the enactments from time to time in force relating to town and country planning.

(9) On a sale by private treaty references to the "auctioneer" shall be read as references to the vendor's agent.

(10) On a sale in lots, the conditions apply to each lot.

(11) "Abstract of title" means in relation to registered land such documents as the vendor is required by Land Registration Act 1925, s. 110, to furnish.

The conditions

1. The Sale: by Auction: by Private Treaty

(1) Paragraphs (2) to (5) of this condition apply on a sale by auction and paragraphs (6) and (7) on a sale by private treaty.

(2) Unless otherwise provided in the Special Conditions, the sale of the property and of each lot is subject to a reserve price and to a right for the vendor or any one person on behalf of the vendor to bid up to that price.

(3) The auctioneer may refuse any bid and no person shall at any bid advance less than the amount fixed for that purpose by the auctioneer.

(4) If any dispute arises respecting a bid, the auctioneer may determine the dispute or the property may, at the vendor's option, either be put up again at the last undisputed bid, or be withdrawn.

(5) Subject to the foregoing provisions of this condition, the highest bidder shall be the purchaser and shall forthwith complete and sign the contract, the date of which shall be the date of the auction.

(6) Where there is a draft contract, or an arrangement subject to contract, or a negotiation in which there are one or more outstanding items or suspensory matters (which prevent there being yet a concluded agreement of a contractual nature), a solicitor, who holds a document signed by his client in the form of a contract of sale in writing and embodying this condition, shall (unless the other party or his solicitor is informed to the contrary) have the authority of his client to conclude, by formal exchange of contracts, or by post, or by telex or other telegraphic means, or by telephone, and in any case with or without involving solicitors' undertakings, a binding contract in the terms of the document which his client has signed.

(7) The date of the contract shall be—

(i) the date, if any, which is agreed and put on the contract, but if none, then

(ii) on an exchange of contracts by post (unless the parties' solicitors otherwise agree), the date on which the last part of the contract is posted, or

(iii) in any other case, the date on which, consistently with this condition, a binding contract is concluded.

2. Deposit
(1) Unless the Special Conditions otherwise provide, the purchaser shall on the date of the contract pay a deposit of 10 per cent of the purchase price, on a sale by auction, to the auctioneer, or on a sale by private treaty, to the vendor's solicitor and, in either case, as stakeholder.
(2) In case a cheque taken for the deposit (having been presented, and whether or not it has been re-presented) has not been honoured, then and on that account the vendor may elect—
either   (i) to treat the contract as discharged by breach thereof on the purchaser's part
or   (ii) to enforce payment of the deposit as a deposit, by suing on the cheque or otherwise.

3. Purchaser's short right to rescind
(1) This condition shall have effect if the Special Conditions so provide, but not otherwise.
(2) If the property is affected by any matter to which this condition applies, then the purchaser may by notice in writing (hereinafter referred to as a "Condition 3 Notice") given to the vendor or his solicitor and expressly referring to this condition and the matter in question, and notwithstanding any intermediate negotiation, rescind the contract on the same terms as if the purchaser had persisted in an objection to the title which the vendor was unable to remove.
(3) A Condition 3 Notice shall not be given after the expiration of 16 working days from the date of the contract, time being of the essence of this condition.
(4) This condition applies to any matter materially affecting the value of the property, other than—
    (i) a matter which was not yet in existence or subsisting at the date of the contract
    (ii) a specific matter to which the sale was expressly made subject, or
    (iii) a matter of which the purchaser had at the date of the contract express notice or actual knowledge, not being notice or knowledge imputed to the purchaser by statute solely by reason of a registration of such matter, or notice or knowledge which the purchaser is only deemed to have had by the conditions.
(5) This condition and condition 15 are additional to each other.

4. Chattels, etc., and separate items
If the sale includes chattels, fittings or other separate items, the vendor warrants that he is entitled to sell the same free from any charge, lien, burden, or adverse claim.

5. Date and manner of completion
(1) The completion date shall be the date specified for the purpose in the contract or, if none, the 26th working day after the date of the contract or the date of delivery of the abstract of title, whichever be the later.
(2) Unless the Special Conditions otherwise provide, in respect of the completion date time shall not be of the essence of the contract, but this provision shall operate subject and without prejudice to—
    (i) the provisions of condition 22 and
    (ii) the rights of either party to recover from the other damages for delay in fulfilling his obligations under the contract.
(3) The purchaser's obligations to pay money due on completion shall be discharged by one or more of the following methods—
    (i) authorisation in writing to release a deposit held for the purposes of the contract by a stakeholder
    (ii) banker's draft issued by a designated bank
    (iii) cheque drawn on and guaranteed by a designated bank
    (iv) telegraphic or other direct transfer (as requested or agreed to by the vendor's solicitor) to a particular bank or branch for the credit of a specified account
    (v) legal tender
    (vi) any other method requested or agreed to by the vendor's solicitor
(4) Completion shall be carried out, either formally at such office or place as the vendor's solicitor shall reasonably require, or (if the parties' solicitors so arrange) by post, or by means of solicitors' undertakings concerning the holding of documents or otherwise Provided that on a sale with vacant possession of the whole or part of the property, if the conveyance or transfer will not, by overrreaching or otherwise, discharge the property from interests (if any) of persons in, or who may be in, actual occupation of the property or such part of it, then (subject always to the rights of the purchaser under Law of Property Act 1925, s. 42 (1)), the purchaser may, by giving reasonable notice, require that on, or immediately before the time of, completion possession of the property or part be handed over to the purchaser or his representative at the property.
(5) The date of actual completion shall be the day on which, the contract being completed in other respects, the purchaser has discharged consistently with the provisions of this condition the obligations of the purchaser to pay the money due on completion Provided that—

(i) for the purposes only of conditions 6, 7 and 8, if but for this proviso the date of actual completion would be the last working day of a week (starting on Sunday) and the purchaser is unable or unwilling to complete before 2.15 p.m. on that day, then the date of actual completion shall be taken to be the first working day thereafter

(ii) a remittance sent by post or delivered by hand shall be treated as being made on the day on which it reaches the vendor's solicitor's office, unless that day is not a working day in which case the remittance shall be treated as being made on the first working day thereafter.

6. Rents, outgoings and apportionments

The purchase being completed (whether on the completion date or subsequently), the income and outgoings shall be apportioned as follows (the day itself in each case being apportioned to the vendor):—

(1) In a case to which proviso (i) to condition 7 (1) applies apportionment shall be made as at the date of actual completion.

(2) In a case in which the purchaser is in possession of the whole of the property as lessee or tenant at a rent apportionment shall be made as at the date of actual completion unless proviso (ii) to condition 7 (1) applies, when apportionment shall be made as at the date of the purchaser's notice under that proviso.

(3) In any other case apportionment shall be made as from the completion date Provided nevertheless that, if delay is attributable to the vendor's failure to obtain the reversioner's licence, where necessary, or if the vendor remains in beneficial occupation of the property after the completion date, the purchaser may by notice in writing before actual completion elect that apportionment shall be made as at the date of actual completion.

(4) Rates shall be apportioned according to the period for which they are intended to provide and rents (whether payable in advance or in arrear) according to the period in respect of which they have been paid or are payable; and apportionment of yearly items (whether or not the same are payable by equal quarterly, monthly or other instalments) shall be according to the relevant number of days relatively to the number of days in the full year.

(5) Service charges under leases, in the absence of known or readily ascertainable amounts, shall be apportioned according to the best estimate available at the time of completion and, unless otherwise agreed, the vendor and the purchaser shall be and remain mutually bound after completion to account for and pay or allow to each other, within 15 working days after being informed of the actual amounts as ascertained, any balances or excesses due.

7. Interest

(1) If the purchase shall not be completed on the completion date then (subject to the provisions of paragraph (2) of this condition) the purchaser shall pay interest on the remainder of his purchase money at the prescribed rate from that date until the purchase shall actually be completed Provided nevertheless—

(i) That (without prejudice to the operation of proviso (ii) to this paragraph) the vendor may by notice in writing before actual completion elect to take the income of the property (less outgoings) up to the date of actual completion instead of interest as aforesaid

(ii) That, if the delay arises from any cause other than the neglect or default of the purchaser, and if the purchaser (not being in occupation of the property in circumstances to which condition 8 applies) places the remainder of his purchase money (at his own risk) at interest on a deposit account in England or Wales with any designated bank, and gives written notice thereof to the vendor or his solicitor, then in lieu of the interest or income payable to or receivable by the vendor as aforesaid, the vendor shall from the time of such notice be entitled to such interest only as is produced by such deposit

(iii) That the vendor shall in no case be or become entitled in respect of the same period of time both to be paid interest and to enjoy income of the property, or to be paid interest more than once on the same sum of money.

(2) The purchaser shall not be liable to pay interest under paragraph (1) of this condition—

(i) so long as, or to the extent that, delay in completion is attributable to any act or default of the vendor or his mortgagee or Settled Land Act trustees

(ii) in case the property is to be constructed or converted by the vendor, so long as the construction or conversion is unfinished.

8. Occupation pending completion

(1) If the purchaser (not being already in occupation as lessee or tenant at a rent) is let into occupation of the property before the actual completion of the purchase, then, as from the date of his going into occupation and until actual completion, or until upon discharge or rescission of the contract he ceases to occupy the property, the purchaser shall—

(i) be the licensee and not the tenant of the vendor

(ii) pay interest on the remainder of the purchase money at the prescribed rate

(iii) keep the property in as good repair and condition as it was in when he went into occupation

(iv) pay, or otherwise indemnify the vendor against, all outgoings and expenses (including the cost of insurance) in respect of the property, the purchaser at the same time taking or being credited with the income of the property (if any)

    (v) not carry out any development within the meaning of the Planning Acts.

(2) Upon discharge or rescission of the contract, or upon the expiration of 7 working days' or longer notice given by the vendor or his solicitor to the purchaser or his solicitor in that behalf, the purchaser shall forthwith give up the property in such repair and condition as aforesaid.

(3) A purchaser going into occupation before completion shall not be deemed thereby to have accepted the vendor's title.

(4) Where the purchaser is allowed access to the property for the purpose only of carrying out works or installations, the purchaser shall not be treated as being let into occupation within the meaning of this condition.

9. Abstract, requisitions and observations

(1) The vendor shall deliver the abstract of title not later than 11 working days after the date of the contract but, subject and without prejudice as mentioned in condition 5 (2), that time limit shall not be of the essence of the contract.

(2) Subject always to the rights of the purchaser under Law of Property Act 1925, s. 42 (1), the vendor may be required by the purchaser to deal with requisitions and observations concerning persons who are or may be in occupation or actual occupation of the property, so as to satisfy the purchaser that the title is not, and that the purchaser will not be, prejudicially affected by any interests or claims of such persons.

(3) The purchaser shall deliver in writing his requisitions within 11 working days after delivery of the abstract, and his observations on the replies to the requisitions within 6 working days after delivery of the replies.

(4) In respect of the delivery of requisitions and observations, time shall be of the essence of the contract, notwithstanding that the abstract may not have been delivered within due time.

(5) The purchaser shall deliver his requisitions and observations on the abstract as delivered, whether it is a perfect or an imperfect abstract, but for the purposes of any requisitions or observations which could not be raised or made on the information contained in an imperfect abstract, time under paragraph (3) of this condition shall not start to run against the purchaser, until the vendor has delivered the further abstract or information on which the requisitions or observations arise.

(6) Subject to his requisitions and observations, the purchaser shall be deemed to have accepted the title.

10. Vendor's right to rescind

(1) If the purchaser shall persist in any objection to the title which the vendor shall be unable or unwilling, on reasonable grounds, to remove, and shall not withdraw the same within 10 working days of being required so to do, the vendor may, subject to the purchaser's rights under Law of Property Act 1925, ss. 42 and 125, by notice in writing to the purchaser or his solicitor, and notwithstanding any intermediate negotiation or litigation, rescind the contract

(2) Upon such rescission the vendor shall return the deposit, but without interest, costs of investigating title or other compensation or payment, and the purchaser shall return the abstract and other papers furnished to him.

11. Existing leaseholds

(1) Where the interest sold is leasehold for the residue of an existing term the following provisions of this condition shall apply.

(2) The lease or underlease or a copy thereof having been made available, the purchaser (whether he has inspected the same or not) shall be deemed to have bought with full notice of the contents thereof.

(3) On production of a receipt for the last payment due for rent under the lease or underlease, the purchaser shall assume without proof that the person giving the receipt, though not the original lessor, is the reversioner expectant on the said lease or underlease or his duly authorised agent.

(4) No objection shall be taken on account of the covenants in an underlease not corresponding with the covenants in any superior lease.

(5) The sale is subject to the reversioner's licence being obtained, where necessary. The purchaser supplying such information and references, if any, as may reasonably be required of him, the vendor will use his best endeavours to obtain such licence and will pay the fee for the same. But if the licence cannot be obtained, the vendor may rescind the contract on the same terms as if the purchaser had persisted in an objection to the title which the vendor was unable to remove.

(6) Where the property comprises part only of the property comprised in a lease or underlease, the rent, covenants and conditions shall, if the purchaser so requires, be legally apportioned at his expense, but completion shall not be delayed on that account and in the meantime the apportionment by the auctioneer shall be accepted, or the property may at the option of the vendor be sub-demised for the residue of the term, less one day, at a rent apportioned by the auctioneer and subject to the purchaser executing a counterpart

containing covenants and provisions corresponding to those contained in the lease or underlease aforesaid.

(7) Any statutory covenant to be implied in the conveyance on the part of a vendor shall be so limited as not to affect him with liability for a subsisting breach of any covenant or condition concerning the state or condition of the property, of which state and condition the purchaser is by paragraph (3) of condition 13 deemed to have full notice, and where Land Registration Act 1925, s. 24, applies the purchaser, if required, will join in requesting that an appropriate entry be made in the register.

12. Vendor's duty to produce documents

(1) If an abstracted document refers to any plan material to the description of the property, or to any covenants contained in a document earlier in date than the document with which the title commences, and such plan or earlier document is in the possession or power of the vendor or his trustees or mortgagee, the vendor shall supply a copy thereof with the abstract.

(2) If the property is sold subject to restrictive covenants, the deed imposing those covenants or a copy thereof having been made available, the purchaser (whether he has inspected the same or not) shall be deemed to have purchased with full knowledge thereof.

(3) The vendor shall not be required to procure the production of any document not in his possession or not in the possession of his mortgagee or trustees, and of which the vendor cannot obtain production, or to trace or state who had the possession of the same.

13. Identity: boundaries: condition of property

(1) The purchaser shall admit the identity of the property with that comprised in the muniments offered by the vendor as the title thereto upon the evidence afforded by the descriptions contained in such muniments, and of a statutory declaration, to be made (if required) at the purchaser's expense, that the property has been enjoyed according to the title for at least twelve years.

(2) The vendor shall not be bound to show any title to boundaries, fences, ditches, hedges or walls, or to distinguish parts of the property held under different titles further than he may be able to do from information in his possession.

(3) The purchaser shall be deemed to buy with full notice in all respects of the actual state and condition of the property and, save where it is to be constructed or converted by the vendor, shall take the property as it is.

14. Property sold subject to easements, etc.

Without prejudice to the duty of the vendor to disclose all latent easements and latent liabilities known to the vendor to affect the property, the property is sold subject to any rights of way and water, rights of common, and other rights, easements, quasi-easements, liabilities and public rights affecting the same.

15. Town and Country Planning

(1) In this condition, where the context admits, references to "authorised use" are references to "established use", or to use for which permission has been granted under the Planning Acts, or to use for which permission is not required under those Acts, as the case may be.

(2) The purchaser shall be entitled to deliver, with his requisitions in respect of the title, requisitions concerning the authorised use of the property for the purposes of the Planning Acts. The vendor in reply shall give all such relevant information as may be in his possession or power.

(3) Where the property is in the Special Conditions expressed to be sold on the footing of an authorised use which is specified, then if it appears before actual completion of the purchase that the specified use is not an authorised use of the property for the purposes of the Planning Acts, the purchaser may by notice in writing rescind the contract, and thereupon paragraph (2) of condition 10 shall apply. But, subject to the foregoing provisions of this condition, the purchaser shall be deemed to have accepted that the specified use is an authorised use of the property for the purposes of the Planning Acts.

(4) Save as mentioned in the Special Conditions, the property is not to the knowledge of the vendor subject to any charge, notice, order, restriction, agreement or other matter arising under the Planning Acts, but (without prejudice to any right of the purchaser to rescind the contract under paragraph (3) of this condition) the property is sold subject to any such charges, notices, orders, restrictions, agreements and matters affecting the interest sold.

(5) Subject as hereinbefore provided, and without prejudice to the obligations of the vendor to supply information as aforesaid, the purchaser shall be deemed to buy with knowledge in all respects of the authorised use of the property for the purposes of the Planning Acts.

16. Requirements by local authority

(1) If after the date of the contract any requirement in respect of the property be made against the vendor by any local authority, the purchaser shall comply with the same at his own expense, and indemnify the vendor in respect thereof: in so far as the purchaser shall

fail to comply with such requirement, the vendor may comply with the same wholly or in part and any money so expended by the vendor shall be repaid by the purchaser on completion.

(2) The vendor shall upon receiving notice of any such requirement forthwith inform the purchaser thereof.

17. Errors, mis-statements or omissions

(1) Without prejudice to any express right of either party, or to any right of the purchaser in reliance on Law of Property Act 1969, s. 24, to rescind the contract before completion and subject to the provisions of paragraph (2) of this condition, no error, mis-statement or omission in any preliminary answer concerning the property, or in the sale plan or the Special Conditions, shall annul the sale, nor (save where the error, mis-statement or omission relates to a matter materially affecting the description or value of the property) shall any damages be payable, or compensation allowed by either party, in respect thereof

(2) Paragraph (1) of this condition shall not apply to any error, mis-statement or, omission which is recklessly or fraudulently made, or to any matter or thing by which the purchaser is prevented from getting substantially what he contracted to buy.

(3) In this condition a "preliminary answer" means and includes any statement made by or on behalf of the vendor to the purchaser or his agents or advisers, whether in answer to formal preliminary enquiries or otherwise, before the purchaser entered into the contract.

18. Leases and tenancies

(1) Abstracts or copies of the leases or agreements (if in writing) under which the tenants hold having been made available, the purchaser (whether he has inspected the same or not) shall be deemed to have notice of and shall take subject to the terms of all the existing tenancies and the rights of the tenants, whether arising during the continuance or after the expiration thereof, and such notice shall not be affected by any partial or incomplete statement in the Special Conditions with reference to the tenancies, and no objection shall be taken on account of there not being an agreement in writing with any tenant.

(2) Where a lease or tenancy affects the property sold and other property, the property sold will be conveyed with the benefit of the apportioned rent (if any) mentioned in the Special Conditions or (if not so mentioned) fixed by the auctioneer, and no objection shall be taken on the ground that the consent of the tenant has not been obtained to the apportionment and the purchaser shall not require the rent to be legally apportioned.

(3) The purchaser shall keep the vendor indemnified against all claims by the tenant for compensation or otherwise, except in respect of a tenancy which expires or is determined on or before the completion date or in respect of an obligation which ought to have been discharged before the date of the contract.

(4) Land in the occupation of the vendor is sold subject to the right (hereby reserved to him) to be paid a fair price for tillages, off-going and other allowances as if he were an outgoing tenant who had entered into occupation of the land after 1st March 1948, and as if the purchaser were the landlord, and in case of dispute such price shall be fixed by the valuation of a valuer, to be nominated in case the parties differ by the President of the Royal Institution of Chartered Surveyors.

19. Preparation of conveyance: priority notices: indemnities

(1) Where the interest sold is leasehold for a term of years to be granted by the vendor, the lease or underlease and counterpart shall be prepared by the vendor's solicitor in accordance (as nearly as the circumstances admit) with a form or draft annexed to the contract or otherwise sufficiently identified by the signatures of the parties or their solicitors.

(2) In any other case the conveyance shall be prepared by the purchaser or his solicitor and the following provisions of this condition shall apply.

(3) The draft conveyance shall be delivered at the office of the vendor's solicitor at least 6 working days before the completion date and the engrossment for execution by the vendor and other necessary parties (if any) shall be left at the said office within 3 working days after the draft has been returned to the purchaser approved on behalf of the vendor and other necessary parties (if any).

(4) Where the property is unregistered land not in an area of compulsory registration and the conveyance is to contain restrictive covenants, and the purchaser intends contemporaneously with the conveyance to execute a mortgage or conveyance to a third party, he shall inform the vendor of his intention and, if necessary, allow the vendor to give a priority notice for the registration of the intended covenants at least 15 working days before the contract is completed.

(5) Where the property is sold subject to legal incumbrances, the purchaser shall covenant to indemnify the vendor against actions and claims in respect of them; and the purchaser will not make any claim on account of increased expense caused by the concurrence of any legal incumbrancer.

(6) Where the property is sold subject to stipulations, or restrictive or other covenants, and breach thereof would expose the vendor to liability, the purchaser shall covenant to observe

and perform the same and to indemnify the vendor against actions and claims in respect thereof.

(7) Paragraphs (5) and (6) of this condition shall have effect without prejudice to the provisions of Law of Property Act 1925, s. 77, and Land Registration Act 1925, s. 24, where such provisions respectively are applicable, and in respect of matters covered by a covenant implied under either of those sections no express covenant shall be required.

20. Severance of properties formerly in common ownership

Where the property and any adjacent or neighbouring property have hitherto been in common ownership, the purchaser shall not become entitled to any right to light or air over or in respect of any adjacent or neighbouring property which is retained by the vendor and the conveyance shall, if the vendor so requires, reserve to him such easements and rights as would become appurtenant to such last-mentioned property by implication of law, if the vendor had sold it to another purchaser at the same time as he has sold the property to the purchaser.

21. Insurance

(1) With respect to any policy of insurance maintained by the vendor in respect of damage to or destruction of the property, the vendor shall not (save pursuant to an obligation to a third party) be bound to keep such insurance on foot or to give notice to the purchaser of any premium being or becoming due.

(2) The purchaser shall be entitled to inspect the policy at any time.

(3) The vendor shall, if required, by and at the expense of the purchaser obtain or consent to an endorsement of notice of the purchaser's interest on the policy, and in such case the vendor (keeping the policy on foot) may require the purchaser to pay on completion a proportionate part of the premium from the date of the contract.

22. Special notice to complete

(1) At any time on or after the completion date, either party, being ready and willing to fulfil his own outstanding obligations under the contract, may (without prejudice to any other right or remedy available to him) give to the other party or his solicitor notice in writing requiring completion of the contract in conformity with this condition.

(2) Upon service of such notice as aforesaid it shall become and be a term of the contract, in respect of which time shall be of the essence thereof, that the party to whom the notice is given shall complete the contract within 16 working days after service of the notice (exclusive of the day of service): but this condition shall operate without prejudice to any right of either party to rescind the contract in the meantime.

(3) In case the purchaser refuses or fails to complete in conformity with this condition, then (without prejudice to any other right or remedy available to the vendor) the purchaser's deposit may be forfeited (unless the court otherwise directs) and, if the vendor resells the property within twelve months of the expiration of the said period of 16 working days, he shall be entitled (upon crediting the deposit) to recover from the purchaser hereunder the amount of any loss occasioned to the vendor by expenses of or incidental to such resale, or by diminution in the price.

Appendix 3
Bibliography

Barnsley, D. G., *Conveyancing Law Practice* (Butterworth 1982)

Cordery, A., *Law Relating to Solicitors*, ed. Graham J. Graham (Butterworth 1981)

Curzon, L. B., *Land Law* (Macdonald & Evans HANDBOOK 1982)

Curzon, L. B., *Law of Trusts* (Macdonald & Evans HANDBOOK 1980)

Dalton, Patrick J., *Land Law* (Pitmans 1983)

Encyclopaedia of Forms and Precedents, Volumes 18 and 19 (Butterworth)

Emmet, L. E., *Notes on Perusing Titles and on Practical Conveyancing* (Oyez 1986)

Farrand, J. T., *Contract and Conveyance* (Oyez 1983)

George, Edward F., and George, A., *Sale of Flats* (Sweet & Maxwell 1984)

Gibson's *Conveyancing*, revising ed. R. A. Donnell (Law Notes Lending Library Ltd. 1980)

Guide to the Professional Conduct of Solicitors, published by the Law Society and issued free to all solicitors

Oliver, M. C., *Company Law* (Macdonald & Evans HANDBOOK 1982)

Riddall, J. G., *Introduction to Land Law* (Butterworth 1983)

Ruoff, Theodore B. F., and Roper, R. B., *Law and Practice of Registered Conveyancing* (Stevens & Sons 1986)

Wontner, J. J., and Quickfall, F., *Guide to Land Registry Practice* (Oyez 1985)

Appendix 4
Examination technique

1. Preparation. The importance of adequate preparation before the examination cannot be over-emphasised. Revision must be planned and the plan adhered to. A crash course in revision compressed into a few days immediately before the examination is no substitute for a proper course of revision. Staying up until the early hours of the night before the examination rarely results in a better examination script, it is much more likely to lead to fatigue and muddled thinking.

Having adequately prepared himself the student can enter the examination with the knowledge that he will be able to tackle the examination paper confidently. He should bear in mind that the purpose of an examination paper is to find out what the candidate knows, not what he does not know. There is therefore, no need to panic, although most students are nervous before an examination.

2. In the examination room. The golden rule for all examinations is to arrive in adequate time, it is as bad to arrive too early as too late. It is also important to read the instructions at the head of the examination paper carefully. If five questions are to be answered and the student mistakenly answers only four his paper in effect will be marked out of 80 per cent not 100 per cent, so that he will have lost 20 per cent of the marks. Timing is equally important; four questions answered in three hours because the student has mistimed his answers and has no time to answer the fifth question again will result in a loss of 20 per cent of the marks, a luxury which most students cannot afford.

3. Types of questions. All questions should be read through carefully before the student decides which questions to answer. The student may expect to be confronted with examination questions that fall into three broad categories.

(*a*) *The book-work question.* For example: "To what extent does the contract for sale merge into the conveyance?" Here the student can easily and quickly identify what is required from him, and provide an account of the doctrine of merger and its exceptions (*see* 17:**6–12**). This type of question should always be attempted, although it may be put in a slightly different form: "A fallacy may possibly lie in the use of the word rescission *per* Bowen, L.J. in Mersey Steel and Iron Co. *v.* Naylor Benzon & Co. (1882). Explain this in relation to remedies for breach of contract for the sale of land." Upon reflection the student will recall the difference between "*rescission ab initio*" where damages for breach of contract cannot be obtained, and the situation which obtains if the rescission follows a repudiatory breach of contract and the innocent party can obtain damages for breach of contract.

(*b*) *The problem question.* For example: "Henry Brown agreed to buy 'Blackacre' from George White for £30,000. Henry Brown paid a deposit of £3,000 and received a receipt from George White's solicitors U. Heep & Co., in the following terms: 'Received from Henry Brown the sum of three thousand pounds. (Signed) U. Heep & Co.' The receipt is dated 26th March 1980. George White died on 2nd April 1980 and his personal representatives inform Henry Brown that they do not propose to proceed with the sale. Advise Henry whether he is likely to be successful in obtaining a decree of specific performance."

(*c*) *The discussion question.* For example: "Discuss what significance the phrase 'subject to contract' possesses in the sale of land." This is by far the most difficult type of question to answer, for here the student has less of an idea of what the examiner requires by way of an answer. While all answers should be carefully planned, this answer requires a greater degree of planning than the other. It gives the better student an opportunity to demonstrate not only his knowledge of legal principles, but also a critical appreciation of them. The student should not be deterred from putting forward a point of view because he is afraid that the examiner may not agree with it. If it is properly presented and argued, there is no reason why the student should lose marks even if the examiner disagrees with the point. However, a discussion question should not be used as a vehicle for a woolly-minded ramble around the question, it will fool no one, particularly not the examiner.

4. Technique in Solicitor's New Finals Examination. The examination in conveyancing falls into two two-hour examinations. The first of these is more practical in nature and the second is very similar in concept to a traditional written law examination paper. It is early days yet to be able to comment with complete certainty on how this examination will work out but the following points may usefully be made:

(a) *The practical paper.* This will consist basically of one question. The form of this will be the presentation to the students of a series of documents from a conveyancing transaction, followed by a series of exercises thereon. Typically, the student may be presented with an epitome of title and asked questions such as to frame requisitions; the procedure to be followed by the parties to complete the conveyance; and post-completion procedures such as registration at HMLR, etc. In answering a question of this nature key points to ensure are:

(i) a methodical approach to perusal of the abstract—the use of mental check-lists is advised to ensure that points such as acknowledgments for production in deeds; certificate of value, correct execution, etc., are not missed;

(ii) clarity of expression and unequivocality in answers—this will be at a premium in showing that a student can deal with problems in a way suitable to the dictates of practice;

(iii) answering the exact question that is asked. This sounds too trivial a point, but will be of immense importance. If asked to frame requisitions and explain the reasons therefore, it is important that requisitions are clearly framed and separated from the legal explanation in the presentation of the answer. It will not be sufficient to outline the legal problems raised by the abstract and discuss them in the way one might in a traditional law degree paper;

(*iv*) having regard in producing answers to the marks allocated for each part of the question. This gives an important guide to the amount of time and detail to be allowed for each section.

(*b*) *The second Conveyancing paper.* This does not present such a challenge to the student in its style of presentation as the practical paper. Nevertheless, it is worth stressing again that depth of analysis is not so important as concise, unequivocal clearly set out answers. The motto for a student in this examination should be sound unequivocal legal advice expressed with clarity and confidence. Further guidance is given in the notes following the specimen paper (p. 341–4).

5. Technique in Fellowship of Institute of Legal Executive's examination. The format of this is one compulsory document question and a number of traditional academic style questions. Thus, the examination technique required is an amalgam of that required for undergraduate examination and the Law Society Finals. Students are advised to obtain specimen document questions and practise answering these, particularly taking account of the guidance given above.

Appendix 5
Specimen questions

The following questions are taken from Part II of the University of London's External LL.B Examination, by whose kind permission they are reproduced.

1. Consider whether an enforceable contract exists in each of the following sets of circumstances:

(i) A and B met together at a social gathering and A orally agreed to sell his house, Redwood, to B for £20,000. The next day, A's solicitors, S & Co., wrote to B as follows: "Dear Mr B, With reference to the proposed sale of Redwood by our client, A, to yourself for £20,000, our client has instructed us to inform you that he has received a higher offer for the property and accordingly will not be proceeding with the sale to yourself. Signed, S & Co."

(ii) After preliminary negotiations resulting in an agreement for the sale and purchase of certain land subject to contract, A and B each instruct their respective solicitors to draw up a contract for signature. Two forms of written contract in identical terms are drawn up by each firm of solicitors and both A and B sign their respective parts and instruct their solicitors to exchange. In the morning of 10th June, it is agreed between the two firms on the telephone that contracts shall be treated as exchanged and B's solicitors post B's part of the contract. Before A's solicitors post off A's part of the contract, however, A telephones and instructs them not to proceed whereupon they write to B's solicitors informing them that no exchange can take place.

(iii) The facts are as in (ii) above except that both A's and B's parts of the contract have been posted before A telephones his solicitors instructing them not to proceed, but in fact the letter written by A's solicitors to B's solicitors is received by B's solicitors the day before A's part of the contract is received by B's solicitors.

On the facts in (iii), would your advice be affected by the existence in the form of contract of a general condition providing that where the exchange of contracts takes place through the post the exchange shall be deemed to be complete when the last part is posted?

2. Smith, a developer, has just agreed to buy ten acres of land from Jones for £500,000. The contract states (in the particulars) that the interest sold is the fee simple free from encumbrances. Before entering into the contract, Smith made enquiries (i) of the local authority and (ii) of Jones (through his solicitors) as to the planning position concerning the land and was told by both that planning permission had been granted permitting residential development of the land at a density of ten detached houses to the acre. In fact, this had, at one time, been true but had been superseded by a later planning permission permitting only six detached houses to the acre and Smith's solicitors have just been informed by Jones' solicitors of this fact. Further, from the abstract of title delivered by Jones' solicitors, it appears that in a conveyance of the land made in 1950 (before the root of title) the purchaser thereunder entered into a restrictive covenant (which was registered and is still enforceable) not to erect any buildings on the land except detached dwelling-houses at a density of not more than six to the acre. On the basis of a development density of six houses to the acre, the land is currently worth £400,000 but with market interest in building land now increasing, it is anticipated that in four months' time it might be worth £600,000 on that basis. However, on the basis of a density of ten houses to the acre, the land is currently worth £600,000 and may, in four months' time, be worth £900,000. The date fixed for completion of the sale is 4th July 1978. Smith estimates that his loss of trading profit on the development as a sixty house development rather than a hundred house development would be £200,000.

Smith's solicitors have notified Jones' solicitors that without prejudice to their rights with regard to ending the contract, Smith would be prepared to consider proceeding to completion on the basis of a reduced purchase price but Jones' solicitors have now informed Smith's solicitors that Smith must choose between withdrawing without compensation or completing at the contract price.

Advise Smith as to the possible courses of action open to him and (in the light of the foregoing facts) their respective financial merits.

3. In April of this year, Percival contracted to purchase a dwelling-house from Victor for £50,000 and paid a deposit of £5,000 to Victor's solicitors as stakeholders. The date fixed for completion was "on or before 1st May 1978". Owing to a change in his personal circumstances, Percival no longer desires to purchase the house and has taken no steps towards completion or otherwise. Advise Percival as to his legal position and the best course of action open to him (with a view to withdrawing from the contract) in each of the following alternative sets of circumstances:

(i) If the contract is an open contract and, on 2nd May, Victor's solicitors wrote to Percival's solicitors saying that as Percival had not completed on the due date, his deposit was forfeited and Victor would be selling the property elsewhere;

(ii) If the contract is an open contract and Victor's solicitors (*a*) on 2nd May served a notice on Percival's solicitors stating that unless Percival completed the purchase within twenty-one days, his deposit would be forfeited and the property would be sold elsewhere, and (*b*) on 24th May wrote to Percival's solicitors saying that the deposit had been forfeited and the contract was to be treated as at an end;

(iii) If (*a*) the contract contains a provision (as in the National Conditions of Sale, 19th Edition) that "on or after the completion date, either party, being ready and willing to fulfil his own outstanding obligations under the contract, may give to the other party or his solicitor notice in writing requiring completion in conformity with this condition" and that "upon service of such notice as aforesaid it shall become and be a term of the contract in respect of which time shall be the essence thereof, that the party on whom the notice is served shall complete the contract within twenty-eight days after service of the notice (exclusive of the day of service)" and (*b*) on 15th May 1978, Victor's solicitors served on Percival's solicitors a notice in writing requiring completion in accordance with the provision.

4. Six months ago, Flashman contracted to sell his house, The Knoll, to Brown for £40,000, completion to take place on 10th June 1978. The solicitors acting in the matter for Brown, Messrs Bumble & Co., took no steps to procure an entry in respect of the contract on any register. On 1st May, Flashman received an offer from Black of £80,000 for The Knoll which Flashman accepted and on 30th May, the sale to Black was completed. On completion, the purchase money (£80,000) was paid to Flashman's solicitors, Messrs Frankenstein, and is still in their hands. Flashman is heavily in debt elsewhere and on the verge of bankruptcy.

Messrs Frankenstein have just informed Messrs Bumble of the above facts concerning the sale to Black. Advise Brown on his possible remedies.

Would your answer be affected if at all material times the title to The Knoll had been registered at H.M. Land Registry under the Land Registration Acts?

5. V's title to certain agricultural land consists of the following:

1935 Vesting Deed for giving effect to a pre-1926 settlement naming T as the tenant for life and P and Q as the trustees of the settlement for the purposes of the Settled Land Act 1925;

1945 Deed of Declaration executed by P, Q, R and S declaring that R and S were the trustees of the settlement for the purposes of the Settled Land Act 1925;

1953 Death of T;

1954 Probate of T's will granted to A and B, the executors appointed by T's will;

1956 Assent by A and B in favour of R and S upon the trusts provided for by section 36 of the Settled Land Act 1925;

1972 Death of R;

1975 Conveyance by S to V, it being recited in the conveyance that V had become solely and beneficially entitled to the land.

Advise P, who has contracted to purchase the land, on the above title ignoring any questions (such as stamp duty) which do not directly arise out of the above facts.

6. (*a*) "Now that the Law of Property Act 1969 s. 23 has reduced the statutory length of title that a purchaser may demand to fifteen years, registration of title has ceased to make any substantial contribution to the simplification of conveyancing."

Discuss.

(*b*) In 1955 A was registered proprietor of Blackacre with freehold title absolute under the Land Registration Act 1925. In 1959 X openly occupied part of Blackacre and began to use a short cut across the remainder. In 1972 A transferred Blackacre to B as a gift. In April 1979 B orally gave Y a monthly tenancy of a cottage on Blackacre; Y has done some decorating and paid rent but has not moved in. Last month B, as beneficial owner, sold and transferred Blackacre to C, who is now registered proprietor.

C has just discovered the above facts relating to X and Y and seeks your advice.

7. (*a*) Where the boundary between two separately owned parcels of land consists of a hedge and ditch, how is the precise line of boundary to be determined (i) where the title is unregistered (ii) where the title is registered under the Land Registration Act 1925?

(*b*) Fiveways Farm lies to the east of the road running from North Rufflings to South Rufflings, except for one field, Soggyacre, which is on the west side of the road. For the last ten years sheep belonging to the adjoining Heavitrees Farm have grazed Soggyacre without complaint from George, estate owner in fee simple of Fiveways Farm.

In consequence Soggyacre has become known locally as belonging to Heavitrees Farm. Last month George conveyed to Harry "All that piece or parcel of land known as Fiveways Farm, To Hold unto Harry in fee simple". A plan, marked "Only for identification" was bound up in the conveyance but not specifically referred to; on that plan Fiveways Farm, including Soggyacre, is edged in red.

Advise Harry whether Soggyacre has passed to him.

8. V agrees in writing to sell a house, which he occupies with his wife as a residence, to P for £20,000, completion to take place on or before the 30th June 1979, and P pays the usual 10 per cent deposit to V's solicitor as stakeholder.

Consider the possible remedies and claims which P may have against V if:

(*a*) on investigating the title, P discovers that the title to the house is vested in V and his wife and V's wife is unwilling to join in the sale;

(*b*) while the title is found, on investigation, to be vested in the name of V, P, on making his search under the Land Charges Act 1972, discovers that, the day after the date of the contract, V's wife had registered a Class F land charge against the name of V and is unwilling to agree to its removal.

9. In 1965 Winifred purchased Greywalls and became estate owner in fee simple (the title being unregistered). In 1968 she sold and conveyed Greywalls to Thomas. Thomas and Winifred married in 1970. Thomas died in 1974 and by his will devised Greywalls to Coke and Littleton, his executors and trustees, upon trust either to sell and to pay the income from the proceeds of sale to Winifred during her life or until her remarriage, or to retain the property and to allow Winifred to occupy Greywalls, again during her life or until her remarriage, and on determination of her interest to hold the trust fund for his three children in equal shares absolutely. In 1975 Coke and Littleton made a vesting assent, under the Settled Land Act 1925, vesting Greywalls in Winifred as tenant for life, and duly handed her the title deeds. Winifred remarried in 1977 but did not tell Coke and Littleton. Consider the validity of the title of Philip, a purchaser of Greywalls, in each of the following sets of circumstances:

(*a*) In 1976 Winifred as tenant for life sold and conveyed Greywalls to Philip, the purchase money being duly paid to Coke and Littleton.

(*b*) The same transaction took place, but in 1978 instead of 1976.

(*c*) In 1978 Winifred suppressed the will and assent and as beneficial owner sold and conveyed Greywalls to Philip, making a title concluding with the conveyance to her in 1965.

How, if at all, would your answer to the above questions differ if the title to Greywalls had throughout been registered under the Land Registration Act 1925, and all appropriate steps as to registration had been taken when the various transactions occurred?

The following is part of a paper, Conveyancing II, set in the Solicitor's Final Examination. Notes on how to prepare an answer follow the paper. The Law Society kindly gave permission for reproduction of the paper—views expressed are, of course, solely those of the authors.

Material provided for question 1: Office copies. Will of Alan Mason.

1. You have been instructed by Mrs Anne Mason to deal with a loan she is obtaining from the County Building Society for the purpose of installing central heating and double glazing in her house. The house was erected thirty years ago and is not in a mining area. She has handed you the land certificate (*see* pp. 343) which she explains she and her late husband were given because the title deeds were lost. She has also handed you her late husband's will which has not been proved. You have also been instructed to act for the building society, and have obtained the above office copies.

(*a*) Explain whether the will must be proved in order to complete the mortgage and what other steps (if any) you will need to take to have the title registered in her sole name.

(*b*) Explain the significance of registration with possessory title and whether this fact will create any problems in dealing with the mortgage.

(*c*) Briefly explain the searches you will make on behalf of the building society.

3. You have been consulted by Harry Robinson and his brother Tom who tell you that they want you to act for them in the sale of a dwellinghouse No. 28 Rookery Lane, Bogginton. You have obtained the title deeds on undertaking from the Bank which holds them as mortgagee. These include a Conveyance to William Robinson

dated 13th May 1954 and a legal mortgage of the same date to the Bank. The Will of William Robinson (who died in 1981) has already been proved by Harry and Tom. This devised the house to William's widow for life without the imposition of a trust for sale, and on her death to Harry and Tom in equal shares and appointed them to be the executors and trustees. The brothers explain that their mother has recently moved from the house to live with Harry and his wife, and all agree that the house should be sold as soon as possible. Tom is going abroad in three weeks' time and will be away for several months and it may be difficult to contact him during this period. He therefore wishes to leave all the formalities to Harry so that there will be no delay.

(a) Briefly explain the alternative ways in which title can be made to a purchaser and who will be the parties to the conveyance in each case. What further documents (if any) will be needed and, in either case, to whom will you account for the proceeds of sale after repaying the mortgage?

(b) Is it possible for Harry or some other person to act on Tom's behalf whilst he is abroad?

(c) What special requirements will you need to bear in mind in relation to the form of discharge to be endorsed on the mortgage?

Notes on Law Society Finals paper

1. QUESTION 1

(a) Explain the effect of registration of joint proprietors—does Law of Property (Joint Tenants) Act 1964 apply to registered land? Effect of there being no restriction—proof of death to Land Registry is required—thus, will does not have to be proved—how is registration of new proprietor effected?

(b) Explain nature of possessory title by contrast to absolute title; explain availability of conversion to title absolute.

(c) List pertinent searches with brief explanation.

3. QUESTION 3

(a) Explain

(i) Sale by tenant for life under SLA 1925; need for and effect of vesting deed.

OFFICE COPY

ISSUED BY THE WEYFORD DISTRICT LAND REGISTRY

H.M. LAND REGISTRY
Edition 1 opened 13.9.1965   TITLE NUMBER LM12037   This register consists of   pages

A. PROPERTY REGISTER
containing the description of the registered land and the estate comprised in the Title

COUNTY	DISTRICT
LOAMSHIRE	LOAMSTER

The Freehold land shown and edged with red on the plan of the above Title filed at the Registry **registered on**
13 September 1965 known as 48 Queen's Road

B. PROPRIETORSHIP REGISTER
stating nature of the Title, name, address and description of the proprietor of the land and any entries affecting the right of disposing thereof

TITLE **POSSESSORY**

Entry number	Proprietor, etc.	Remarks
1.	FIRST REGISTERED PROPRIETORS Alan Mason and Anne Mason both of 48 Queen's Road, Loamster, Loamshire, registered on 13 September 1965	
	Note to Candidates The charges register is blank and has not been reproduced. The filed plan may be treated as not relevant to the question and has not been supplied. The note to the proprietorship register explaining the nature of a possessory title has been omitted for the purpose of this question.	

Printed LIF 8/78

Register Model III

Any errors struck through are no longer subsisting

ISSUED BY THE WEYFORD DISTRICT LAND REGISTRY SHOWING THE SUBSISTING ENTRIES ON THE REGISTER ON 1 FEB 1983
UNDER S.113 OF THE 1925 ACT THIS COPY IS ADMISSIBLE IN EVIDENCE TO THE SAME EXTENT AS THE ORIGINAL

G1   C103

THIS IS THE LAST WILL AND TESTAMENT of me ALAN MASON of 48 Queens Road Loamster retired Draper.

I HEREBY REVOKE all previous wills and APPOINT my wife Anne to be the sole executrix of this my will and I GIVE to her the whole of my estate absolutely.

SIGNED by the Testator ALAN MASON
as his last will and testament
in the presence of us both who
being present at the same time
have hereunto subscribed our
names as witnesses:-

Alan Mason

Judy Henson,
54 Markham Crescent,
Grantchester.
Housewife.

Tom Henson,
54 Markham Crescent,
Grantchester.
Joiner.

(*ii*) Sale by personal representatives in that capacity—recitals on sale by personal representative.

(*b*) Trustee power under Trustee Act, s. 25 and effect of Powers of Attorney Act 1971, s. 9.

(*c*) Need to avoid receipt acting as transfer instead of discharge, LPA 1925, s. 115(2).

The student is advised to work through other questions in the same way, setting out the basic framework required to give an answer. It will be found that what is required to produce a good answer in this exam is the ability to state fundamental principles clearly and concisely, to apply a little common sense and not to be afraid to commit yourself to a straightforward answer.

Generally in the Law Society Finals the papers are quite lengthy—however, the answers required are short and direct. It is essential in writing your answers not to rush to judgment. Allow yourself thirty minutes at least to read the paper, re-read the paper, make notes on it, plan your answer and only when the scheme of your answer is absolutely clear should you begin to write. When you do, make your points in simple sentences, in ordered paragraphs and do not be afraid to adopt a layout or numbering which gives your answer form and is easy for the examiner to follow.

Appendix 6

Law Society practice rules and codes of practice

1. The Law Society's Formulae for Exchanging Contracts by Telephone/Telex

Formula A *(for use where one solicitor holds both signed parts of the contract):*

A. A completion date of   19   is agreed. The solicitor holding both parts of the contract confirms that he holds the part signed by his client, which is identical to the part he is also holding signed by the other solicitor's client and will forthwith insert the agreed completion date in each part.

Solicitors mutually agree that exchange shall take place from that moment and the solicitor holding both parts confirms that, as of that moment, he holds thenceforth the part signed by his client to the order of the other. He undertakes that day by first-class post **or, where the other solicitor is a member of a document exchange (as to which the inclusion of a reference thereto in the solicitor's letterhead shall be conclusive evidence) by delivery to that or any other affiliated exchange** or by hand delivery direct to that solicitor's office, to send his signed part of the contract to the other solicitor, together, where he is the purchaser's solicitor, with a banker's draft or a solicitor's client account cheque for the deposit amounting to £........ .

Formula B *(for use where each solicitor holds his own client's signed part of the contract):*

B. A completion date of   19   is agreed. Each solicitor confirms to the other that he holds a part contract in the agreed form signed by his client and will forthwith insert the agreed completion date.

Each solicitor undertakes to the other thenceforth to hold the signed part of the contract to the other's order, so that contracts are exchanged at that moment. Each solicitor further undertakes that day by first-class post, **or, where the other solicitor is a member of a document exchange (as to which the inclusion of a reference thereto in the solicitor's letterhead shall be conclusive evidence) by delivery to that or any other affiliated exchange** or by hand delivery direct to that solicitor's office, to send his signed part of the contract to the other, together, in the case of the purchaser's solicitor, with a banker's draft or a solicitor's client account cheque for the deposit amounting to £........ .

These formulae indicate the matters agreed and the undertakings given. If one of these formulae is adopted, all that is necessary for the solicitors to record is a note in substantially the following form:

eg 'Completion date of   19   agreed. Law Society's Exchange Formulae A or B adopted [variations if any]. Banker's draft or a solicitor's client account cheque for £...... to be paid. Date and time of the conversation. . .'.

Notes

1 The circumstances in which Formula B is applicable (*ie*, where each party's solicitor holds his own client's signed part of the contract) are, and perhaps should be, exceptional. It is recognised, however, that there may be occasions when it is essential to make a contract effective before the part signed by the purchaser can be sent to the vendor's solicitor. Formula B is, therefore, included to cover such cases.

2 The risk of effecting exchange of contracts without a deposit first having been paid in accordance with the terms thereof was demonstrated in the case of *Morris* v. *Duke-Cohan & Co* (1975) 119 SJ 826. It is therefore provided as a first alternative that in the cases to which

the formulae apply where the deposit, or any part thereof, is still outstanding, payment should be made by banker's draft.
3 Any variations in the formulae applicable are a matter for agreement between the solicitors in the particular case. Any such variations should be carefully recorded in the notes of the telephone conversation or in the exchange of telex messages and should be confirmed in the letters enclosing the part contracts.

2. The Law Society's code for completion by post (1984 edition)

Preamble

The code provides a procedure for postal completion which practising solicitors may adopt by reference.

First, each solicitor must satisfy himself that no circumstances exist that are likely to give rise to a conflict between this code and the interests of his own client (including where applicable a mortgagee client).

The code, where adopted, will apply without variation except so far as recorded in writing beforehand.

The Code

1 Adoption hereof must be specifically agreed by all the solicitors concerned and preferably in writing.

2 On completion the vendor's solicitor will act as agent for the purchaser's solicitor without fee or disbursements.

3 The vendor's solicitor undertakes that on completion, he:
(1) will have the vendor's authority to receive the purchase money; and
(2) will be the duly authorised agent of the proprietor of any charge upon the property to receive the part of the money paid to him which is needed to discharge such charge.

4 The purchaser's solicitor shall send to the vendor's solicitor instructions as to:
(1) documents to be examined and marked;
(2) memoranda to be endorsed;
(3) deeds, documents, undertakings and authorities relating to rents, deposits, keys, *etc*; and
(4) any other relevant matters.

In default of instructions, the vendor's solicitor shall not be under any duty to examine, mark or endorse any documents.

5 The purchaser's solicitor shall remit to the vendor's solicitor the balance due on completion specified in the vendor's solicitor's completion statement or with written notification; in default of either, the balance shown due by the contract. If the funds are remitted by transfer between banks, the vendor's solicitor shall instruct his bank to advise him by telephone immediately the funds are received. The vendor's solicitor shall hold such funds to the purchaser's solicitor's order pending completion.

6 The vendor's solicitor, having received the items specified in paras 4 and 5, shall forthwith, or at such later times as may have been agreed, complete. Thereupon he shall hold all documents and other items to be sent to the purchaser's solicitor as agent for such solicitor.

7 Once completion has taken place, the vendor's solicitor shall as soon as possible thereafter on the same day confirm the fact to the purchaser's solicitor by telephone or telex and shall also as soon as possible send by first class post or document exchange written confirmation to the purchaser's solicitor, together with the enclosures referred to in para 4 hereof. The vendor's solicitor shall ensure that such title deeds and any other items are correctly committed to the post or document exchange. Thereafter, they are at the risk of the purchaser's solicitor.

8 If either the authorities specified in para 3 or the instructions specified in para 4 or the funds specified in para 5 have not been received by the vendor's solicitor by the agreed completion date and time, he shall forthwith notify the purchaser's solicitor and request further instructions.

9 Nothing herein shall override any rights and obligations of parties under the contract or otherwise.

10 Any dispute or difference which may arise between solicitors that is directly referable to a completion agreed to be carried out in accordance herewith, whether or not amended or supplemented in any way, shall be referred to an arbitrator to be agreed, within one month of any such dispute or difference arising between the solicitors who are party thereto, and, in default of such agreement, on the application of any such solicitor, to an arbitrator to be appointed by the President of The Law Society.

11 Reference herein to vendor's solicitor and purchaser's solicitor shall, where appropriate, be deemed to include solicitors acting for parties other than vendor and purchaser.

Notes

1 The object of the code is to provide solicitors with a convenient means for completion, on an agency basis, that can be adopted for use, where they so agree beforehand, in completions where a representative of the purchaser's solicitors is not attending at the

office of the vendor's solicitors for the purpose.

2 As with The Law Society's formulae for exchange of contracts by telephone/telex (republished in [1984] *Gazette*, 18 January, 82), the code embodies professional under-takings and is, in consequence, only recommended for adoption between solicitors.

3 Cl2 of the code expressly provides that the vendor's solicitor will act as agent for the purchaser's solicitor without fee or disbursements. It is envisaged that, in the usual case, the convenience of not having to make a specific appointment on the day of completion for the purchaser's solicitor to attend for the purpose will offset the agency work that the vendor's solicitor has to do and any postage he has to pay in completing under the code, and on the basis that most solicitors will from time to time act both for vendors and purchasers. If, nevertheless, a vendor's solicitor does consider that charges and/or disbursements are necessary in a particular case, as such an arrangement represents a variation in the code, it should be agreed in writing beforehand.

4 Having regard to the decision in *Edward Wong Finance Co Ltd* v. *Johnson, Stokes & Master (supra)*, cl 3(2) of the code requires the vendor's solicitor to confirm, before he agrees to use the code, that he will be the duly authorised agent of the proprietor of any charge upon the property (typically but not exclusively the vendor's building society) to receive that part of the money paid to him which is needed to discharge such charge.

5 Cl 9 of the code expressly provides that nothing therein shall override any rights and obligations of parties under the contract or otherwise.

The above notes refer only to some of the points in the code that practitioners may wish to consider before agreeing to adopt it. It is emphasised that it is a matter for the solicitors concerned to read the code in full, so that they can decide beforehand whether they will make use of it as it stands or with any variations agreed in writing beforehand, whether or not they are referred to in the above notes, as the case may be.

3. Law Society Practice Rule 2

The Solicitors' Practice Rules, 1936/72

2 (1) A solicitor or two or more solicitors practising in partnership or association shall not act for both vendor and purchaser on a transfer of land for value at arm's length or for both lessor and lessee on the grant of a lease for value at arm's length.

(2) Provided no conflict of interest appears and the vendor or lessor is not a builder or developer selling or leasing as such this rule shall not apply if:

(a) the parties are associated companies; or

(b) the parties are related by blood, adoption or marriage; or

(c) both parties are established clients (which expression shall include persons related by blood, adoption or marriage to established clients); or

(d) on a transfer of land the consideration is less than £1,000; or

(e) there are no other solicitors in the vicinity whom the client can reasonably be expected to consult; or

(f) two associated firms or two offices of the same firm are respectively acting for the parties provided that:

(i) the respective firms or offices are in different localities, and

(ii) neither party was referred to the firm or office acting for him from an associated firm or from another office of the same firm; and

(iii) the transaction is dealt with or supervised by a different solicitor in full-time attendance at each firm or office.

Index

M&E Handbooks

Law

Business and Management

Advertising/F Jefkins
Basic Economics/G L Thirkettle
Basics of Business/D Lewis
Business and Financial Management/B K R Watts
Business Mathematics/L W T Stafford
Business Systems/R G Anderson
Data Processing Vol 1: Principles and Practice/R G Anderson
Data Processing Vol 2: Information Systems and
   Technology/R G Anderson
Economics for 'O' Level/L B Curzon
Human Resources Management/H T Graham, R Bennett
International Marketing/L S Walsh
Marketing/G B Giles
Marketing Overseas/A West
Modern Commercial Knowledge/L W T Stafford
Modern Marketing/F Jefkins
Office Administration/J C Denyer, A L Mugridge
Operational Research/W M Harper, H C Lim
Production Management/H A Harding
Public Administration/M Barber, R Stacey
Public Relations/F Jefkins
Purchasing/C K Lysons
Retail Management/R Cox, P Brittain
Selling: Management and Practice/P Allen
Statistics/W M Harper
Stores Management/R J Carter

Accounting and Finance

Auditing/L R Howard
Basic Accounting/J O Magee
Basic Book-keeping/J O Magee
Company Accounts/J O Magee
Company Secretarial Practice/L Hall, G M Thom
Cost Accounting/W M Harper
Elements of Banking/D P Whiting
Elements of Insurance/D S Hansell
Finance of Foreign Trade/D P Whiting
Investment: A Practical Approach/D Kerridge
Management Accounting/W M Harper
Practice of Banking/E P Doyle, J E Kelly
Principles of Accounts/E F Castle, N P Owens

Humanities and Science

European History 1789–1914/C A Leeds
Land Surveying/R J P Wilson
Sociology 'O' Level/F Randall
World History: 1900 to the Present Day/C A Leeds